Strategic Change Management in Public Sector Organisations

Strategic Change Management in Public Sector Organisations

DAVID BAKER

*Case studies researched and written by
Kathryn Taylor*

Chandos Publishing
Oxford · England

Chandos Publishing (Oxford) Limited
Chandos House
5 & 6 Steadys Lane
Stanton Harcourt
Oxford OX29 5RL
UK
Tel: +44 (0) 1865 884447 Fax: +44 (0) 1865 884448
Email: info@chandospublishing.com
www.chandospublishing.com

First published in Great Britain in 2007

ISBN:
978 1 84334 141 3 (paperback)
978 1 84334 191 8 (hardback)
1 84334 141 7 (paperback)
1 84334 191 3 (hardback)

© David Baker, 2007

British Library Cataloguing-in-Publication Data.
A catalogue record for this book is available from the British Library.

Typeset by Domex e-Data Pvt. Ltd.
Printed in the UK and USA.

For Barry
A great change manager, and a good friend

Contents

List of boxes, case studies, figures and tables

Boxes

Case studies

Figures

Tables

List of abbreviations

ACAS	Advisory, Conciliation and Arbitration Service
AI	Appreciative Enquiry
BOS	Bristol Online Surveys
BPR	Business Process Re-engineering
BS	Balanced Scorecard
CCSU	Council of Civil Service Unions
CEO	Chief Executive Officer
CI	Continuous Improvement
CPD	Continuing Professional Development
EFQM	European Foundation for Quality Management
FE	Further Education
GOSW	Government Office for the South West
HE	Higher Education
HEFCE	Higher Education Funding Council for England
HR	Human Resources
HRM	Human Resource Management
HSA	Hard Systems Approach
ICT	Information and Communications Technology
IiP	Investors in People
IPA	Involvement and Participation Association
JISC	Joint Information Systems Committee
LSW	Learning South West
NHS	National Health Service
OD	Organisation Development
RSP	Regional Skills Partnership
SHRM	Strategic Human Resource Management
SIS	Systems Intervention Strategy

SSM	Soft Systems Methodology
SWESA	South-West Enterprise and Skills Alliance
SWRDA	South-West Regional Development Agency
TMS	Team Management Systems
TQM	Total Quality Management
UK	United Kingdom
UKHE	United Kingdom Higher Education

Acknowledgements

I would like to thank Tim Boyes-Watson, Chief Executive, Learning South West, for permission to reproduce his recent strategic planning documents; the South West Enterprise and Skills Alliance/Regional Skills Partnership, for allowing me to reproduce documentation; June Whetherly, for putting me in touch with a number of people who had undertaken change management projects; and all the people interviewed for the case study elements of the book. I would also like to thank Wendy Clements, my secretary, for her help and support throughout the preparation and writing period; Dr Glyn Jones of Chandos Publishing, for his forbearance while I completed the text; Gareth Haman, my copy-editor; and Jonathan Kendon, for preparing the Index. Above all, I am especially grateful to Kathryn Taylor, my research assistant, without whom this book would simply not have been completed.

Note on the case studies

The case studies that appear throughout this book are all 'real-life' examples. Where permission was given to 'go public', real names have been used. In a number of cases, however, while those interviewed were happy to have their case studies included in this book, anonymity was requested. In such cases names have been changed in order to respect these wishes.

Preface

We live in an increasingly turbulent world. Environments have become much more competitive; expectations, attitudes and moralities have been transformed. The speed at which change occurs or is required has increased markedly since the Industrial Revolution of the eighteenth century, when the need for innovation borne of a desire to improve competitiveness in the manufacturing industries became apparent. Social improvement came to the fore as an equally important imperative for change in the nineteenth century. Change driven by fashion is arguably a more recent phenomenon, though one that is as influential on approaches to management as it is to what people wear or what they eat.

Public sector organisations – just like their private sector counterparts – have to respond to change and increased turbulence; those institutions that anticipate and embrace change constructively and creatively will be the ones that are most likely to develop rather than decline. But how should they best respond? Is change actually manageable? I argue that it both can and must be managed if desired improvements or enhancements are to be implemented efficiently, effectively and in a sustainable way. Managing change is about altering the way individuals, groups and organisations do things. But there is no magic formula, no single way of doing it. This book aims to cover all the major aspects of change management for those working in public sector organisations, and can be seen as a companion volume to my earlier work, *The Strategic Management of Technology*, from which it draws in certain areas, and notably in the forecasting, risk and project management techniques, duly re-written, updated and re-contextualised. *Strategic Change Management* summarises key theories and approaches to change management, and includes worked descriptions of some of the key techniques used in change management processes and programmes, with reference to case studies drawn from a range of environments such as the public sector, not-for-profit organisations and others. This book argues that leadership skills and managerial approaches, structures and techniques are required if any change is to be successful, with the responsibility for change resting firmly with those who lead and manage the organisation undergoing change, but with a deep involvement of all the key stakeholders. It is therefore written primarily from the point of view of the change manager, and aims to look at both the strategic aspects of change management and the ways in which a strategy, once formulated, might then be implemented to the best effect.

David Baker,
Plymouth,
October, 2006

About the author

David Baker was born in Bradford, West Yorkshire, in 1952. His first love was the church organ, which he began playing from the age of 12. By the time that he was 16, he was an Associate of the Royal College of Organists. He gained his Fellowship the following year. In 1970 he was elected Organ Scholar of Sidney Sussex College, Cambridge, graduating with a First Class Honours degree in Music three years later. He took an MMus degree from King's College, London in 1974. He then moved into Library and Information Services, taking a Master of Library Studies degree in 1976 and a PhD in 1988. Both of these degrees were from Loughborough University. After a number of library posts at Nottingham, Leicester and Hull Universities and a lecturing role at Loughborough, he became Chief Librarian of the University of East Anglia, Norwich, in 1985. He was promoted to Director of Information Strategy and Services in 1995, and Pro-Vice-Chancellor in 1997. He became Principal of the College of St Mark and St John, Plymouth, in July 2003 and, in addition, was appointed Professor of Strategic Information Management there in July 2006.

David Baker has published widely in the field of Library and Information Studies, with thirteen monographs and some 100 articles to his credit. He has spoken at numerous conferences, led workshops and seminars and has undertaken consultancy work in most countries in the European Union, along with work in Bulgaria, Slovenia, Ethiopia, Kuwait, Nigeria and the Sudan. In recent years, his particular professional interest has been in the strategic management of technology. He gained an MBA degree from the Open University in this subject area in 2002. He is a member of the Board of the Joint Information Systems Committee (JISC) and chairs its Content Services Committee, also having led a number of large technology-based projects in the LIS sector, both in relation to digital and hybrid library development and content creation for teaching and learning. His other key professional interest and expertise has been in the field of human resources, where he has been active in major national projects. When not working he enjoys watching cricket, walking, archaeology, history, creative writing and music – both as listener and performer.

The author has previously published *The Strategic Management of Technology* (2004) with Chandos.

Introducing change and strategic change management

Introduction

This chapter looks at change management overall, while recognising that management in general is typically about change – not least because change is necessary simply to survive in the modern, turbulent world, and the skills and approaches needed for change management are practically the same as those needed for any kind of management. It considers the nature and types of change and what it is in the particular context of the not-for-profit organisation. The key drivers of change and organisational readiness to respond to them are also considered. The chapter then aims to define change management and consider its constituent parts. Change management should be underpinned by an overarching strategy that provides a rationale for the change, a vision of the future state when the changes have been made, an indication of how the changes are to be made, over what time period, and by whom. Overall, the chapter therefore looks at strategic change management.

Change

Change is about becoming different through some kind of process, whether managed or unmanaged. Individuals, groups and organisations of all shapes and sizes alter from one state to another, over a period of time. Our environments, cultures, countries and even our world are in a constant state of flux or flow. Change is no single 'event' but an ongoing process that may seem like, or be punctuated by, a series of occurrences or activities that are perhaps perceived as finite, time-limited moves from one steady state to another, but in fact are not; change is continuous. 'Change is a pervasive phenomenon and the effects of even relatively minor changes in policy and attitude can appear in many guises' (Cooke, in Slowey, 1995).

Change is brought about through some form of metamorphosis or transformation process. It may be made actively in a planned way, or it may seem to occur naturally or organically, with an individual or an organisation adapting or evolving. It may happen slowly and imperceptibly, or seemingly as a revolutionary or discontinuous change that transforms an organisation, a society or even a whole country almost overnight. Basic attitudes to change in world societies vary: some may argue that change is random, lacking any predetermined attributes or outcomes; others assert that change is part of a cycle, and the same or similar circumstances or events re-occur over a period of time. Change is not, in itself, inherently good or bad.

The organisation

This book focuses on change at the level of the organisation, though change at the individual, group and levels broader than the organisation are closely linked and must also therefore be considered. An organisation can consist of two or more people, or have tens of thousands of employees spread all over the world; its budget can be up to hundreds or billions of pounds; its aim to manufacture, produce or serve, whether for public good, profit or both. 'There are many different forms of organisation, which can be typified as being primarily related to the way in which they coordinate themselves, the degree of their centralisation or decentralisation, and the aspect which the organisation considers to be of primary importance' (Sutherland and Canwell, 2004).

The organisation will typically have a longer-term strategy or plan, core aims and objectives, a management structure, and policies and rules by which it carries out its operations. It will have 'a life of its own', above and separate from that of the people that it employs; this 'life' or culture will incorporate a set of attitudes, codes, boundaries, groupings and alliances. Some institutions, such as universities, are hybrid organisations, containing a number of diverse parts. 'However, even across the most disparate of communities ... it is possible to argue that there will be shared objectives derived from an overall focus' (Huxley, 2005). At the same time, it should be noted that it is the members of an organisation that have to react to change as much as the organisation itself.

Not-for-profit organisations

The particular emphasis in the book is on public sector and other not-for-profit organisations. These come in all shapes and sizes. Sutherland and Canwell (2004) suggest the following categories:

Box 1.1   Types of not-for-profit organisation

- special interest organisations;
- government entities;
- educational or medical organisations;
- charities;
- religious groups;
- social groups.

In the private sector there is a clear objective: earning a profit. In the public sector, it is a case of a more broadly-based concept of 'adding value'. But it is often difficult to be clear about what that 'value' really is. Much depends upon the relative importance of the key stakeholders (discussed elsewhere in this book). For example, government may have a different view of the added value of public services from the end users. In addition, while not-for-profit organisations do not aim to 'make money' for shareholders through profits that yield dividends, they often aim to make an operating surplus or margin – perhaps to reinvest in the further development of the organisation and its core activities. As a result of pressure from the bodies that provide the bulk of the funding for these organisations, many aim to generate income in order to become less reliant on government or other funding sources, whether through the selling of products and services to customers (in the same way that a commercial organisation would do) or by the 'levering' of funding from sponsors or donors. Sutherland and Canwell (2004) list the main ways in which not-for-profit organisations differ from commercial ones (i.e. those that aim to make a profit):

Box 1.2 **Ways in which not-for-profit organisations differ from commercial (for profit) ones**

- Their outputs and results are often intangible and therefore difficult to measure.

- They may not be unduly influenced by their clients or customers.

- Financial contributors may well have different priorities from those of the customers or clients that the organisations actually serve.

- Many of the employees are such in name only, as they are volunteers.

- These volunteers may be subject to external influences and other commitments that could affect their commitment to the organisation itself.

- There are more constraints on finances, as not-for-profit organisations tend not to have access to credit facilities. They cannot offer shares on the market and therefore have fewer debt management options.

They also identify specific challenges relating to the management and development of such organisations:

Box 1.3 **Specific challenges in managing and developing not-for-profit organisations**

- Goal conflicts – as they often lack unifying central goals (such as profitability).

- The management and planning have to take into account inputs of resources, as they have a direct impact upon what the organisation is able to output.

- There is considerable political infighting in many organisations as a result of either conflicting or ambiguous objectives.

- Many of the organisations are controlled by professionals, who may not have managerial expertise but are recognised as being experts in their field.

- Many not-for-profit organisations are centralised to ensure that maximum value is achieved from the inputs.

The necessity for change

The pace of change has increased significantly in recent years within both private and public sectors and is set to quicken even further in a highly competitive environment, where all organisations will have to fight to develop even faster to stay in existence in a new atmosphere of 'hyper competition' (Aupperle and Karimalis, 2001). Increased competition has, at least in part, been caused by greater internationalisation. The education sector, for example, crosses national boundaries in a way that it did not even 20 years ago, whether in collaboration over knowledge sharing and common structures, or competition for staff, students, funding and prestige. 'We've always lived through and worked with change, but the scale and the pace of the changes we're facing now are, I think, unprecedented; we're challenged to change on every front and there's a sense that the pace is gathering'.[1]

There are a number of reasons – discussed in detail below – why change is necessary or desirable. Any organisation must ensure that it continues in the future by remaining viable, typically through being successful in core aims that continue to be relevant within the environment in which the organisation operates. The organisation's priorities in doing this will vary depending upon the industry, sector, external environment and current position.

Box 1.4	Key drivers for change

- the user;
- competition;
- diversity and diversification;
- legislation;
- human resource management;
- technology;
- finance.

The user

In recent years, the emphasis has been increasingly on the customer or user of the organisation, both within the private and the public sectors.

People 'vote with their feet' because there is a greater choice; service users are increasingly demanding because their expectations have been raised, not least by having to contribute themselves towards the cost of many of the services provided. Even the public sector is not immune and projects and services fail when they do not take account of what the 'customer' or the 'user' wants. Witness the £50m e-University initiative in the UK, which failed badly 'largely because it took a supply-driven rather than a demand-led approach'.[2] 'Market forces', then, give the user a greater role within the organisation and drive greater competitiveness between organisations to the point where competitive forces are driving internal change – whether it be based on cost reduction, quality improvement or product and service development. 'Organisational change has proceeded at a different pace in different countries and different institutions; arguably, this may mean that some ... are better placed than others to respond to new realities' (Middlehurst, 1999).

Competition

Increased competitiveness is one of the major drivers for change, as already noted; 'after the primary change driver behind change initiatives, most frequently the customer... the actions of competitors provide a major impetus behind organisations' attempts to implement innovation and change practices' (Solomon, 2001). In Higher Education within the UK (UKHE), for example, the sector is increasingly subject to market pressures: 'the challenge ... will be to adapt to a dynamic new environment where lucrative national and international markets arising from the growing importance of lifelong learning are likely to be contested strongly by traditional universities, new forms of universities, and by non-university providers. For the sector to operate successfully, it must be able to develop a response which builds on its strengths and acknowledges its weaknesses' (Cunningham et al., 1997).

This 'marketisation' has not only led to greater competition between universities to attract the best candidates to apply for their courses, but also students now see themselves as 'paying customers' and demand more from those who are providing the educational experience. Marketisation has also led to 'massification' and segmentation, where the sector has developed into sub-sectors, each with their particular markets and critical masses, with a greater need to perform to a high standard and to be seen to be doing so. This in turn has led to greater job fluidity within particular sectors and more interaction with other sectors, as new people have come in from outside higher education to change it towards a more market-oriented approach.

Many institutions have found themselves under intense financial pressure as a result of these environmental issues and developments. 'For universities, the changing patterns of business are not only of interest as a basis for noting the potential for parallel institutional change, but also as a warning of the changes that will affect day-to-day working patterns and employment prospects for staff and students' (Middlehurst, 1999). Sporn (1999) lists a range of internal responses that external change – including government pressure – has triggered in public sector education: re-engineering of processes, a focus on quality management, strategic planning, financial accounting and technology transfer. This has resulted in the growing importance of management, shifts from collegial to corporate institutions, the embracing of commercial activities and the emergence of the entrepreneurial public sector organisation, as exemplified by Middlehurst's comparision of HE and business.

Table 1.1 Parallels between business and HE

Business	HE
More efficient and effective customer service	More efficient and effective service to students
Enhanced sales and marketing reach – through leverage of trusted brands into new markets	New educational markets and possibilities for collaboration and branding
Lower purchasing costs	Lower purchasing costs
Increased speed to market – through tighter development and supply chain integration	Shorter development times for programmes – potential for 'real time' learning
Ability to outsource processes – without loss of coherence in product or service development	Potential to disaggregate and outsource processes: curriculum design, delivery and assessment
Growth of new intermediaries, system integrators	Growth of education service companies, brokers, consortia
New companies, virtual companies	New university models, virtual universities

Source: Middlehurst (1999).

Diversity and diversification

Diversity and diversification are two major drivers of change. Most societies are increasingly diverse in terms of ethnic, social and cultural mixes, and reflecting that diversity within an organisation can bring a richness of thinking and approaches as well as being increasingly necessary on the grounds of legal compliance. Large organisations – or some of those with a particular mission such as certain types of educational establishment – span ethnic or cultural boundaries and need to recognise such differences. Embracing this kind of diversity may necessitate fundamental shifts in the prevalent attitudes and cultures of the organisation. Diversity will therefore need to be embedded in order to ensure that people are included rather than excluded.

Diversification can relate not only to the workforce, but also to the products or services being offered, and organisations may see a cessation and substitution of activity, a change of direction within an existing area or an expanded portfolio, or some variation between the three options, as a way of responding to external circumstances, whether on a permanent basis or as circumstances demand.

Legislation

While the user is a key stakeholder, whose wants, needs and preferences will shape if not drive change, there are other 'dominant' stakeholders who also have large parts to play in driving or forcing change; the strategic aspirations of governments, for example, are major forces for change, whether or not such change fits in with the core needs of user stakeholders. Legislation is typically used as a way of meeting governmental aspirations and organisations may have to make changes in order to keep up to date and stay within the law. Legislation may encapsulate changes in the society over which the law will have effect, or represent a shift in culture or 'public opinion'.[3] In many societies, for example, the population is an increasingly diverse one, and new or revised laws are designed to reflect those societal changes, for example to allow for equality of opportunity. Organisations will not only have to respond to the cultural and societal changes in order to reflect the environment in which they operate, but may also be legally obliged to make changes even if they perceive little or no benefit to their particular organisations in so doing.

Human resource management

Legislation, culture and social change come together in approaches to employee relations or human resource management more generally, with the approaches to managing and leading people being ever more varied. Moreover, people are increasingly recognised as a core strategic asset for an organisation, to be treated as such. For example, 'the modernisation of the H[uman] R[esources] function in higher education in recent years has been remarkable. In the space of a few years, HR has shifted from an administrative support function to a valued strategic activity' (Higher Education Policy Institute, 2005). There has been major restructuring of whole industries and sectors in recent years as a result of a whole range of imperatives – including the financial: 'one implication of declining attendance is that the Church [of England] cannot continue to support 43 independent dioceses each replicating many functions, although some sharing is taking place. The whole structure needs a radical rethink to fit twenty-first century circumstances' (Brierley, 2005a).

The rhetoric and the reality of equality of opportunity is a major challenge for organisations of all shapes and sizes. On the one hand, relevant legislation has to be observed; on the other, the more subtle cultural changes that a diversifying workforce brings must be managed and harnessed to best effect. The rise of women to senior positions and the changed gender balance in many organisations may have altered the concept and approach to management, attitudes to change, and the types of change most desired and embraced – as well as being a major change itself. Experience to date of a more diversified workforce suggests that typical male roles – and the role of men – may need redefining, with a consequent change in the view of leadership and the role of 'the leader', discussed later in this book. Similarly, cultural and ethnic diversity needs to be represented within the organisation; but representation has to be as the result of a belief in diversity rather than a token for it. As such, diversity has to be embraced by the whole organisation and different voices listened to so that people do not feel discriminated against.

Poor employee relations can also be a driver for change, with a realisation that unless the position improves the organisation will eventually fail both in terms of its ability to change and more generally. On occasion, change in this area has followed significant conflict between management and workforce, and communication has been vital to improving relations. Partnership at Nottinghamshire Healthcare NHS Trust (Involvement and Participation Association, 2004) followed a period of unrest. Wills (2004) describes a partnership between Barclays and Unifi arising 'on the back of damaging industrial action in 1997, crisis in management and the union's ability to pose a real threat to the implementation of change'.

Technology

Technological development can often be the driver for change – as well as the facilitator of it. For example, 'the global internet challenges the very structure of industries and their supply chains and many existing approaches in regulation. Internet-centred convergence represents a major discontinuity in the evolution of both commerce and society (Department of Trade and Industry, 1998). 'New technologies permit richer, more complete and often instantaneous interactions' (Solomon, 2001). Academic and public libraries, for example, have already been significantly transformed by the advent of the Internet and the ability to provide resources in a 'martini' environment (anytime, any place, anywhere – a slogan from an old advertising campaign) to people who may never visit a physical building, but use resources intensively in their own homes or offices. They – and most other organisations – will need to respond to future technology challenges such as increased automation of processes and systems, mass digitisation, system integration, funding innovative development, re-skilling staff and a whole range of other demands brought about by new or improved technology (Baker, 2004, 2006).

Technology has the power to revolutionise the way an organisation does its business, such as by increasing productivity or reducing the workforce: 'working patterns are part of the change equation, but changes in the nature of work are equally significant. Technology is altering the relationship between knowledge areas and disciplines, and is also exponentially increasing the growth of knowledge and decreasing its shelf-life' (Clark, 1998); it is also 'rapidly shifting the balance of what is regarded as a 'routine' procedure, requiring a certain level of skill (and training) and what is regarded as complex professional activity. And even such complex activities can be displaced from the realm of professionals to the operations of expert systems and intelligent agent software (as in the flying of aeroplanes)' (Middlehurst, 1999).

The pace of technology innovation is increasing, and organisations are under greater pressure than ever before to put in place structures to deal with constant and pervasive technology changes that in turn require new or enhanced skills and active strategic management processes (Baker, 2004). But the potential of new technology applications is only fully realised if the organisation can embrace all the other changes – in roles and responsibilities, hierarchies, networks, and even physical estate. Adopting and adapting to new technology almost inevitably leads to a review of organisational structures, where the power of electronic communication, for example, enables a greater degree of 'connectivity' and networking across traditional boundaries and hierarchies. Technology should ideally be the enabler as much as the driver, and technology application will not be successful if it is not part of a broader strategic change management approach.

Finance

Finance is a major reason for change, even in public sector organisations. A commercial organisation has to make a profit, a return on investment for its shareholders. A public sector organisation may not have to make a surplus in the same way, but it will have to stay within its budgets and manage them efficiently, and make the most effective use of available resources in the interests of those who fund and pay for the organisation's activities. Similarly, a not-for-profit organisation will be looking to maximise the share of the resource that is used to fulfil its aims. In most institutions, the largest single budget item will be staffing, and financial pressures may well be a major driver of change in working practices or organisational structures as a result. In many parts of the public sector, an increasingly 'market' approach to the provision of services means that the price at which services are offered is a key driver for change. British universities, for example, have to come to terms with an environment in which students may be significantly influenced in their choice of institution by how much it will cost to study there.

Types of change

A number of types and levels of change are possible, from the small to the large, and the incremental to the discontinuous. Change can be developmental, and is largely concerned with change through improvement. According to Greiner (1972), organisations grow, as they develop, through five stages, each prompted by some form of crisis because the organisation cannot continue to cope without some form of change.

Nelson and Winter (1990) suggest that organisations evolve in the way that the natural world evolves, through selection (relating to the organisation's internal routines and their effectiveness), mutation (relating to changes in those routines to improve performance) and the struggle for

Table 1.2 Developmental change: the stages

Creativity	Growth is based on ideas and creativity. The organisational structure is simple and concentrated on enterprise. But as the organisation grows it cannot cope without a clearer sense of direction.
Direction	Further growth is possible through the development of a functional structure that provides systems and procedures that focus direction and 'smooth out' creativity. But the structure cannot accommodate issues of autonomy and individuality.
Delegation	Decentralisation provides autonomy, allowing more localised (and quicker) decision-making, with staff having more opportunity to exercise initiative. But as internal 'business units' start to form, there will be fragmentation, inconsistency and possibly a crisis of control.
Co-ordination and monitoring	A divisional structure balances central control with devolved autonomy, though there are issues of levels of bureaucracy required to maintain overall co-ordination and achieve consistency of approach.
Collaboration	A matrix structure allows cross-organisational teams to complete tasks.

Source: Greiner (1972).

existence (relating to the fact the organisations typically operate in a competitive environment): 'change begets change in part because institutional culture begins to change' (Corvey and Leitzel, 2004).

Transitional change 'seeks to achieve a known desired state that is different from the existing one' (Sutherland and Canwell, 2004; see also Amado and Ambrose, 2001), through three basic phases, as described by Lewin (1947), who developed the concept of 'unfreezing' an organisation, making changes and then 'refreezing' the organisation at the end of the change process at its new, improved level.

Transformational change is concerned with fundamental improvement in the way in which the organisation operates. It necessitates strategy development, planning and commitment throughout the organisation. Anderson and Anderson (2001) summarise seven steps in transformational change:

Table 1.3 **Transformational change: the stages**

Define the change strategy	The organisation assesses the need for change and its preparedness for it, the most likely change configuration and how the process of change will be managed and controlled.
Gain management commitment	The change manager will need to create 'ownership' within the management, developing a shared strategic vision that drives the change and provides a focus for the management team both individually and collectively.
Create a change strategy	The change manager will need to develop a strategy for making the change pertinent and relevant to all the staff, especially through a coherent communications strategy.
Build commitment from the workforce	Potential resistance to change will need to be identified and a rationale for persuading staff of the need for, and benefits of, change will need to be determined.
Develop a new culture	New values will need to be created and new behaviours encouraged that are supportive of the new vision of the organisation.
Reconfigure the organisation	Roles will be redesigned, competences developed, structure created and appointments made.
Manage performance	Performance measures will be developed that are in alignment with overall and individual objectives.

The state of the organisation may require a 'big bang' change that acts as a 'shock to the system'. In such cases, the organisation has to embrace radical and perhaps discontinuous change in order to survive. This is typically a 'turn round' situation, for if the existing direction continues then the organisation will eventually collapse. This is a form of crisis management – 'an unavoidable situation where ... survival or well-being is threatened by an unexpected problem' (Sutherland and Canwell, 2004). The well-managed organisation will have developed a risk register and contingency plans for dealing with the unexpected or the high risk, but there may be situations when the position is so critical that an individual, or a small team, must take strong, central and directive control in order to make rapid decisions (Fink, 2000). Turn rounds, then, are to be favoured when change must occur quickly and recovery is essential. There will be a need to gain management control of the organisation, in particular over decisions and resources. There will be a need to establish early and strong credibility with the stakeholders, to determine what the strengths and weaknesses of the organisation are and to eradicate the latter (including poor performing staff) as early as possible. When fundamental change is required, a full-scale approach is more likely to bring the desired 'turn round' than a piecemeal approach.

Organisational readiness for change

At its best, the organisation as a living organism will support more formal structures that encourage learning, development, innovation and renewal; at its worst, it will be a series of invisible and disparate 'sub-systems' that are not necessarily working together for a common good or goal. Effective change will not easily be possible unless these sub-systems are removed, preferably as an integral part of the changes themselves, for the organisation has to work as a whole, otherwise any change is likely to be undermined in the longer term. This requires real, open networks, both within the organisation and outside it, in terms of its external links with its key suppliers and stakeholders.

Those leading and managing change will need to assess what kind of organisation it is that provides the 'backdrop' for a change management project and associated processes. Is it a strong organisation or a neurotic one? Does it need wholesale change and restructuring, or is it only a case of refining, enhancing and updating what is basically sound? Some organisations are better at adapting to change – typically by changing themselves – than others. Those that do it best tend to be the ones that survive and thrive. At times, even a successful organisation will need to make fundamental changes, whether they relate to what is done or how it is done. There will be a need to determine new responsibilities, roles and priorities within the organisation. Even the maintenance of a given and desired state or 'status quo' may require underlying change, for while an individual or an organisation may wish to remain as before, surrounding environments or external pressures may necessitate a different approach. Universities, for example, 'are changing because their world is changing and perceptions of their functions, role and utility change with it' (Duke, 2002). Here, a 'challenging external environment ... [has] led to questions about internal change and, indeed, to broader questions about the whole shape and purpose of universities' (Middlehurst, 2004).

The concept of the learning organisation, where change is a 'way of life', is discussed elsewhere in this book. There certainly seems to be widespread agreement that the ability to learn, develop and adapt on an ongoing basis is crucial to the survival of any organisation: '[change] is vital for our survival and future. We won't have one unless we constantly improve and develop' (Wetherly, 1998). This need to learn is typically driven by an even more crucial requirement to improve and innovate in order to remain efficient, effective, competitive and successful. The more innovative the organisation tries to be, the higher the risk of failure, especially where novel approaches are being trialled for the first time. Much depends upon the nature of the industry or sector, the key competitors, the current climate, the perceived threats and the desired future position. The acceptable level of risk will need to be determined. This is likely to be lower in the public than in the private sector.

Change management

A simple definition of change management could be: 'the controlled implementation of required changes to some system'.[4] The 'system' in question may be an organisation encompassing not just 'mechanical' systems or processes but people and services, in which case a broader definition is more appropriate, such as:

Box 1.5   Change management: a definition

Change management is the process, tools and techniques to manage the people-side of the change processes, to achieve the required outcomes, and to realise the change effectively within the individual change agent, the inner team, and the wider system.[5]

The emphasis in these definitions is on the management of a process that has one or more planned alterations to the existing state that are deemed to improve the system that is the subject of the changes. Change management is seen as a series of activities that bring about some desired improvement or enhancement to an existing system or organisation. Change at the organisational level will typically be wanted or required in order to make the organisation faster, more sustainable, more coherent or more effective or efficient in its work.

Managing change is a task that can either be embraced proactively, with changes made in a systematic and planned way, or reactively, with external changes (over which there may be little internal control) being responded to by the organisation. The question is one of acceptance or intervention: accepters 'carry out the minimum of tasks necessary to cover themselves under ... [the] law'; interveners 'cover a much wide range of activities ... [diversifying] in new directions' (Senker, 1990). Organisations that choose to take a particular approach, and pursue opportunities, are far more likely to be successful than are those that are carried along by circumstances.

Some argue that 'change management is a nonsense ... [that it] fails because of its focus on management. The notion that you can manage change is an absurd one.'[6] Change is the result of, and/or results in, uncertainty. Uncertainty means unpredictability, so that there is no simple, easy or 'correct' approach to change; it therefore cannot be managed as such. Those who hold this view tend to argue that overseeing successful change within an organisation is about good leadership rather than effective management and that it is therefore not a process but an approach. However, even in the smallest organisations, changes are likely to be fundamentally interlinked and even interwoven. A change made in one part of an institution is likely to have an impact on other parts of the organisation if not beyond it.

Change management and leadership embrace context, content and process, and it is necessary to learn how to manage all those aspects and to fit them into one coherent whole. Whatever the nature, scope and extent of change proposed, it is important to ensure that the organisation looks beyond its immediate needs to the wider environment, and frames its change strategies and policies round the 'bigger picture', even if this means taking longer and planning further, and involves a more complex reality. Some form of change management structure or process will help to ensure that changes made in one particular area have a positive rather than a negative effect elsewhere, and any local positive outcomes are potentially replicated in other areas.

Strategic change management

For successful change to occur, and for real long-term advantage to be gained from it, then, there is a need for a coherent and extensive strategy that draws in all aspects of the environment within which the organisation is active. A systematic, well-ordered and properly constructed change management project will provide a 'route map' for change that will help to identify the required changes, the best order for implementing them and the pace at which they should be implemented, the key opportunities for success and the likely 'danger' areas where failure is most likely, the key prerequisites and the gaps that need to be filled before the project can proceed. Later chapters of this book look at change management structures and route maps for change that offer a framework within which changes can be put into the most efficient and effective order, ensuring as far as possible that pitfalls are avoided and opportunities taken and that the pace of change is that which is most appropriate for the particular context in which the change management process is taking place.

Defining strategy

A strategy is the outcome of some form of planning – 'an organised process for anticipating and acting in the future in order to carry out the [organisation's] mission' (Siess, 2002). Corrall (1994) defines strategic planning as:

| Box 1.6 | Strategic planning: a definition |

[Strategic planning is] essentially a process of relating an organisation and its people to their changing environment and the opportunities and threats in the marketplace; it is a process in which purposes, objectives and action programmes are developed, implemented, monitored, evaluated and reviewed ... [It is] particularly concerned with anticipating and responding to environmental factors, taking responsibility for change, and providing unity and direction to [an organisation's] activities. It is a tool for ordering one's perceptions about future environments in which one's decisions might be played out.

As Stueart and Moran (1998) point out:

> Planning is both a behaviour and a process; it is the process of moving an organisation from where it is to where it wants to be in a given period of time by setting it on a predetermined course of action and committing its human and physical resources to that goal.

It is important to recognise that there has to be a close fit between the high-level strategy and the actual day-to-day operations on which an organisation depends for survival. Tensions can arise between strategic and operational management, with the one emphasising the long-term, the other the immediate requirement. In practice, operational management should be at least partly concerned with what will happen more than twelve months ahead, while strategic management cannot be solely about what life will look like in five years' time.

Why is strategy so important in change management?

Collins and Porras (1994) found that organisations with a clear-defined purpose and a strong set of shared values do better than others within their sector: 'they exhibit vastly superior financial performance, better reputations, superior endurance records, and resilience to changes in leadership'. Crawford (1991) gives four reasons why strategy is so important in an organisational context. It focuses team effort; it brings integration across the organisation; it enables senior managers to delegate, in the knowledge that the strategy gives them and the rest of the workforce a framework within which to operate; and it requires the leadership of the organisation to be proactive rather than reactive. 'If it is necessary to state what a project's focus will be, chances are the investigation of the opportunities will be more thorough. And, if the strategic statement must include all critical guidelines, then its author had better study the selected opportunity thoroughly. In other words, having to write out strategy helps create better managers'.

Strategic planning will also need to take account of the organisation's capabilities, as against those of the rest of the sector. Sutherland and Canwell (2004) define capabilities as 'the key skills

| Box 1.7 | The importance of strategy |

- gives a focus;
- integrates;
- enables delegation;
- provides a framework;
- requires proactivity;
- demands data gathering and analysis.

which allow organisations to utilise and coordinate their resources ... at an optimum level in order to maximise their productivity and profitability'. Strategy, then, has to be worked out anew for each set of circumstances in which a strategic approach is required. There is nevertheless a wide range of generic techniques that can be applied in different circumstances and a number of these are discussed in later chapters. They encompass the key elements of strategy formulation, planning and implementation and include forecasting, scenario planning and risk management.

Summary

This chapter has introduced the idea of change, the concept of change management and strategy and its development, all in the context of the organisation in general and the not-for-profit organisation in particular, noting the especial challenge of managing in this latter kind of environment. It has looked at the key drivers for change and provided definitions and an outline typology of change and the major stages in change as part of a process of development or transition within an organisation. It has introduced the idea of organisational readiness for change and the concept of the learning organisation. The chapter also focuses on the management of change and the benefits of an organised, systematic approach to introducing change within the organisation. The chapter argues that it is only when there is a clear strategic direction, based on information, analysis, debate and agreement, that change management is likely to be successful in the longer term.

Notes

1. Pam Taylor, quoted in (2005) *Engage* 2(6).
2. House of Commons Education and Skills Committee, 2004–5. *UK e-University*. Third report, p. 3.
3. In the UK in recent years, the following laws have had a significant impact on the ways in which both private and public sector organisations operate: Telecommunications Act (1984); Data Protection Act (1998); Human Rights Act (1998); Freedom of Information Act (2000).
4. *http://en.wiktionary.org/wiki/change management*
5. *http://www.change-management-toolbook.com*
6. P. Birch, as quoted in *Leadership matters* (3): 8.

References

Amado, G. and Ambrose, A. (2001) *The Transitional Approach to Change*. London: Karnac Books.

Anderson, D. and Anderson, L.S.A. (eds) (2001) *Beyond Change Management: Advanced Strategies for Today's Transformational Leaders*. New York: Jossey Bass Wiley.

Aupperle, K. and Karimalis, G. (2001) 'Using metaphors to facilitate co-operation and resolve conflict: examining the case of Disneyland Paris'. *Journal of Change Management*, 2(1): 23–32.

Baker, D. (2004) *The Strategic Management of Technology*. Oxford: Chandos.

Baker, D. (2006) 'Digital library futures: a UK HE and FE perspective'. *Interlending and Document Supply*, 34(1): 4–8.

Brierley, P. (2005a) *Opportunities and Challenges for the Church of England Over the Next 15 Years: Some Statistical Trends and What They Imply for Church Leaders*. London: Christian Research.

Brierley, P. (2005b) *12 Trends in British Society: Some Statistical Trends and What They Imply for Church Leaders*. London: Christian Research.

Clark, B. (1998) *Creating Entrepreneurial Universities: Organisational Pathways of Transformation*. Oxford: Pergamon.

Collins, J.C. and Porras, J.I. (1994) *Built to Last: Successful Habits of Visionary Companies*. New York: Harper Business.

Corrall, S. (1994) *Strategic Planning for Library and Information Services*. London: ASLIB.

Corvey, C. and Leitzel, J. (2004) 'Integrated planning and change management at a research university'. *Change*, 36(1): 36–43.

Crawford, C.M. (1991) *New Products Management*. Homewood, IL: Irwin.

Cunningham, S., Tapsall, S., Ryan, Y., Stedman, L., Bagdon, K. and Flew, T. (1997) *New Media and Borderless Education*. Report 97/22, Higher Education Division. Australia: DETYA.

Department of Trade and Industry (1998) *Converging Technologies: Consequences for the New Knowledge-Driven Economy*. London: Future Unit, DTI.

Duke, C. (2002) *Managing the Learning University.* Buckingham: Society for Research into Higher Education and Open University.

Fink, S. (2000) *Crisis Management: Planning for the Inevitable.* Parkland, FL: Universal Publishers.

Greiner, L.E. (1972) 'Evolution and revolution as organisations grow'. *Harvard Business Review* 50(4): 37–46.

Higher Education Policy Institute (2005) *Mission Critical? Modernising HRM in HE.* Oxford: The Institute.

Huxley, L. (2005) 'What is organisational development?' *In Practice* 6: 1–4.

20. Involvement and Participation Association (2004) *Informing and Consulting Your Workforce: Nottinghamshire Heathcare NHS Trust.* IPA case study 7, series 4.

Lewin, K. (1947) 'Group decision and social change'. In *Readings in Social Psychology*, eds T.M. Newcomb and E.L. Hartley. New York: Henry Holt, pp. 340–4.

Middlehurst, R. (1999) 'New realities for leadership and governance in Higher Education?' *Tertiary Education and Management*, 5: 307–29.

Middlehurst, R. (2004) 'Changing internal governance: a discussion of leadership roles and management structures in UK universities'. *Higher Education Quarterly* 58(4): 258–79.

Nelson, R.R. and Winter, S.G. (1990) *An Evolutionary Theory of Economic Change.* Boston, MA: Harvard University Press.

Senker, J. (1990) *A Taster for Innovation: British Supermarkets' Influence on Food Manufacturers.* Bradford: Horton Publishing.

Siess, J.A. (2002) *Time Management, Planning and Prioritisation for Librarians.* Lanham: Scarecrow.

Slowey, M. (ed.) (1995) *Implementing Change from Within Universities and Colleges – 10 Personal Accounts.* London: Kogan Page

Solomon, E. (2001) 'The dynamics of corporate change: management's evaluation of stakeholder characteristics'. *Human Systems Management* 20(3): 257–66.

Sporn, B. (1999), 'Towards more adaptive universities: trends of institutional reform in Europe'. *Higher Education in Europe* 24(1): 23–34.

Stueart, R.D. and Moran, B.B. (1998) *Library and Information Centre Management.* Englewood, CO: Libraries Unlimited.

Sutherland, J, and Canwell, D. (2004) *Key Concepts in Strategic Management.* Basingstoke: Palgrave Macmillan.

Whetherly, J. (1998) *Achieving Change Through Training and Development.* London: Library Association Publishing.

Wills, J. (2004) 'Trade unionism and partnership in practice: evidence from the Barclays-Unifi agreement'. *Industrial Relations Journal* 35(4): 329–43.

Case study 1.1   Change in the UK

'Infant mortality has greatly reduced over the last 50 years, our diet has improved, and medical science has pioneered many life-enhancing changes. As a consequence our expected length of life has increased: a man born in 1951 could expect to live 66 years and a woman 71 years, while those born in 2001 can expect to live to 76 and 81 respectively. Another effect ... is that the number of centenarians is rapidly increasing, with the government predicting the number to reach 39,000 in England and Wales by 2036 and 95,000 by 2066.

The traditional concept of 'family' is currently changing quite dramatically. It used to be considered as a married couple, with or without children, and Government figures showed that in 1980 90 per cent of families were thus constituted. By 2005 this percentage had dropped to 65 per cent, and if present trends continue, by 2020 will be down to 35 per cent ... the proportions of both cohabiting couples and lone parents are increasing quite rapidly.

In 1961, 51 per cent of married couple households in Great Britain had at least one dependent child. In 2001, that was true of only 39 per cent of such households and will be down to 34 per cent by 2011. In 2011 there will be 715,000 fewer children 18 or under in the country than there were in 2001. That decline is made of two principal changes:

- A 17 per cent reduction in the number of dependent children in married couple households (2001 to 2011)

- A 41 per cent increase in the number of dependent children in lone parent households

Fewer children stems partly from the fact that more women are remaining childless than formerly, partly that women tend to start their family later, but mostly from the fact that they are having smaller families.

Girls do better than boys in exams, for example: in 2004 24 per cent of As awarded at A level were to girls, compared to 21 per cent to boys, and 20 per cent of A or A* GCSEs were for girls compared to 15 per cent of boys.

15 per cent of people expect to move in the coming year, although actual moving experience suggests only 10 per cent will in fact do so ... younger people move more than older people.

In the 1970s the number of people leaving the UK each year exceeded the number coming to these shores. Since the mid 1980s this has changed, and the number of immigrants has exceeded emigrants ever since. Some are asylum seekers, some are refugees, others are students coming to join their family or those seeking work. The latter are often needed to help with the general skills shortage in the UK. Almost half the migrant workers settle in the Greater London region ... The Government's Actuary Department, which is responsible for population projections, estimates that the net increase to our population for the foreseeable future will be at an average rate of 130,000 persons a year, a million every eight years, almost entirely immigrants.

Case study 1.1   Change in the UK (*Cont'd*)

One of the consequences of admitting many people from other countries to the UK is that those of religions other than Christianity increase in number. In the 2001 Population Census that showed that 72 per cent were Christian, 6 per cent of the population said they belonged to another religion. This latter percentage is likely to grow while the Christian percentage is likely to decline ... Those with no religion (which includes those not answering the religious question at all) were 22 per cent in 2001, but might well be 40 per cent by 2020 ... The growth of the other religions...is not uniform, as the Muslims are set to outpace the other non-Christian religions. Thus of the 8 per cent other religions in 2005, the Muslims were 38 per cent, but by 2020 this percentage could become 46 per cent, as the Muslim numbers swell from 1.5 million to 2.8 million.'

Source: Brierley (2005b).

Structure and culture

Introduction

This chapter is concerned with both organisational structure and organisational culture. Organisational structure and organisational strategy are inextricably linked. The best fit between structure and strategy, control and empowerment is not an easy one: 'choice of organisational structure has been recognised as leading to a problematic relationship between the respective desires for managerial control, organisational efficiency and responsiveness to external conditions and intended markets' (Thornhill, 2000). Creating and firmly establishing a new structure able to meet the demands of the organisation and its change agenda has to be balanced against the potential challenge of the organisation itself – or at least parts of it – being disengaged because they do not gain, or at least do not perceive themselves as gaining, from the restructuring process or its outcomes. At KPMG, for example, restructuring 'was the last thing that was needed as it often raises anxieties, leads to politicking and distracts from the real issues'; rather, the company needed to focus on a more fundamental review of itself, and most importantly its core values – what it actually stood for (Thornbury, 1999).

Organisational culture – sometimes referred to as 'the way we do things around here' – is a crucial factor in facilitating or denying change. An otherwise faultless change management process is still likely to fail to deliver its desired outcomes if insufficient account is taken of the culture – of the organisation, the sector or industry, the region and even the country in which the changes are taking place. Similarly, 'power' politics are endemic within organisations; often, the importance of viewing change as a political and a cultural process rather than a logical sequence of steps is overlooked. An understanding of an organisation's power structure or political 'make up' will also be key to being able to manage any changes well (Atkinson, 2003). In all but the smallest or the newest organisation, a culture or cultures will already be well embedded. These cultures – and the associated values, concepts, procedures and practices that have grown up with the organisation – are likely to have a strong impact on the extent to which other changes will be possible because they will seriously affect the willingness and even the ability of the workforce to learn and therefore adapt to new circumstances, structures and approaches.

Structure

An organisational structure encompasses relationships, both formal and informal. This 'internal institutional architecture – how [organisations] are constructed and organised – is heavily influenced by certain underlying principles and shaped by the nature of the activities that they undertake' (Middlehurst, 1999).

| **Box 2.1** | Key activities determining institutional architecture |

> ■ role and activities;
> ■ organisational and management frameworks;
> ■ finance and staffing arrangements.

Any and every organisation needs a structure. A good, fit-for-purpose structure will enable changes – continuous or discontinuous, small or large – to be made effectively and efficiently. There is no one perfect structure. What has worked in the past will not necessarily work in the future: changed environments and challenges will require different solutions. The key is to find a structure that works for the organisation as it needs to be, and that will allow it to operate in the future. The following need to be considered when determining the type of structure that will be most appropriate:

Organisational structure can help or hinder, support or block change. A fit-for-purpose structure that is appropriate to the changed circumstances and which facilitates and supports the desired changes and the process by which they are implemented will make a significant difference. Because of this, the structure of an organisation, especially when allied with the beliefs of the people who manage and control that structure, can result in a

Box 2.2   Key determinants of best structure

- type of organisation;
- past experiences;
- level of employee autonomy;
- previous experience of change;
- strength of inter-staff relationships.

powerful shaper of – and possibly opposition to – change. Structure even involves physical (re)arrangement – often a powerful aspect of change that needs to be carefully considered – and the location and relocation of people within an organisation can be important with regard to communications, dynamics and perceptions and beliefs about roles and hierarchy.

There is no single, perfect structure, just as there is no single correct approach to change management. When undergoing a period of change, structures might need to be similarly changed on a temporary basis in order to enable change to happen, for example a project management structure being overlaid on to the main, operational one. Structures need to be evaluated on a regular basis and, when and where necessary, reorganised or redesigned to make sure that they are the most appropriate for the given circumstances, context and environment. The internal environment can be controlled and developed, for example with regard to broader participation and a drive for continuous improvement; the external environment is a given – albeit a changing one – and trends need to be taken into account (but cannot be controlled) in designing new structures. For example, an increasing 'customer' focus (fee-paying students in universities is one such trend) needs to be matched by structures that incorporate market research, strong feedback mechanisms and staff development and training that emphasises the importance of the service user.

Types of structure

A basic description of organisational structure relates to the extent to which power and decision-making are centralised or decentralised. The more centralised, the fewer, more senior people are in control of what happens within the organisation.

Box 2.3   **Organisational structures and restructuring: key questions for the change manager**

- Is the structure the most appropriate one for the organisation, and if not, is restructuring in fact the main or, indeed, the only change required?
- If more widespread change is necessary, how might the organisational structure have to be changed – whether temporarily or permanently – in order to allow significant change?
- How durable will either the current or any new structure be in terms of longer-term change and its facilitation within the organisation?

In a decentralised organisation, decisions are taken at a 'lower' level, away from the higher management, with power and decision-making having been delegated to divisions, departments, groups or teams. The rationale for such an approach is that the people making the decisions are nearer to the 'front line' and therefore better able to make good decisions in the context of their knowledge and know-how, based on the reality of the situation that they are in, and also that they can respond rapidly without recourse to more senior levels of management for permission to proceed. It is also argued that, because staff feel more empowered, they will be better motivated and more effective in their work (Smart, 2002). In organisations that have a degree of delegation, there are likely to be business or decision-making units to which power and responsibility can be formally delegated,

Figure 2.1   **The centralised–decentralised axis**

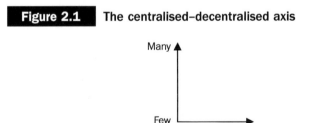

Centralised – Decentralised

typically with a budget attached to their operations. These cost centres may well have their own service level agreements or performance targets, against which their effectiveness within the organisation (and possibly outside it, if external comparisons are taking place) can be judged. The larger the organisation and the more delegated its decision-making structures and processes, the more likely that parts of the organisation will have their own hierarchies, systems and cultures, causing problems with the span and nature of control at the centre of the organisation, and the replication and duplication of effort in terms of certain activities. One approach to this issue is to have certain functions centralised (such as estates or human resources), with other, more specialist, activities devolved to decentralised groups.

Structural change has happened in the light of changing attitudes and fashions with regard to how best to organise work activity both in the public and private sectors. There has been a marked trend, for example, away from centrally managed or co-ordinated and hierarchical structures towards a broader range of flatter, arguably more flexible ways of arranging a business or activity. Restructuring – changing an organisational structure in some way – is both a means of changing and a change in itself. Decentralised structures, for example, have been seen as a necessary prerequisite of a more user- or customer-responsive organisation; in that sense, the new structure is a means to an end. Flat structures are typically intended to break down barriers and improve 'lateral' communication and networking across different parts and elements of the organisation; in this context, they are also perhaps more a change as an end in itself, though the new structure is usually designed to facilitate increased responsiveness within the organisation and develop flexibility in the face of further change. Structural change is often seen as a way of empowering staff to be both more involved and more committed to their work and the organisation of which they are a part.

Team structures have become increasingly popular, one of the key arguments being that a top-down, directive approach from senior management to a deferential workforce will not work in terms of the complex challenges facing organisations in the twenty-first century. There is a fear that in more mechanistic organisations, those in power will not change when change is necessary, and the structure (and possibly the direction) of the organisation will become increasingly outdated because it remains the same for too long. Team approaches fit with 'flatter', non-hierarchical structures, where information generation and dissemination, discussion and decision are across rather than down the organisation. Managing a flatter structure is challenging, and still requires control and order, good communication networks, strong managers and responsible staff working in an understood and accepted environment and culture if it is to succeed fully.

ICT and structure

Information and communications technology (ICT) developments can have a significant influence on organisational structure. In particular, the use of such technology can change significantly the way information – and hence, power – are distributed across the organisation (Baker, 2004). Take the impact of electronic mail on communication networks within and between organisations: employees feel more empowered, and traditional and more hierarchical structures are 'flattened', because interaction between staff is levelled. ICT systems thus open up significant possibilities for change, with the prospect of teleworking and 'virtual' organisations operating across previous boundaries, whether physical or structural, cultural or spatial.

Structural change in this context may be evolutionary, for example the gradual increase in the use of electronic mail as the main medium of (written) communication, or significant and revolutionary, as with the rapid development of online systems that obviate the need for face-to-face interaction such as is seen with electronic publishing. The key challenge here is the extent to which the organisation can manage the technology proactively rather than just react to it, especially given the rapid changes that ICT developments engender. Poor technology implementation could actually restrict broader change, as when the structure has to be changed to suit the technology rather than the other way round because the technology does not have the flexibility or the fitness for purpose for the institution. Training in the effective use of the technology must be an integral part of any ICT implementation project, not least as a way of ensuring positive attitudes to the ICT as part of (structural) change.

Culture

Culture can be defined at a number of levels. Overall national culture plays a very large part in determining the success of major change initiatives, even at the organisational level. The 'cultural atmosphere' of a nation is something that changes over time and, according to Lewin (1947), can be changed itself; however, though at the same time, 'traditions' can have a long lifespan and may be a barrier to fundamental change if this is introduced too rapidly or in the wrong context, because there is a residual belief that the 'old ways' are better. Organisations that are innovating may need to try to get society 'onside' if they are making changes, or at least recognise the current common values across the environment within which they are operating. Otherwise, they may flounder once their proposed changes or innovations are implemented: a changing organisation may suffer for its initiative if society disagrees or is moving in a different direction. Deep, detailed and sensitive knowledge of the contextual culture within which change is being managed is of paramount importance if success is to be achieved.

Culture may also vary between regions or countries, though it is important to avoid stereotypes in this context. To what extent, for example, can or should one generalise about 'British' cultural attitudes in the workplace, such as valuing tradition or respectability; respect for, and comfort with, hierarchy; or an unwillingness to bring unsuitable or unsavoury topics 'out into the open'? In larger organisations and sectors, different cultures are likely to have an impact. Culture will also vary from sector to sector. In commerce and industry, for example, the profit motive is likely to be a greater driver for change and a basis of the prevailing culture than in the public sector. Culture – nationally, regionally, locally and organisationally – is changing all the time and what may be an acceptable way of working and managing within one culture or era may not be acceptable in another. For example, participation and democracy in the workplace are now key, accepted, aspects of organisational structures and behaviours with a strong focus on empowerment and a downplaying of bureaucracy and hierarchy.

Organisational culture

The term 'organisational culture' is widely used. 'Edgar Schein originally proposed the notion that organisational culture is framed by what a business assumes to be true about itself and the environment in which it operates. He also suggested that culture is unconscious, but can be learned and reinforced when problems are repeatedly solved using the same approach' (Sutherland and Canwell, 2004). Writers on management may differ (Martin, 1992) about whether culture is something that an organisation has or is something that the organisation actually is, and the extent to which culture is the 'glue' that holds together an organisation through consensus and even integration. The organisation as a social system is made up of a whole series of symbols, rituals, myths, stories and shared history that can certainly exert a strong influence on the people who form a part of the organisation, though while there are these commonalities and similarities, there are also differences, disagreements and conflicts that also shape the organisation and its culture (Hughes, 1996).

Even the very smallest organisations are likely to have a whole set of cultures, from 'top' to 'bottom'. There is, for example, the senior staff's view of the organisation, based on a strategic and managerial approach and typically led by the 'chief executive', who will 'set the tone' for much of the management team's behaviour and attitude, though it will also inherit inbuilt cultural traits. One key decision for senior managers is the extent to which this inheritance is acceptable in terms of their aims and ambitions for the organisation. Another important aspect of managing culture change is the dynamics of particular groups within the organisation and the extent to which those dynamics work for or against the organisation, either as it currently is or as it wants to be in the future.

In any case, people behave differently in different situations (for example between work and home, in public and in private). Lewin (1947) developed the 'field theory', where behaviour is the function of both the person and the environment, with personal characteristics and social situation interacting to produce a particular set of responses and actions that will not be reproduced if any of these variables (environment, function, characteristics, situation) change. Culture change, then, will result from one or more changes in these elements. Changes in the environment, for example, will alter how individuals – and the particular group(s) to which they belong – feel; understanding how, and what, changes affect people may help the change manager to steer change in certain, desired, directions.

Organisational culture is typically based on a set of values that are tacitly understood and accepted. The staff may not speak about or against these values, but they work within them. These values will tend to emphasise and reinforce tradition, and hence limit future options for change. In consequence, a good deal of literature on the subject of management argues that the key task is to change culture so that it is properly 'aligned' with the aims and objectives of the organisation – particularly as expressed in the specific goals of a change management programme. The expectation will be that the staff of the organisation will not only be in sympathy with all the key elements of long-term strategy (mission, values, aims and objectives) but also that they will actively support the implementation process through involvement in programmes and projects and changes in their own behaviour. This alignment of strategy with staff, of managers with managed, is meant to be beneficial for all concerned: 'employees with strong commitment tend to be highly productive and loyal, while those [organisations] with low levels [of commitment] tend to have higher incidence of turnover, absenteeism, stress-related health claims and other workforce problems' (Ward and Davies, 1995). '[Organisational] success can be traced most directly back to a very strong culture, founded on a set of beliefs and values' (Deal and Kennedy, 1982). This 'social model' of the organisation assumes that everyone can think, adapt and develop both themselves and the organisation as a whole.

Types of culture

Different types of culture may be more productive than others, depending upon the overall environment and what needs to change – or, indeed, remain the same. There are many ways of categorising organisational cultures. One broad set of groupings relates to process and role, power, task and reward. In reality, of course, most organisations contain a combination of cultures.

Table 2.1   A broad typology of organisational culture

Type	Comment
Process and role (bureaucratic culture)	Where a bureaucratic process or role culture is prevalent, the organisation is unlikely to adapt to change easily, not least because it either does not foster a workforce or management where the need for change is perceived or, when the need is perceived, the response is not sufficiently speedy. Change is only likely to occur as a relatively long-term process, with feedback on the effectiveness of any change being at a slow pace. While a slow and long-term change process may not in itself be wrong, it will be necessary to ensure that the speed of change is sufficiently fast to keep pace with what is going on in the 'outside world'. A bureaucracy that does not keep checking on external environment factors will become increasingly detached from the 'real world'. Bureaucracies are seen as increasingly unhelpful at times of major change, with hierarchical structures being a major blockage to staff empowerment – widely regarded as an essential prerequisite where major change is required.

Table 2.1   A broad typology of organisational culture (*Cont'd*)

Type	Comment
Power (strong central or hierarchically-based culture)	A power-based culture may enable rapid and radical change to take place, though such a culture is likely to be centred upon only a small number of people or even one person. Reliance on such a small number could be dangerous if they leave or lose influence, and in any case they may not be able to carry the broader workforce with them, so that their changes are not fully embedded in the longer term.
Task (project and goal-oriented culture)	Task cultures are just that: they focus on 'getting the job done' and are, at their best, flexible and sensitive to the needs of the organisation and its changing environment, though they can also be internally competitive.
Reward (recognising and rewarding talent and success)	Reward cultures foster personal success and ambition, with the 'bright sparks' especially being recognised and rewarded.

Sutherland and Canwell (2004) talk of 'adaptive cultures' where the organisation is 'forward-looking and [tends] to be guided by positive change'. As a result, as the external environment changes, the organisation is more able to respond positively. Sutherland and Canwell list the key differences between organisations with high-performance adaptive cultures and those without.

Sub-cultures

There will then be a whole range of other cultures or sub-cultures within the organisation, often operating independently of each other. These cultures may be based on managerial sub-units or 'departments' within the organisation, or on groups of staff undertaking the same function or on the same grade (as for example secretarial or technical staff), or they may revolve around like-minded people (such as an ethnic or religious group within the larger workforce). The management team is likely to be concerned with changing the culture of the organisation and the rest of the workforce where the current prevalent environment is not seen as conducive to the achievement of the goals set by that senior team. Other

Table 2.2	Adaptive and non-adaptive cultures
Organisations with high-performance adaptive cultures	**Organisations without high-performance adaptive cultures**
Ability to maintain a fit between the culture and the business context	Short-termism
Active support within the organisation to identify problems	Emphasis on structure and systems
Active support within the organisation to identify problems and find workable solutions	Inability to focus on multiple stakeholders
Feeling of confidence amongst employees	Biased perception of the competition
Trust	Inability to deal with negative suggestions or observations
Risk taking	Feeling of invulnerability
Proactivity	Alternative strategies ignored

groups may have different reasons for supporting – or opposing – change. Sub-cultures can lead to significant resistance within an organisation, especially if they demonstrate a coherent (if implicit) and well-embedded structure underneath a managerial one. In higher education, for example, there is typically an administrative structure that can be both supportive of, and/or antagonistic to, the academic culture and aspirations of the institution; and vice versa (Middlehurst, 1999; Duke, 2002). Successful change management processes will need to recognise these sub-cultures, however harmful or antagonistic they may be towards the proposed changes. Indeed, it is often important to ensure that these sub-cultures are brought out into the open so that the challenges and blockages that they may present can be properly tackled and subversion avoided.

Power

Power is an important aspect of the organisation, its structure and its culture. 'Power equates to the ability to command. [It] not only conveys the ability to direct operations, but also allows those with power to delegate to those at lower levels of the organisational structure to exercise power on their behalf. Clearly power can also be exemplified through the hierarchical structure of an organisation. This reflects the power structure within the organisation, notwithstanding any functional inter-dependencies between those with power and those with the ability to control the business operations' (Sutherland and Canwell, 2004). A description of the organisation's structure – typically in the form of a chart – will show where the 'legitimate power' or formal authority is within the organisation, but may not necessarily plot where the real power lies (Greenleaf et al., 2002). Informal power may be delegated by those with formal power on a particular basis – such as a working party or a task-and-finish group – or may be acquired over a period of time by a member of staff by virtue of their length of service, experience or expertise in a particular area that gives them a reputation and respect within the organisation. Informal power may also come through a representational role – as for example in the case of trades unions. Pettinger (2004) summarises the sources of power within an organisation:

Table 2.3   **Sources of power within the organisation**

Source	Description
Physical	Dependent on the ability to dominate others
Traditional	Based on accepted customs and practices
Expert	Focused on specialist knowledge in a given environment
Charismatic	Revolving around a charismatic or high-profile person
Resource	Ability to pay for change and buy influence
Pressure groups	Proposing a particular viewpoint and persuading others to adopt it
Cluster or specialist groups	Made up of people with a common purpose, specialism or view within the organisation – as for example all those opposed to a particular change
Trade unions	A particular form of cluster group, with its members' interests as the driving force
External agencies	Including statutory bodies that may have a hold over the organisation in what it does and how it does it
Stakeholder groups	All with particular interests and views on how the organisation should operate and in which direction

The challenge of changing organisational cultures

Organisational cultures tend to be firmly embedded and may be difficult to alter, not least because there is often more comfort in staying as we are than making any changes in a well-established and understood cultural environment. On the other hand, the traditions of an organisation are important and should not just be disregarded without due consideration for the consequences and the (dis-)advantages of change. Some embedded cultures are likely to underpin an environment that is so antipathetic to that required in order for change – and especially radical change – to succeed that some form of culture change programme is necessary. Top management needs to be adaptable in such circumstances, looking to remove both obvious and hidden barriers by spanning both organisational and cultural change. This requires a widespread and objective view that is focused on the broadest and deepest possible integration of social, political, managerial, human resource and strategic elements. It has to be realised that these all interact and have an impact on each other, and on the way in which specific changes within organisations must be developed and undertaken.

Is it actually possible to change cultures within an organisation, so that everyone works to a common goal? It should be noted that the question is about changing culture, not getting rid of it. All organisations will always have some form of culture or cultures. The issue is whether or not the prevalent one provides the best environment for the desired changes to be successfully embedded. If culture is something that the organisation has, then changing – or at least manipulating – that culture or cultures is likely to be possible. If the culture is the organisation, then it is unlikely that the culture – or any kind of major culture change – is likely to be fully managed or completely altered, other, perhaps, than by a major change by the majority of those who form the culture that makes up the organisation. There is no doubt that people can affect the way an organisation works or a project is implemented, but it is not necessarily the case that the workforce can ever be the sole, or even the prime, driver of fundamental culture change. However, the manager needs to be aware of the circumstances and situations where people in general can influence change within an organisation through the dominant culture of which they are a part; and, as already noted, organisational culture is usually a heterogeneous mix of sub-cultures, some spanning the organisation and others prevalent in only one area or group of staff. It will be important to determine which cultures – or parts of cultures – are to be changed, or which are being altered to fit in with others, and why.

Approaches to culture change

There are a number of potential components for culture change. Culture change will often require a fundamental rethink of traditional perceptions, as for example in further and higher education, where support staff have often been labelled as 'non-academics' even though they contribute much to the academic experience and, as a result of the changing and innovative use of technology often play the key role in the delivery of education. Ideally, the change manager should aim to establish a culture that sees potential change as normal and acceptable – the 'learning organisation' discussed in more detail elsewhere in this book. Such an organisation is deemed to be capable of taking control of change rather than being directed by it.

However, there is no single, 'correct' way in which an organisational culture or cultures can or should be changed. An organisation will have to determine the current focus and structure of its predominant culture or cultures and the necessary changes to that culture. It is unlikely that a single approach or mechanism will change something as ingrained and pervasive as an organisational culture; what may work in one environment could well be unsuccessful in another because of the significant differences between two organisations, even ones operating within the same sector. However, organisations need to be fair and correct in all that they do. Culture change policies need to be comprehensively and properly planned, and consistently executed, so that they achieve the reforms that they set out to introduce and embed. Culture change, like any other change process, will require consistency and commitment among those in management.

The change manager will need to decide on the desired results and on a realistic timescale for achieving them. In this context, external timescales – whether of the society at large or the industry sector – will be important. A low rate of culture change is not in itself a negative position to be in, provided that the organisation can survive external pressures that ideally would necessitate a faster pace of change in the meantime. Culture change may be happening naturally within the organisation – whether from internal or external factors – and accelerating an existing change may therefore be possible. Even so, there will be a limit to the extent that major culture change(s) can be accelerated.

If an organisational culture has to be altered or even radically changed, then the change manager must have good reason to do so, such as a strong business case: 'culture change in organisations is often conducted solely on idealistic grounds, so it is not surprising when programmes run out of momentum. At KPMG, there were plenty of solid reasons why we should change our culture and, throughout the process, we constantly made links with issues, strategic goals and bottom-line performance in the global firm' (Thornbury, 1999).

Culture change will always need to be handled through good management and with sensitivity. It will be necessary to build up a comprehensive picture of the organisational and social context in which changes are to be made, and in particular where the culture itself is to be transformed; sound knowledge of current conceptions and beliefs and an understanding of the reasons why they are held is crucial. Understanding why certain cultures hold sway can help change managers to determine the rationale and the strategies that will enable them to change those cultures, in favour of a new culture, to best effect. The customs and norms, the ceremonies and events of the organisation need to be examined and reviewed in detail, for they say much about its organisational culture. It will also need to be borne in mind that culture – at all levels – is constantly changing, and the change manager needs to be aware of developments and alterations in the relevant environments when introducing change.

If the desired culture change is to be achieved, then it will be necessary to consider the extent to which it is possible to manage the views and beliefs of the workforce and to mould them into the shape that the change managers need in order to ensure that the staff culture is brought into line with the organisation's requirements. If people can be encouraged – or even 'made' – to believe in a preferred and single overall organisational culture, then the most effective way of doing so is by aiming to ensure that the resulting culture is a full and proper reflection of all sections of the workforce. But going beyond the ways in which employees behave to attempt to change how they think and feel is a major task, and one that has ethical as well as practical considerations. If cultural ideas and beliefs are inherent, then it is likely to be very difficult to change them in any way other than superficially. The older and more traditional the organisation, the more it may struggle in the sense of coming to terms with, and implementing, culture change – for example, in higher education, where there is often a 'weighting' against women, younger people and people from different ethnic communities (Middlehurst, 1999).

Legislative observance can be used as a means of changing culture, for example in relation to equality of opportunity, though it is one thing to observe the 'letter' of the law and another to follow its 'spirit'. Changes in rules and policies can help to eliminate old cultures and establish new ones, but there will also be a need to set goals and introduce measurements in order to ensure that culture change really is taking place. However, legal guidelines can help to engender a positive and encouraging attitude, provided the legal requirement can be translated into a recognition across the institution that the change is desirable.

Recognising diversity

Cultural heterogeneity can strengthen an organisation rather than weaken it. It is argued (Martin, 1992; Middlehurst, 1999) that a diverse workforce will provide a better, more successful model for an organisation, because it needs to succeed in an increasingly diverse society and, it is also argued, it will be more flexible and able to cope with change by virtue of its diversity, with the broadest range of skills, experiences and attitudes available to the organisation as it faces future challenges. For example, in recent years, there have been positive moves to embrace and increase diversity in terms of the gender, social and ethnic backgrounds of the workforce – making diversity the right, normal, accepted, embedded situation in the workplace. This is likely to make the goal of a homogeneous work culture less possible, regardless of whether or not it is actually desirable.

Openly recognising and encouraging cultural diversity is more likely to result in a healthy approach to change management than is a superficial and tokenistic agreement on a single overarching – but emotionally unsupported – single culture model regardless of the on-the-ground reality. 'In our experience [in New Zealand] women are more likely to provide creative ideas for bringing about change in key areas and these are often a challenge to the traditional ways of operating; women managers ... are ideally placed to fulfil a role as critic and conscience' (Brooks and MacKinnon, 2001). Without a sufficiently diverse senior management team, the leaders of culture change themselves may be working within an inadequate knowledge base. Take the example of women in senior positions within higher education: 'what has counted and still counts as knowledge has been severely gendered, so that women's relationship to knowledge and its production and reproduction has been diminished and devalued. For the most part universities, dominated as they are by men as academics and managers, do not produce neutral, still less emancipatory, knowledge' (Brooks and MacKinnon, 2001).

Encouraging and ensuring diversity is itself a change management challenge. Organisations need to ensure that the best possible people are employed at all levels of the organisation, and training and development programmes may be needed to ensure that this objective and the aspiration to ensure an appropriately diverse workforce are complementary without compromising the legislative framework – notably in relation to positive action and positive discrimination. If women and people from black and multi-ethnic backgrounds are to be employed, they must be valued rather than underestimated or looked down upon; the blockages to their career development and promotion within the organisation will also need to be tackled.

Culture change in context

It is important to ensure that a management process concentrating on culture change is not undertaken in isolation; it must form part of a larger change programme: 'culture change cannot stand alone ... it has to be part of an overall set of mutually reinforcing organisational improvement activities ... the purpose of culture change is to provide a coherent set of attitudes and values to underwrite an overall programme of organisational change' (Williams et al., 1993).

Before embarking on any kind of change management programme, it is crucial to ensure clarity of purpose in terms of what the organisation is aiming to achieve. While the key aims and objectives will vary between organisations – or even within organisations in terms of different types of project – unless the overall direction is clear, then poor decisions and implementation pathways are likely to be made or chosen. Knowledge of the organisation needs to be comprehensive and detailed, as well as strategic, and encompass qualitative understanding of the social and 'political' dimensions as well as the quantitative analysis of its strengths and weaknesses.

Senior managers must recognise that a superficial conformity to the desired (by the management) organisational culture may mask significant antipathy (Duke, 2002). Nowhere is this phenomenon of 'espoused theory versus theory in use' more marked than when the workforce is only paying lip service to an ideal in which they do not really believe. Real culture change is only likely to take place if the process takes into account – and combines – the cultural ideals and aspirations of both management and workforce. A process that stresses only the cultural values of the employer is unlikely to be fully embraced by the employees. In some organisations, those who need to change most in order for a culture to be altered may be the management, rather than the workforce at large.

It may be possible for the change manager to exploit the strengths of different and even conflicting cultures in order to create a stronger organisation that is more capable of responding to the challenges and pressures that make change necessary. Staff may respond more positively to change if they can nevertheless feel the security, safety and consistency of a bureaucratic culture without that feeling stopping a more competitive, task-oriented overlay to that culture developing, and while a personal rewards dimension may also be added to that overlay, it may be difficult to combine that mix of cultures with a strong, centralised, power-based approach. On the other hand, a 'merged' culture of professional discipline and an entrepreneurial ethic could be a 'winning combination' in present-day public sector environments: a 'responsible freedom' that empowers staff to develop their own initiative and innovate is unlikely to result in either chaos or stultification if it is clear where the boundaries lie.

People change

Good people skills and techniques will be essential in the management of culture change. The less acute the divergence between management's and employees' ideas, the more likely the changes proposed and implemented will be long lasting. Change managers will need to limit the extent to which they try to change a culture if there is the potential for widespread resistance because the existing dominant culture or cultures are very strong. It may be more practical and effective to concentrate on changing behaviours rather than attitudes in some circumstances, provided that such an approach is perceived as relevant and constructive by the organisation at large. Staff in general, and middle management in particular, may be incentivised to support culture change with rewards and recognition being linked only to new ways of working and the goals of the (culture) change programme.

Personnel or Human Resource Management (HRM) specialists within the organisation have an important role to play in managing culture change, helping to make sure that it is both sustainable and widespread, given their dual role as a 'management' department on the one hand and a major interface with the workforce on the other. Much will depend on the position and reputation of the HR department within an organisation – and particularly the extent to which it is adaptable and flexible as well as effective and efficient – and on its relations with the workforce and their representatives. If HR staff are trusted and respected, then they can both facilitate dialogue and communication, working to marry top-down approaches with bottom-up ideas and aspirations.

Training and development – and in particular experiential training – is an essential element in the effective management of culture change. Longitudinal rather than short-term training is likely to be particularly important in helping culture change. This requires the organisation to take a necessarily long-term view of the change process, and to be willing to spend more time and resources and to put up with a degree of disruption in order to benefit from later culture change by taking a long-term view of the development of the workforce and how it can influence change within the organisation. 'Profit' in a cultural sense can be a very long-term aim, but, once reached, the rewards can be significant.

Summary

This chapter has considered structure and culture, two key environment factors that determine the extent to which change can be introduced and managed successfully within the organisation. At times, changing the existing structure or the prevalent culture is the major aspect of the change itself; at other times, structure and culture either provide a 'backdrop' to the change management project or process and/or restructuring, and culture change is only one element of a much bigger change programme.

The chapter looked at the institutional architecture that underpins the organisation and considered the key determinants of the best, most fit-for-purpose structure, while recognising that there is no single, ideal, structure that can help (or hinder) change. The key is to evaluate the structure in the context of both internal and external environments and what needs to be achieved. There are merits in both centralised and decentralised structures, depending upon the particular circumstances in which the organisation finds itself and the extent to which rapid, major change is required. The more empowering a structure is, however, the more likely that long-term change will succeed. Devolved structures can nevertheless challenge the senior management in terms of consistency of approach and the development and maintenance of a single, unifying organisational culture. Structural change can be evolutionary rather than revolutionary, and restructuring 'by stealth' is possible, not least when technology change is one of the main drivers.

Culture is a major factor in an organisation's ethos, activities, outlook and potential for success through change and development. Most organisations will in fact possess many cultures, all of which have to be recognised if not actually changed. A single individual is likely to belong to more than one culture, depending upon the particular environment or context, whether at work or home. An organisational culture is likely to be intangible and even indefinable, though it will be ever-present. Changing culture to match strategy is a key, ideal, goal of change management, but it is typically difficult to achieve completely. Different types of culture will favour particular types of behaviour, approach and even people; the key is to aim for a culture or cultures that are capable of adapting to changed and changing circumstances. The change manager will need to identify where the sources of power – informal as well as formal – are within the organisation, and deal with them, harnessing individuals and groups that have a particular power base positively as far as possible, or negating that power where it is having a detrimental influence on the change management process. Changing culture is ultimately about changing people, their place within the organisation, their attitudes and behaviour – arguably the greatest single challenge that the change manager will face. There will always need to be a very good reason for culture change, and the broader context must also be taken into account at all stages.

References

Atkinson, P. (2003) 'Reality testing: strategies for a political and behavioural change process'. *Training Journal*, 22(6).

Baker, D. (2004) *The Strategic Management of Technology*. Oxford: Chandos.

Brooks, A. and Mackinnon, A. (2001) *Gender and the Restructured University*. Buckingham: Open University.

Deal, T. and Kennedy, A. (1982) *Corporate Cultures*. Harmondsworth: Penguin.

Duke, C. (2002) *Managing the Learning University*. Buckingham: Society for Research into Higher Education and Open University.

Greenleaf, R.K. (2002) *Servant Leadership: a Journey into the Nature of Legitimate Power and Greatness*. Mahwah, NJ: Paulist Press.

Hughes, D. (1996) 'NHS managers as rhetoricians: a case of culture management?' *Sociology of Health and Illness* 18(3): 219–314.

Lewin, K. (1947) 'Group decision and social change'. In *Readings in Social Psychology*, eds T.M. Newcomb and E.L. Hartley. New York: Henry Holt, pp. 340–4.

Martin, J. (1992) *Cultures in Organisations: Three Perspectives*. New York: Oxford University Press.

Middlehurst, R. (1999) 'New realities for leadership and governance in Higher Education?' *Tertiary Education and Management*, 5: 307–29.

Pettinger, R. (2004) *Contemporary Strategic Management*. Basingstoke: Palgrave Macmillan.

Smart, J.K. (2002) *Real Delegation: How To Get People To Do Things For You and Do Them Well*. New York: Prentice Hall.

Sutherland, J, and Canwell, D. (2004) *Key Concepts in Strategic Management*. Basingstoke: Palgrave Macmillan.

Thornbury, J. (1999), 'KPMG: revitalising culture through values'. *Business Strategy Review* 10(4): 1–15.

Thornhill, A., Lewis, P., Saunders, M. and Millmore, M. (2000) *Managing Change: a Human Resource Strategy Approach*. Harlow: Financial Times/Prentice Hall.

Ward, E.A. and Davies, E. (1995) 'The effect of benefit satisfaction on organisational commitment'. *Compensations and Benefits Management* 111(3): 35–41.

Williams, A., Dobson, P. and Walters, M. (1993) *Changing Culture – New Organisational Approaches*. Second edition. London: Institute of Personnel Management.

Case study 2.1   **Developing library networks for NHS staff: the evolution of the London Library and Information Development Unit (LLIDU)**

Keywords: *external environment, constant change, strategic planning, change and continuity, healthcare, libraries.*

1. The context

The National Health Service (NHS) is always changing. In 1995, the North East and North West Thames regions merged to become the North Thames region and their two library co-ordinating units merged to form the North Thames Regional Library and Information Unit (NTRLIU). The libraries within the region were small and the librarians professionally isolated, whilst the networks were dispersed and fragmented with funding disparities between different services and professions. The libraries also operated within a fast-changing NHS.

Recognition of the need to modernise and reform the NHS was leading to major changes in the way health services were funded, managed and delivered. The first official policy guidance on health libraries for over 30 years was issued in 1997. In this, a number of drivers for change were evident: for example, the need for equity of provision within and between professions and for expansion of provision to include all NHS staff, the need to move from printed to electronic sources and to embrace IT, the need to take account of changes in education and training and the need to move towards greater partnership-working.

As part of this drive, it was decided that library budgets should be held centrally. Librarians were no longer answerable only to the hospitals that had provided their funding; their services were instead effectively subcontracted through the NTRLIU, and a number of stakeholders started to take an interest.

2. Implementing strategic change

The changes to be implemented necessitated a lot of work, both to develop the library and information services in line with new strategy and demands, and to develop fuller understanding and 'buy-in' among staff. To help with the implementation of a region-wide, collaborative strategy, and to develop a more coordinated and equitable service, the Library and Information Development Unit (LIDU) was set up in 1999 under a Regional Director of Education and Training, himself a former Dean of Postgraduate Medicine.

LIDU, supported by strong leadership from the Director, helped colleagues to deal with culture and role change by facilitating projects which contributed to developing a multidisciplinary approach to library provision, closer links with regional R&D and IT and service level agreements with Higher Education libraries. They also worked to rationalise and develop partnerships that would extend the range of services available to NHS staff and to increase the use of information technology in the sector. Leadership, partnership and communication strategies were coordinated through the Unit. What is more, as change agents, LIDU's staff helped to create a system of empowerment and continuous learning among and librarians and others, including healthcare professionals.

Case study 2.1   **Developing library networks for NHS staff: the evolution of the London Library and Information Development Unit (LLIDU) (*Cont'd*)**

The Director acted as a champion for the change management programme. Two important outcomes of this were:

1. LIDU gained two new posts – one in IT and one in Training and Development. Training and development, including lifelong learning, was particularly important, because the librarians needed new skills to manage change and to deal with the needs of a changing NHS workforce as well as to become competent and confident in the use of IT.
2. Libraries moved from a solely medical to a multi-disciplinary focus. This represented a huge and difficult culture shift, with library staff and users unused and sometimes unwilling to share facilities. Here, the Director's medical background was helpful as he used his influence and knowledge to explain the reasons for change, especially to senior medical staff.

3. Devolution
As LIDU continued to evolve, it worked with Education Consortia to set up more local groupings of libraries who served NHS staff. These Consortia held significant education and training funding and, in return for investment in libraries, insisted on stronger marketing and business development strategies for libraries to help ensure long-term sustainability. Individual Consortia projects built local capacity and complemented region-wide projects to develop networked information systems, linking libraries and librarians together.

Even so, despite an innovative programme of active and keen change management, getting buy-in from librarians and users was often hard, especially regarding Internet and IT development. Both groups were interested in what would bring local benefit but were wary of general change, which might cause loss locally. Consequently, change had to be transparent, using consultation and involvement to gain ownership.

4. Further change
Just as LIDU was becoming established, further change occurred within the NHS in 2000. Regions were abolished and Workforce Development Consortiums (WDCs) were introduced. London was split into five WDCs. LIDU was prepared for this, having written - using input from librarians and users - a major strategic and developmental review anticipating the change (entitled *The Libr@ry is Open*). This review was used to ensure that all the libraries would be ready for the changes when the time came. Its existence also meant that those leading the change from the very top would be aware of the contribution that Library and Information Services could and should make to their agendas.

By 2001, LIDU had itself evolved into the London Library and Information Development Unit (LLIDU). The Unit focused on getting everyone involved,

Case study 2.1   **Developing library networks for NHS staff: the evolution of the London Library and Information Development Unit (LLIDU) (*Cont'd*)**

for example by the launch of a new and ambitious partnership project, Knowledge Access 24 (24-hour access for NHS staff to clinical research information), and by the creation of a new integrated, Electronic Knowledge Access Team (EKAT) who eventually became responsible to the London Health Library Partnership (LHLP) of WDC coordinating librarians.

These changes affected LLIDU, which closed in 2003 when the need for its regional level strategic role ceased. EKAT continued operational work under the aegis of the LHLP. The library networks continue to change, develop and flourish even though change is beckoning yet again.

Lessons that can be learnt from the experiences of LLIDU include:

1. Do not get mired in a 'blame' culture, where those implementing change blame those on the ground for their scepticism and lack of cooperation and those on the ground blame those implementing change for not listening to and understanding their concerns. Seek to move forward and show people the advantages of the change to them and the wider community.

2. Understand that change is a constant, and that there can be no resting on laurels if one process is successful.

3. Secure funding to carry out the required changes.

4. Provide clear, strong leadership, including leadership in partnership.

5. Understand the context of change – especially political imperatives, power structures and funding streams.

6. Cultivate new skills suitable for a political environment – for example, influencing, persuasion and advocacy.

7. Win over a powerful and senior manager into the role of a champion.

8. Sell the change to people affected by it, and show them how they can benefit from it (or at least how the pros outweigh the cons).

9. Provide training and development, so that staff have the skills to deal with anything new brought in by the changes.

10. Be kind to yourself and others: some people exposed to change may be bruised in the process while others flourish. Encourage and support others to make small steps as well as big leaps. Change can make people grow both as individuals and in their profession.

3

Building blocks

Introduction

This chapter is concerned with the 'building blocks' of change management – those essential prerequisites and elements without which any change project is likely to be unsuccessful. It looks at why change may be needed and the importance of having or developing environmental knowledge before determining when, where and how to change. It suggests that a planning framework, good timing and realistic timescales are key elements of success in change management, as are the allocation of sufficient resources and a willingness to change direction or even backtrack if the change is not working out as intended, with a regular 'virtuous' change management evaluation cycle ensuring that problem indicators are identified early enough to take remedial action.

The chapter then looks at a range of attributes required of the organisation and its management: commitment, consistency, integrity and trust, good communications and staff motivation, the latter attribute assisted by involvement, engagement, encouragement and empowerment of the workforce wherever possible. The need for, and appropriateness of, 'top-down' and 'bottom-up' approaches, and the question of balancing change and continuity within the organisation are also considered. Any major change management project is likely to meet at least some opposition, and the reasons for resistance to change and how to respond to it, including through conflict management, are considered.

Rationale for change

There must be a reason or purpose for wanting to change. The simpler and clearer the basic goal of the change management process is, the more likely it will be to 'take hold' within the organisation, not least because the rationale for why change is necessary should be easier to communicate. If the reason why change has to happen cannot be explained and justified, then it is likely that the need for change has not been thought through properly and fully and the proposals will not be easy to implement because those affected by them will not see why they should co-operate. Ideally, the change management process should be aiming to achieve a single goal, such as 'to stay in business' or 'to be top of the league table', or 'to improve efficiency by 20 per cent'. In reality, there will be a number of goals that need to be identified, agreed and delivered in order to make the overarching aim achievable.

Box 3.1   **Key questions in decision-making**

1. Have I defined the objective?
2. Do I have sufficient information?
3. What are the feasible options?
4. Have I evaluated them correctly?
5. What is the best possible outcome?
6. What is the worst possible outcome?
7. Is 5 worth 6?
8. Can I live with 6?
9. Does the decision feel right now that I have begun to implement it?

Maintaining or developing an organisation in which strategic thinking can flourish is a critical success factor in change management – and, indeed, management in more general terms. So too is the visionary ability and capacity of the organisation's leadership in particular. In recent years, the need to adapt to rapidly-changing circumstances and to marry operational needs with strategic needs and thinking has led to the formulation of the concepts of organisational development and the learning organisation, discussed elsewhere in this book. Strategies for deciding on changes and getting them implemented must be developed. These strategies should be based on principles that will help to make the best decisions and get them accepted by those affected. The strategy may be concerned primarily with internal (adapting structures/processes to strategies) or external (finding environmentally appropriate strategies)

Box 3.2   Key decisions to take before embarking on a change
management project

- What is the overall direction of the organisation?
- What are the specific needs of the organisation?
- What needs changing?
- What should be kept the same?
- How will the new arrangements work once they are in place?
- Will the result be increased efficiency and effectiveness?
- Where and how should resistance be anticipated?
- When and where should the organisation be determined to change, or what is the 'bottom line'?
- When and where should the organisation be flexible in implementing change?
- Will the revised organisation be able to keep up to date naturally and organically in future, changing with changing circumstances, responding and anticipating changes in the overall world in which it operates in order to enhance its position and increase its rates of success, as determined by both internal and external performance indicators?

Box 3.3   Factors to be taken into account in the
decision-making process

The Situation:
  Time available
  Values
  Knowledge
  Experience
  Complexity or specialised nature of the problem
  Traditions
  Culture
The Organisation:
  Values
  Traditions
The People:
  Knowledge
  Experience
  Culture

change, or (more likely) both. Focusing on outcomes rather than inputs will help both the management and the organisation more generally to remain on course during a period of change. Wherever possible there should be sufficient flexibility in the change management strategy to allow for new approaches to emerge, even if not originally planned. This will facilitate the involvement of the workforce in the direction and implementation of the change as the project progresses, providing space and opportunity for all parties to learn something.

Environmental knowledge

No organisation exists in isolation. Any changes that are planned will have to be made in the context of the overall environment in which the organisation operates in order to ensure that it is better placed for future success within that environment. It is therefore essential that there is a full and clear picture of the environment and the opportunities and threats that face the organisation, and the options and constraints that need to be considered when deciding on what changes need to be made, as well as when and how they should be introduced. Without such knowledge, either an incorrect change will be made, or a correct change will be implemented in an inappropriate way: 'a valuable tool may be applied in a situation for which it is not appropriate, or it may be applied suboptimally' (Iles and Sutherland, 2001b). External benchmarking will be particularly useful in this respect, for it can assist the change manager in asking key questions about existing approaches and attitudes, and enables the organisation to see where it is currently positioned in relation to its key markets and the rest of its sector, where it could be, and where it needs to be, though 'it must also be remembered that improving a service is not about changing all practices but evaluating practices and identifying the best practice with the aid of benchmarking' (Lowry and Lewis, 2004).

Such evaluative approaches also bring into the organisation the 'realities of the marketplace' in public sector organisations, where there may still be a tendency to ignore environmental realities, even though there is increased pressure to change as result of greater competition and market-like changes to the environment in which such organisations operate. Given the importance of governments in shaping the future development of public sector organisations, it is especially important that there is a two-way dialogue with this important, if not dominant, stakeholder, not least so that those in power understand that change will not occur easily, effectively or deeply if it is seen as being led solely by external forces: 'the more strategy in this area comes to be perceived as being prepared to meet external requirements, the less it will gain the acceptance necessary for implementation' (Newton, 2003).

In order to plan ahead then, it is important to know about previous activity in the area and to analyse the key factors that are likely to influence future success or failure. Without knowing the environment accurately enough, it will be impossible to determine a change management strategy that will be truly effective. The analysis of the external environment will need to be matched by a similar analysis of the internal environment. Both analyses will need to identify the key stakeholders, their needs and wants, and their relative strengths and interests. Legal, technological, political, economic and social opportunities and constraints will need to be identified, analysed and balanced against each other – a significant challenge given that they may contradict each other. The internal analysis will need to consider the organisation's capacity for, and capability to, change, and the gap between the present position and that required to implement the required changes effectively. Without a full analysis of both internal and external positions, with awkward or difficult questions ignored, any change strategy will be superficial or skewed.

Box 3.4   **Organisational context**

Organisational context is crucial in determining:

- how different change strategies work;
- what effect different aspects of leadership have on the process; and
- what types of leadership are necessary to succeed – having the right people and using the right tools/techniques for the situation at hand.

The organisation will need to take due account of its position – within the market in the case of a commercial organisation, and the rest of the sector in the case of a public one. This knowledge should include wider society in its key aspects – economic, social, physical, mental – rather than just the specific areas where the organisation operates, for societal attitudes and values will shape and influence what changes are possible and desirable, as for example the ever-more important drive towards 'green' solutions and sustainable development. This is particularly relevant where an organisation is customer-, user- or people-based and led. The broader the involvement of people in developing such 'market' intelligence, the more likely it will be that the organisation will be able to formulate the best strategies for change, not only because the richest possible picture will have been drawn but because it will have been achieved through a high degree of consensus. In addition, the best environmental knowledge – especially in relation to long-term trends – will allow the organisation to anticipate and even help to create the future.

Marketing information can then be used to present the desired and required position of the organisation to its sector, its markets and society more broadly. In this context, major changes in brand or image will need to be handled with care. Users or customers may have a particular view of the organisation, and may find it difficult to adjust to that organisation providing something different from what they expect and what they are used to. If a change of direction is decided, then it is crucial to ensure that there is a marketing strategy that prepares the market for the proposed new approach. In the public sector, of course, marketing may be to those who fund the organisation rather than those who use it, and the strategy may therefore relate to a demonstration of the organisation's fitness for purpose against the objectives of the funding source(s) and in the context of their value systems.

The key challenge is to ensure that the internal changes are matched and synchronised with what is happening externally, so that changes made at organisational level can be made for the longer term. Where the external environment is volatile, it will be important to ensure that internal approaches are either flexible or tentative, or both, in order to avoid a potentially debilitating series of changes in quick succession. Even the most stable of environments may change, and contingency plans should always be built in as a response to continuing environmental analysis and future forecasts.

Frameworks

Providing a framework within which change can be managed is important. It is likely to be easier to see what needs changing if order is more prevalent than uncertainty or even chaos. It is therefore essential to use a particular approach to change management in order to provide a framework or a point of reference, not only to give the change manager a mechanism for managing change effectively, but also to provide those less constantly involved in the planning and implementing of the change management project a way of remaining up to date. It is particularly important when new staff – especially at more senior levels – join an organisation, to ensure that they do not assume that the approaches and techniques that worked for them in their previous organisations will be as effective in their new one. It is almost never possible to superimpose previously thought-out policies or approaches directly onto a new organisation.

Adopting a particular framework cannot be a mechanistic process. There will be times when the direction of, and/or the approach to, change will itself have to be changed, particularly if key drivers – notably external factors – alter in unforeseen ways. As with all aspects of change management, much will depend upon the particular circumstances and the underlying environment. The planning framework should anticipate such change and be flexible enough to cope with altered states, while retaining control and an ability to continue in line with the overall agreed strategy.

Timing

Knowing when to make which changes is one of the most important aspects of successful change management. When does one act and when not? Good timing is crucial, whether relating to the formulation of the change policy or the many aspects of its implementation. 'It's not about doing it fastest. We do have deadlines but it's about doing it right for your institution' (Neathey, 2005). Eason (1984) talks about the importance of determining the 'window of opportunity' – in his case with particular reference to the available time for consulting and involving people in developing a strategy for change – which, once closed (that is, the strategy is set) cannot easily be altered. This argues, of course, for the window being as large as possible and open for as long as possible, not least because, as Eason points out, the learning process that is an integral part of change will almost inevitably lag behind the events that initiated the change in the first place.

Timing change correctly can be difficult because the external environment is too volatile to allow for neat planning. The ability to predict changes within the relevant sector and change or evolve just ahead of, rather than behind, the rest of that sector is essential, though difficult. On the other hand, being too proactive can mean that changes are either made too hastily and possibly therefore ineffectively, or they are made too quickly and further change has to ensue sooner rather than later because the external environment has changed again. The 'interim' change may or may not have been necessary, but if it was made, then it is important to ensure that significant resources are not expended wastefully because further rapid change is subsequently necessary. It is important to ensure that the change manager stays ahead of the changes being made, avoiding a situation where a set of changes have not been fully implemented and evaluated before the next round of changes are desired or necessary. This is a difficult challenge, and the timing of change is crucial, as well as the phasing of it.

At times, rapid change may be the best – and perhaps the only – way forward. There may be a crisis within the organisation (such as is engendered by serious financial difficulties), the external pressure to change may be irresistible, other sudden changes in either the environment or the circumstances relating to the organisation may come to the fore almost overnight, or a new chief executive may, with benefit, take the opportunity to make rapid changes early in his/her tenure of office as a way of capturing the 'occasion' of the appointment or the 'honeymoon' period. Rapid, big bang or turn-round change is more likely to be centralised or top-down. Such change will be in the hands of a few people only. The other key stakeholders – and notably the workforce – may be willing to support such an approach, especially in times of crisis, but it will not necessarily be one that will be acceptable as part of a normal managerial role.

Change may be necessary to avoid stagnation in an age of changing external circumstances: even if the organisation appears to be performing well, it will become relatively worse off if it does not adjust where possible and certainly in advance of any predicted future change in circumstances, or even a crisis point.

Anticipating decline and acting at a 'peak' point in the organisation's life will pre-empt enforced change brought about by the need to react to decline. This will allow the change manager to capture the energy, interest and strength of the organisation and its workforce when it perceives itself to be successful; in decline, the change manager is more likely to be working in a climate of blame, depression and enforced change, including job losses. All change is likely to bring problems – 'teething troubles' – and making changes when the organisation is successful is likely to mean that it can better withstand these initial difficulties in the change management project and its associated processes.

It is important to ensure that key elements of the change management process – such as dissemination, feedback and involvement – are timed as well as planned. The same is true of training – a workforce that is not trained at the appropriate time to take on the new challenges brought about by the changed environment will not be able to play a positive part in the change management process. Too soon, and the training will not be applicable and the new skills cannot be put into practice; too late, and there will be inefficiency and low productivity.

Time

Knowing when to make change and at what pace is one thing. Making sure that there is sufficient time to make the change properly is another. Time to prepare, time to make the changes, and time to evaluate them once made: these time requirements all need to be taken into account. Short or unrealistic timescales are a major reason for failure in change management projects, often leading to a 'vicious circle of: no time – no improvements – more need for improvements – more failure – no time. Rather the organisation should aim to 'adopt a longer life cycle, with a ... multifunctional perspective' (Clegg and Walsh, 2004), not least because trying to find immediate solutions can inhibit more long-term change and fundamental learning. At the same time, people have differing ideas of time and organisations may be under pressure to change more quickly than they would prefer, especially where the external environment or even the sector itself is moving quickly. 'Customers', in particular, have increasingly high expectations of public services and systems, and are unlikely to tolerate steady development and in particular the lack of it. Staff also may be impatient for change, perhaps because they see improvements elsewhere that they wish to see introduced in their own organisation or because they themselves want a more rapid personal development than is currently on offer.

Allowing 'sufficient' time may only be possible if change is being embraced in a proactive rather than a reactive way and is not, perhaps, critical in terms of timing. If change is required in response to a grave need, then there is likely to be only a limited choice in terms of how much time is devoted to preparing for change. However, most writers with experience of change management stress that even the most time-critical of change management projects requires the change manager to talk and listen to people, spending more time with them when the initial turn round has taken place and the immediate 'crisis' is over. 'Usually, organisations fall into hectic activism when crisis is visible and touchable ... [But] at Lufthansa, Jurgen Weber gave his management team 'time out' [that] led to thought-through action plans rather than through haste' (Bruch and Stattelberger, 2001).

The key to success, then, is to ensure that change is not pushed through more quickly than is required, but at a pace that is consistent with the various drivers for change. Unless the need for change is urgent and therefore immediately necessary, it is likely to be much more beneficial to spend more time both planning the changes and communicating with, and involving, staff and other key stakeholders. For example, Jones et al. (2005) found that 'readiness for change acted as a mediator in the relationship between employees' perceptions of a human culture orientation and their subsequent usage of the new computing system. A similar pattern of results was found in relation to reshaping capabilities ... premature implementation may not produce intended outcomes simply because employees are not psychologically ready'.

Slowing down the pace of change should be a deliberate decision rather than one taken by default; that decision should also be clear and communicated, otherwise momentum may be lost and the change process will appear inefficient and superficial. Time may also be needed to remove, alter or improve any elements of the organisation, so that the potential for failure is minimised. While change cannot be rushed through if it is to be truly effective, opportunities may arise that need to be seized and the clever change manager will want to take advantage of them. Good planning – by use of planning frameworks – will ensure that opportunities can be used to move the change management programme forward as part of a process of measured opportunism rather than a reckless game of chance.

Resource allocation

Any change management project has to have a resource attached to it. The precision with which resources are invested will be as important as the scale of the investment. The level of resource required will vary depending upon the type and nature of the changes. Resources might be financial, but they are also likely to include time and commitment, especially of the senior staff that are ultimately responsible for developing and implementing the change management strategy. The appropriateness of the level of resource to be made available will be a particular issue in major innovation projects, when research and development may well require a particularly intensive investment. Resource allocation is an operational issue, and one that is typically addressed as part of programme and project management. Where major costs are involved, the balance of spend between 'the centre' and departments may pose problems when attempting to institute organisational change. Indeed, particularly where institutions are highly devolved, with departmental cost centres, policies derived from strategic institutional management will generally need to be championed by senior managers who will work hard to 'sell' the advantages to the various sections of the organisation. Even if the departments are not required to pay from their own budgets, they pay indirectly via a 'top slice'.

In the particular context of change management projects, resource allocation must look both to continuing operation of the organisation as it currently stands but also to what is necessary for it to be running as required in the future. The change manager, then, must understand what is necessary both for successful change and immediate survival, with sufficient resources to tackle both. More importantly, however, there needs to be a dynamic allocation of enterprise time, competencies, money and executive energies to realise the future vision, underpinned by structures and feedback mechanisms as necessary.

Changing direction

Change managers must be willing to backtrack if necessary. If a proposed change does not work, or generates significant criticism that is relevant and fair, then a good approach will be to 'think again', still with a view towards making the changes but perhaps in a different way. A decision to change direction must only be taken after serious consideration: too much alteration may look like uncertainty, and lead to bemusement or even chaos within the organisation. On the other hand, not taking account of changes in context or requirement or the sensible objections and counter-proposals of others and rigidly following an out-of-date or inappropriate notion of change will be seen as foolish inflexibility rather than strong management – and rightly so if it results in ineffective change that leaves the organisation no better off (and possibly in a worse position) than before. But if there is a backtracking on the project, it is important to say why this has happened and to discuss the reasons for it, rather than to pretend that the whole experience did not happen at all. Rather than return to the status quo, the organisation should go to 'back to the drawing board', formulating fresh plans that learn from the project and move towards a better way for the change, assuming that the change is still needed, while recognising that it is foolish to stick blindly to change for the sake of 'saving face' when the chosen direction is obviously flawed.

The higher the risk identified in the change management project, the more there will be a need to have an 'exit strategy', where the change manager plans for the worst case scenario – actual abandonment of the proposed changes – though aiming to obviate any negativity by not believing that such an outcome will ensure because the risk is being managed and contingency plans are in place to cope with every eventuality. Constant iteration and evaluation (see below) will enable the change manager and the organisation more generally to decide whether a project is still on track, and should also help to identify why things are going wrong and what can be done to rectify the problem. If the worst projected outcome from this formative evaluation of the project suggests that the situation will deteriorate significantly, even with contingency plans in place, and/or the best possible outcome from the project no longer looks very good, or desirable, then the change manager will need to recommend a change of focus or direction.

Iteration

Change management has to be about iteration – of ideas, proposals, plans, and many other aspects of strategy, policy and operation – in order to decide on the best courses of action by analysing them thoroughly at all stages of the process and to be successful (Donaldson, 2005b). At all times, the change manager should keep thinking about the change and the change management process, and in particular evaluating its effectiveness and appropriateness, constantly asking others' opinion on 'how things are going'. Above all, if the worst possible outcome is that the process is leading to an ever-deteriorating situation, and the best possible outcome no longer looks very attractive, appropriate or realistic, then the good change manager should be prepared to accept and admit that it is probably time to change focus. At its most basic, change management should encompass a virtuous circle of: decision – communication – implementation – evaluation (see Figure 3.1).

Figure 3.1 Virtuous change management evaluation cycle

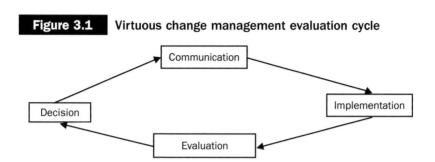

Within this cycle, the manager must continually build acceptance of change, and aim for continuity in the change management programme and associated processes. Two-way communication, where the change manager asks, listens, reviews, responds and, as necessary, alters approach or direction, is essential. So too is a firm grasp of both internal and external environments and 'market' forces. Long-term change almost inevitably happens incrementally, so success is likely to be cumulative rather than instantaneous. Periodic success should gradually persuade the workforce that the changes are working and that the momentum should at least be maintained. A clear direction, strong structures and a consistent approach are important in this context.

Commitment

A strong commitment to the proposed changes by the senior management of the organisation is essential. The position and level of

Box 3.5 The importance of clear commitment

A clear commitment from the most senior management in the organisation to embrace the joint working process is essential. Where the initiative is being taken solely by the personnel or human resources department, ACAS has found that doubt among worker representatives over the true commitment of senior management can remain. Similarly, in workplaces that are relatively autonomous parts of larger organisations, a perceived lack of commitment within the parent company to the joint approach tends to present barriers.

Source: ACAS – Advisory, Conciliation and Arbitration Service (1999).

involvement of key individuals has a major impact on the extent to which commitment is perceived by staff. The importance of building trust and commitment cannot be overstressed:

While commitment from senior managers is important to success in change management, the commitment of the organisation at large is also crucial. For example, a study of private sector partnerships by Oxenbridge and Brown (2004) revealed what they termed 'the uneven diffusion of partnership working among internal stakeholders: that is, a lack of commitment at different levels of the organisation', which can jeopardise successful working:

> In all cases, senior-level managers, union officers and/or stewards had together developed and promoted the co-operative relationship. However, in most cases there was a lack of commitment to co-operative working among other managers: either beyond British borders at parent company level, or at workplace, middle or local management.

Commitment is not just about remaining determined to see through the change management process to a successful conclusion and 'backing' those who are leading that process, albeit without being dogmatic, inflexible or unresponsive to the staff and the organisation at large if major problems arise; it is also about being trustworthy in terms of the commitments given to those affected by the changes being implemented as a result of the process. For example, if the senior management of the organisation has promised a new structure and way of working that will offer more delegation to first-line managers, then – unless there is a very good defensible reason – that management cannot change its mind, even if the initial results of the new order worry the heads of the institution. Change of this fundamental kind takes time, and the workforce at large will be confused if policies keep being altered as a result of panic reaction to adverse outputs from the process.

Consistency

Change is more likely to succeed if it is done in a unified way. For example, a restructuring exercise will be more successful if it is done holistically rather than in a fragmented way, while policy changes, for example, will be embedded more fully and properly if they are iterated across rather than down the organisation. This could be challenging when the change has to take effect over a long timescale, especially when there are external pressures to make policy shifts. Where altering direction in a change management project is inevitable, it is essential that structures and mechanisms are in place to ensure that the necessary shifts are adopted fully within the organisation. Internal and external communications will be of particular importance in such contexts.

Consistency of approach and treatment is important across all the areas that are part of the same change management project and process. This should include uniformity, or at least the adoption of uniform methods in all relevant areas. A consistent, standardised approach across the area where the change management is taking place is likely to help the process to be successful. This is not to say that a rigid approach should be adopted; rather a framework is provided within which the parameters of change – what is and is not intended, what is and is not possible – are clearly demonstrated to all those involved. Standardisation must never lead to the loss of motivation or creativity; organisations that seek and need to change must be open to new ideas. However, common guidelines, language and structures can help people to work, develop, change and communicate. Technology is one area where standardisation brings benefits. Those unwilling or unable to use the Internet, for example, might be encouraged if there are simple, easy and standard guidelines for use in place. Lifelong learning – especially through the use of Information and Communications Technology (ICT) – will also be easier to integrate in a continuous way with individual and group careers and professional development if common, standardised approaches are in place.

Integrity, truthfulness, openness, ethical standards

The organisation has to have integrity in all that it does, ranging from the way it treats people to the way it spends its money or allocates its resources. This is as true for general management as for managing change in particular.

If there is a lack of trust within the organisation when it is in a steady state, then it is unlikely that there will be a higher degree of trust when change then occurs. A high level of trust, based on integrity and openness, is an essential prerequisite of an effective and successful

Box 3.6   The importance of openness

It's what you do that's important ... If management commits to it and acts in the right way then over time you build trust and openness and you'll get there ... you will have open dialogue, be straight as possible, not mislead, and will allow people to make a statement or to take a position without reacting to it as anything other than a position at the time ... Both sides contribute. For examples, with the reward agenda, both sides have produced models that are going through the pay modeller to see the consequences, with the attitude that neither side has a perfect answer to the issue and it doesn't matter whose model is finally selected; what matters is having people who understand the issue working on the problem as that way they'll produce the best model.

Source: Neathey et al. (2005).

change management project. Managers need to be truthful about the change process. It is necessary to avoid cynicism and deceitful behaviour in order to avoid engendering the feeling amongst staff that it is all merely a fad or a façade. Managers also need to demonstrate commitment to change and to what they are saying to the staff. Promises need to be kept and decisions implemented consistently rather than being broken or overturned in an arbitrary way. 'Following through' on what is said by the senior management is crucial: 'the importance of congruence between espoused values, purposes and actual behaviour' (Duke, 2002) cannot be overemphasised. It is easy, and tempting, to oversimplify under pressure of time, or fear of giving people bad news or making unpalatable decisions. It is particularly important to be truthful whenever options for change are restricted. Change managers may need to stress the lack of alternatives, however much what is being proposed and what is required is resisted by the workforce. The organisation, and its senior and change managers, will need to work to certain ethical standards – preferably articulated – through an ethical policy, which the workforce can see in operation as well as on paper. Ethical policies will encourage the organisation to look more to longer sustainability, as well as the need to be ethical for people to buy into institutional values and even for people to be willing to work for it.

Communication

'The prospect of change often feels threatening. It is important therefore that organisations explain their intentions to involve staff to all members of their workforce in a clear and positive manner' (Department of Health, 2003). Effective communication throughout the change process is therefore a 'must' (Donaldson, 2005b). No change management project ever failed because the management over-communicated. It is also good management in any circumstance. 'A fundamental reason [for communicating] is to show respect for all the stakeholders of change. A likely outcome is that people will be more responsive to [that] change' (Whetherly, 1998). Without effective communication, change will be slower and less effective; the change project may break down altogether through misunderstanding, misinformation, lack of crucial knowledge and an air of secrecy or exclusiveness, with the potential for reinventing the wheel, repeating processes or even working in conflict' (Donaldson, 2005b). Cross-cultural or international communication is becoming increasingly important as countries become ethnically more diverse and as activity within both private and public sectors becomes more global, and the need to be sensitive to different cultures ever more crucial as a result.

Communication must start well before the changes actually take place, and must continue throughout the process and beyond the main period of transformation. It must also be a two-way process, especially in the early stages, when the reasons for change are being established. Wherever possible, the change should be phrased as a tentative decision, with the potential for a certain amount of alteration in the light of suggestions from those on the 'receiving end' of the change management process. Feedback from employees must be encouraged and listened to; if the ideas are used, credit must be given (Whetherly, 1998). If not, the manager should explain why the idea was not used. Improved communications may, of course, be one of the desired improvements in a change management project. Those who are in charge of the change management process need to have – or develop through training – effective communication skills. The ability to communicate well also includes the skill to listen and empathise.

Communication of the rationale for change must be clear and consistent, open and honest, with opportunities for all to contribute. The outline and the detail – what is going to change, when and how the changes will be made – must also be communicated clearly, thoroughly and regularly. The change manager must be able and willing to 'sell' any

Box 3.7   **The communication continuum**

- Manager makes decision and announces it.
- Manager 'sells' decision.
- Manager presents ideas and invites questions.
- Manager presents tentative decision, subject to change.
- Manager defines limits; asks group/others to make decision.
- Manager tells staff to function within defined limits without reference back.

decision to change to those affected by what is proposed, not least by being enthusiastic about the change and its benefits. Being truthful can be a challenge for the change manager. Some truths may be unpalatable and there may be a temptation not to tell the staff in order to avoid resistance, or because the senior management is in a hurry to make the changes with too little time available to deal with feedback. Change managers must also therefore be truthful with themselves, accepting the full potential impact of the changes to be made and not running away from the more difficult aspects of them. Whenever there is a 'low point' in the process, a good change manager will remain proactive and engage with the people and systems that can shape the changes – for good or ill – rather than becoming reactive and thus almost certainly unable to control what is happening even within the organisation. Sutherland and Canwell (2004) talk of the importance of clarity of expectations as 'an integral part of enhancing communications, information-sharing and delegation based on sound planning'.

Communication techniques and approaches

Both formal and informal communication networks – including 'the grapevine' – will need to be used. While formal channels will always be the basis of any communication process, it should be noted that informal networks will carry messages too, and care will be needed to ensure that the 'gossip' channel does not distort what the change manager is trying

| Box 3.8 | The importance of clarity of expectations |

Clarity of expectations is an integral part of the structuring of tasks and the setting of deadlines. Clarity of expectations refers to managers being precise regarding their instructions and communications in respect of ensuring that subordinates comprehend what is expected of them and what the likely outcome of a task is expected to be from the point of view of the performance.

Source: Sutherland and Canwell (2004).

to get across. Many people's first news of a change may be through the grapevine unless the senior management positively and proactively use the best communication channels. Grapevines foster and encourage rumour, which is almost always negative rather than positive, whether in terms of the organisation, the management or the change process.

Because change management is an unpredictable process that may need to be altered or that can be derailed, it is important to provide discussion points – both in terms of physical space and time – so that appropriate iteration and, as necessary, redirection can occur. Boddy and Paton (2004) recommend meetings and discussions and the establishment of roles and structures that make communication, decision-making and problem solving much easier, by 'providing a forum in which people [can] raise and debate issues, enabling rapid and well-informed communication between the players', for even if people have different ideas, at least everyone gradually develops a similar understanding of what is going on.

Ensuring that there are points of contact for employees throughout a major change project will aid communication. Reference is made elsewhere to the role and importance of change agents, and key people should be identified who are noticeable (and hence noticed), approachable, and significant enough within the organisation to have influence and respect. These 'middle' people can act as two-way conduits with regard to suggestions, complaints, feedback, monitoring and evaluation of the change projects and its associated processes. They can also keep the change in the forefront of people's minds, encouraging the workforce to work harder at achieving success and ensuring that fears and problems can be identified and dealt with more quickly and easily.

A mixture of verbal and written techniques used as effectively and widely as possible is likely to be the best way of combating 'misinformation'. It will be important to use language that the entire workforce can understand and which cannot be misinterpreted. Appropriate use of language can help to explain changes in positive and attractive ways; inappropriate language could signal danger to those being addressed. The language of senior management may not be accepted by the rest of the organisation, for example, and words can have different and powerful meanings to different people (Chreim, 2005). Different 'narratives' about the organisation at different levels may compete with each other and get in the way of open communication, blocking uniformity of approaches, ideas and cultures.

It is therefore important to define the terms being used within the rhetoric of change – for example the word 'innovation' – otherwise people may end up going in different directions because the words that sum up the proposed changes were never properly explained. Aupperle and Karimalis (2001) argue that metaphors can be used as a positive means of communication at times of change. They perceive that the metaphor can be used to provide an image from which to work on dealing with key change management issues, providing a stimulus to action provided there has been a good analysis of overall conditions as the basis for the development of the language: 'within an organisation, metaphors can provide a crucial, dynamic contribution as a creative iterative tool that facilitates understanding and speeds up learning', dealing with connections and relationships and knocking down barriers by using concepts that people can understand and feel a part of, and every day ideas and language to make the idea of 'change' seem less frightening, alien and different. Organisations are complex, and the changes that need to take place often even more so; metaphors are a way to deal with this without making the reality any less true. The approach requires that the metaphors are relatively simple and short – flexible and easy to grasp on the one hand, but not too simple, controversial, insulting or ambiguous on the other. Even if the language encompasses ambiguity or conflicting ideas, it must be understood by all in the same way, not only to help draw people together and to provide a common understanding, but also to provide a common reference point from which everyone can work within a framework that provides a sense of coherence, direction, process, and measures of success and wholeness.

Similarly, non-verbal communications – such as touch, space, posture, appearance, facial expression, eye contact, gesture, tone and timing – will all have to be carefully considered, especially in a multi-cultural or multi-national context. Thinking carefully about how best to communicate with staff and other key stakeholders will help the change manager work out more generally how these people are thinking and feeling and how they should therefore be treated, and this can help to construct an organisational identity or culture and a belief in change as well as to represent it.

Box 3.9	Communication and consensus

The Advisory, Conciliation and Advisory Service (1999) suggests that the 'smooth flow of communications' is aided by reaching consensus during joint working by doing the following:

- listen: pay attention to others;
- encourage participation;
- share information;
- don't agree too quickly;
- don't bargain or trade support;
- don't vote;
- treat differences as a strength;
- create a solution that can be supported;
- avoid arguing blindly for your own views;
- seek a win-win solution.

Motivation

'Change is assisted by a climate of enthusiasm and participation; resistance is a result of fear, prejudice, anxiety and ignorance' (McCalman and Paton, 1992). If change is perceived as something negative or shameful that should be hidden away or not admitted to as being real or necessary, then the organisation will have significant problems, with staff disliking and even fearing what is proposed and being unwilling and perhaps unable to comply with, let alone support, what is proposed and required. Ideally, change should not be forced on people. Otherwise, strong resistance will probably occur. If, on the other hand, change can be embraced constructively, positively and openly within the organisation, even if members of the organisation regard the change (at least initially) as undesirable, then it can become a force for good.

Box 3.10   Defining motivation

Motivation implies the instilling in employees of a drive to take action. In human resources terms this means inducing, or providing an incentive to, employees to perform to the best of their abilities ... At its most basic, motivation needs to be sustained by employers in order not only to ensure continued high performance and productivity, but also to create a situation where employees have a positive attitude towards work, a commitment to the organisation and, above all, a belief that their individual roles are not only valued but of crucial interest to the organisation.

Source: Sutherland and Canwell (2004).

A particular challenge, then, for change managers – and managers in general – is to determine how best to motivate staff. The change manager will need to learn what motivates them most in order to help them perform during and after the change management process. The change manager should not assume that the views of one group are those of others, or that the views of the one are the views of the many, even within a single group. A multiple set of responses is likely to be evident. This will include the tailoring of policies, practices, language and employee input to groups identified as having different sets of motivators in order to ensure the best levels of motivation for change. Sutherland and Canwell (2004), quoting 'behavioural theory', suggest that 'particular behaviours can ... be reinforced in order to ensure that the correct response in certain circumstances is largely guaranteed ... [by using] praise and discipline, and perhaps reward ... [though] ... praise is a far more potent form of reinforcement than criticism or punishment and ... feedback is of prime importance in order to ensure behaviour modification.'

In an environment where there is a high level of motivation and job satisfaction, it will likely be easier to implement change than in an environment where the opposite is the case. Staff that feel well cared for and supported are themselves likely to be more supportive when change occurs. It is argued that well-designed jobs are a particularly good way of ensuring that the workforce is motivated and satisfied. Staff who can 'multi-task' are also more liable to embrace change, especially where this entails a degree of disruption – they will be more flexible, adaptive and stimulated by doing something different, even if only on a temporary basis.

| Box 3.11 | Key questions on motivation |

- What are the core needs of staff?
- How do they wish to see them best met?
- What types of incentive or reward are most likely to be productive in a given set of circumstances?
- What are staff's individual and collective personal and professional goals?
- How do these fit in with those of the organisation?

Involvement and engagement

There is a great deal of evidence to show that involving people affected by change in the change management process helps to develop commitment, interest, motivation and a positive attitude (Department of Health, 2003). It is important to treat all staff involved or affected by the change management process as individuals and to keep them informed throughout the process. 'Though it is often perceived that change should be inspired and led by management, ideally an organisation will be able to embrace the creativity and initiative of everyone' (Whetherly, 1998). 'The overall challenge ... that of creating and sustaining an organisation where staff at all levels are encouraged and enabled to give of their best, and are no longer "cogs in the machine"'.[1] By making sure that staff feel involved and interested in the future of the organisation, they are more likely to take responsibility for the outcomes of the change management process and even to initiate some of the changes themselves. The opportunity to make change a part of a continuous improvement process is likely to be enhanced in consequence. Taking a considered risk in the interests of a potentially major, but beneficial, change is more likely to be seen as worthwhile too. Wide involvement should include everyone likely to be affected by the changes, rather than just a small 'tight' group of people – especially important in more hierarchical organisational structures, where there may well be only a few people at middle management level.

Engagement can be described as a particular form of involvement. 'Engaged employees are encouraged to use their natural talents in order to assist the business in having a competitive edge. Employee engagement ... involves mobilising the talent, energy and resources of employees' (Sutherland and Canwell, 2004). Encouraging people to improve their own position, performance and potential will make them more supportive of change and more willing to work for, rather than against, the change management process. The change management process should give staff opportunities for training and development that will help both them and the organisation to develop. These opportunities may include the facility to gain qualifications whilst being taught those new skills necessary for the implemented changes to succeed fully. Monetary reward is also an important motivator.

Involvement and engagement can be accomplished in a number of ways. Staff surveys, open meetings, working parties, focus or small groups, briefing sessions and studies of and visits to other comparable

---

Box 3.12 Benefits of employee engagement

- It contributes to the development of a healthy and sustainable business.
- It assists the business in identifying the needs of customers, and their solutions.
- It creates opportunities for dialogue with the business's stakeholders.
- It provides leverage for the business in the sense that it strengthens relations with stakeholders and leads to partnerships.
- It uses resources efficiently.
- It allows for the development of personal skills.
- It assists in bringing any form of corporate culture into sharp focus, building morale, loyalty and pride in the workforce.
- It assists in the establishment and maintenance of the business's reputation.

Sources: summarised from Axelrod (2003), Buckingham and Coffman (2001) and Sutherland and Canwell (2004).

organisations are all approaches that will help the change manager to be successful. Where the groups are intended to do some of the work of formulating, implementing and evaluating change, it is important to ensure that they have a proper and well-understood remit, group members with well-defined roles and a good mixture of those who are keen on change (in general and in relation to the specific project) and those who are sceptical, if not actually resistant. The size of all types of group will be important – the larger the group, the more opportunity there will be for strong characters to dominate activities and the less conducive the atmosphere to those who are less assertive but whose views are no less important.

Box 3.13   **Ways of involving staff**

- staff surveys;
- open meetings;
- working parties;
- focus or small groups;
- briefing sessions;
- studies of visits to other comparable organisations.

Encouragement

People who are informed, listened to, heard, involved, trained and developed are likely to be more encouraged to support change than those who are not. Encouragement should be a part of individual and group development, and include the freedom and the environment within which they can speak out both for and against proposed changes and make suggestions and proposals for alternatives or enhanced approaches that will be taken seriously by the change managers. Encouragement can be through the standard support mechanisms of organisational development, such as appraisal and performance management systems, which should aim to ensure that staff do their best and realise their full potential. People who are working in such a context are more likely to be supportive of change. Encouragement can also take the form of more formal reward and motivation: promotion, pay increases or improved conditions are the obvious ones, though the gaining of new skills and qualifications that make the workforce both more effective in the changing environment and more marketable more generally are other ways of motivating staff. As already noted, they are also essential for the organisation to succeed in its drive to make necessary changes.

Empowerment

Consistent, deep and high-quality involvement and encouragement should involve empowerment, where people feel that they are at least one set of partners – along with the change managers and the other key stakeholders in charge of the change. There is a need to determine the appropriate level of empowerment in given situations, where 'empowerment' gives staff the freedom 'to control their contribution within the organisation ... This means that they are given the authority and responsibility to complete tasks and attain targets without the direct intervention of management. The benefits of empowerment to the organisation are that it reduces the importance of repetitive administration and the number of managers required at the various levels of the structure. Streamlining management levels often increases the effectiveness of communication. From the employees' point of view, empowerment increases their creativity and initiative, as well as their commitment to the organisation, by allowing them to work with autonomy' (Sutherland and Canwell, 2004). On the one hand, an empowered workforce is more likely to feel involved in the organisation and its change management programme than a disempowered one, with ideas and creativity harnessed at all levels. On the other hand, empowerment without a clear framework of responsibility may be a negative factor, with a sense of disintegration of order and additional worries and uncertainties at a time when the environment is an uncertain one anyway. In order for staff to take advantage of empowerment, and in order to ensure that they play a full and positive role within the change management process, they need to be trained and developed.

Bottom-up and top-down approaches

A key element of any change management project is determining the balance between a 'bottom-up' and a 'top-down' approach. What is the correct balance between personal freedom within an organisation and working to a pattern or an approach (pre-)determined by management? There may be occasions when the change has to be decided at the more/most senior levels of the organisation, especially when combined with a strong change management structure. It should not be assumed that change can be forced or brought in from the top down, however. Staff 'on the ground' will always help to shape (or hinder) changes. Nor is it possible to use the traditional hierarchy within the organisation to force change, if the change is to try to alter the structure of the organisation: using the structure to change the structure will not work. Senior management cannot talk about structural change or a more inclusive culture change if they continue to use traditional hierarchies to bring about that change (for example, if they do not use consultation and involvement or do not engage others); if in reality the new structure has the same power structures as the old one, and employees have no more real say, then they are more likely to change on a superficial level only.

The role of the employee, then, is seen as being crucial in the effective management of change, and many organisations adopt at least some form of 'bottom-up planning', the assumption being that its opposite, a top-down approach, is less satisfactory because 'it does not seek to incorporate the ideas or positions of the subordinate managers of those carrying out the tasks ... [and does] not tend to involve ... staff in the decision-making process' (Sutherland and Canwell, 2004).

| Box 3.14 | Defining 'bottom-up' planning |

A form of consultative management style. The planning system encourages employee participation in both problem solving and decision-making. In effect it is a form of empowerment, which aims to encourage flexibility and creativity across the organisation. Bottom-up planning is also closely associated with organisations which have a flat structure. In other words, the hierarchy of the organisation has few tiers of management, allowing employees far greater access on a day-to-day basis to key decision-makers within the organisation.

Source: Sutherland and Canwell (2004).

Change versus continuity

Any change management process will need to determine the nature and extent of the change to be made. A key challenge for change managers is to choose the best approach for the particular circumstance, taking account of timing, the environment, the requirement and the current position. In reality, change management processes are often a mixture of the really different, the subtly altered and the recycled (Eccles, 1996), for in all but the most radical change management situation, there will be a need to balance change with continuity. 'Despite their contrasting nature ... change and permanence should always be envisaged together' (Muratbekova-Touron, 2005).

Without the identified change, the organisation will not deem itself capable of maintaining its position, however good its traditions and previous record of success are. At the same time, without some form of continuity from the organisation's past, there will be a strong chance that at least some parts of that organisation will face a crisis or loss of identify or purpose that may cause negative reactions to the change. It can be argued that one of the main reasons for change is to preserve the best aspects of the organisation – to change in order to remain the same: this can often be a powerful argument when persuading people to alter the ways in which they work, not least as something on which to 'anchor' change, to rally people behind and to help explain the need for something new and different.

This balance between old and new can extend to staff recruitment, with the employment of newer (possibly younger) people being matched by the retention of good, long-serving staff. It will be important to make sure that employees understand the reasons behind and the need for the changes and, ideally, that they believe in and support those changes, not least because the proposals are based on analysis and a study of alternatives, are appropriate for the particular circumstances that the organisation finds itself in and that it genuinely appears they will bring future benefit. Before the change process begins, let alone ends, there will need to have been a widespread involvement of all those affected by the changes taking place and a testing and measurement of the changes to see if they really are bringing – or are likely to bring – advantage and improvement. In reality, of course, few organisations are likely to have static periods for very long in rapidly-changing external environments, or where the organisation wishes to lead and innovate in its particular sector or area. However, at the same time, the other option of totally continuous change is just as unrealistic and even dangerous, for there will need to be a reasonable degree of acceptance and embedding of one set of changes before the next set can effectively occur. A sensible framework must recognise that stability and continuity are also important (Huy and Mintzberg, 2003).

At its best, the overlap between change and continuity will give solidity and sustainability to the change management process. At its worst, this overlap will result in a damaging mix of the least satisfactory of the old and the most dangerous of the new, with additions and alterations seeming to be piecemeal rather than planned. Hales (2005), for example, talks of front-line managers who have been given extended rather than new job descriptions, retaining a strong supervisory role rather than having become totally detached and more 'managerial'/strategic, and still subject to an 'authority gap' between the supervisory and the managerial levels on the one hand and the workforce on the other. Hales found that even in times of change, job styles and some of the ideas that underpin them can be surprisingly tenacious, with, for example, a lack of trust of 'the workers meaning that the first-line managers have to continue in [a] supervisory role, despite the restructuring process'.

There will also be a need to determine the extent to which change within an organisation is itself continuous – a long-term way of working – or a temporary state only, where a specific time of alteration is bounded before and after by periods of stability. Should the organisation always be looking for the next change to make, or be content with a 'status quo' until something alters elsewhere that requires it to change? In many environments, the suggestion that there can be periods of stability is not in fact a realistic one: the external environment may simply not allow a particular situation or approach to remain in force within the organisation; indeed, change, however small and seemingly innocuous, may set larger and irreversible changes in motion; on the other hand, it is dangerous for change managers to be obsessed with the idea of dramatic, turbulent change as the way forward. Some writers (Abrahamson, 2000, for example) suggest that organisations should alternate major change initiatives with carefully-paced periods of smaller organic changes in order to give 'dynamic stability'. In addition, change certainly need not always be overt to be successful. Implicit changes have their place, especially when part of a process of building the organisation's ability to change generically as well as specifically.

Managing resistance

Any change may bring about difficulties for people, however enthusiastic they may be, and a period of organisational instability can be unsettling and worrying for individuals and groups. People are not – in general – deliberately awkward, and resistance does not in itself make them bad employees. They want to know that change really is going to be better for them and the organisation, or they are so used to a particular arrangement that they cannot see the value of things being done any other way. Change frequently moves outwards through an organisation rather than up and down a hierarchy. Many challenges will therefore present themselves at the same time, with resistance occurring on the way out from the centre of the organisation. So there may, for example, be a tension between old-style thinking in terms of how a traditional hierarchy works and the implementation of new structures, the danger being that the change manager introduces new approaches on the erroneous assumption that the old structures have already been replaced, when they are still in place, at least in the 'hearts and minds' of those resisting.

It is inevitable that there will be resistance, and the good change manager will understand this and work with people's fears and concerns and other drivers of resistance and antagonism towards change, because the workforce is a critical factor in the extent to which change is successfully implemented: their happiness and willingness to engage with what is proposed is essential. Therefore the change manager needs to take time and effort to embrace and soften the resistance, pre-empting it by anticipating and planning for it, building the potential for antagonistic reactions into the change management planning process. Working with, rather than against, resistance will best be done through communication, involvement, training and good management.

Key reasons why change is resisted in organisations include: lack of awareness of the need for change; fear of redundancy; uncertainty of the future need for present skills or their ability to gain required new ones; feeling of comfort with the 'status quo'; feeling of having to do more with the same resources or for the same pay; lack of understanding or knowledge; lack of capacity; fear of being downgraded; and unawareness that they are actually resisting. All these issues can be tackled by the change manager: retraining can be offered where redundancy is a possibility; awareness and understanding can be increased and enhanced through effective communication, as noted elsewhere; incentives – including monetary rewards, better job prospects or enhanced working conditions – can be offered and explained, though

| Table 3.1 | Reasons for resistance |

Poor appreciation of the need for change.
View that change is secondary to other concerns.
Poor understanding of the proposed solutions.
View that the solution proposed is not appropriate.
Disagreement as to how the change should be implemented.
Embarrassment/unwillingness to admit that improvements could be made.
Fear that the change will result in loss of skill, role, kudos or even job.
Lack of trust in the change manager or the organisation (perhaps based on previous poor achievement).
Assumption that resources needed for the change will be insufficient or inadequate.

rewards, if used, need to stay in line with wider policy, be meaningful and make a difference; giving those resisting change reasons why they should support what is proposed; planned allocation of work in order to avoid overburdening staff; or a concerted communication campaign to persuade staff that any additional workload required is temporary.

The ways in which resistance is handled will vary depending on whether it is only a few people who are 'against' the changes, or if it is in fact a majority of those who need to be convinced, and why people are resisting what is proposed. The change manager needs to identify who will be the 'losers' as a result of any change, in order to prepare for and pre-empt their possible resistance. Where small numbers are involved, individual programmes of training and development, supported by appraisal schemes, may be the best way forward and should provide them with new skills that can help to help them embrace change more positively and effectively. Where people are resistant because of feeling personally threatened, tackling the fear 'head on' but sympathetically could be the best way forward. When redundancies are necessary, they should be handled carefully, giving those leaving the organisation help with regard to their future careers and lives.

Whether the numbers involved are few or many, it is important to listen to criticisms and not to belittle resistance: those who oppose the changes may have good points to make, if allowed to make them. It is important to remember that a good organisation allows for differences of opinion and is more likely to be united overall if this is the case,

| **Box 3.15** | **Key questions to ask when aiming to persuade others** |

- Who are the winners?
- Who are the losers?
- Who has the information?
- Who has the power?
- Where will the resistance to change come from and why?

provided that the overarching aims and objective are common to all. The good change manager will accept that while there may be a majority view, the minority, whether or not they resist the changes, will not agree with what is happening. However they need to be kept involved in the process in order to aim to pacify them and to diffuse their possible aggression or resistance.

Conflict management

Conflict management, then, is likely to be a necessary ability, especially where resistance and opposition to change is found. Sutherland and Canwell (2004) describe it as involving 'situations where there may be opposition, incompatible behaviour and antagonistic interaction, or the blocking of individuals from reaching their goals. Conflict behaviour can range from questioning or doubting, to a desire to annihilate the opponent.' Conflict is almost inevitable within an organisation, or between sub-groups, or even between organisations, and especially where there is significant change. It should be remembered that disagreement is not necessarily a negative aspect of change and the effective change manager will accept and foster open, creative tensions within the organisation as part of a process of gaining consensus and agreement as to both longer-term direction and ongoing implementation of change. Indeed, conflict may be a necessary part of the open discussion and debate that is such an important element in successful change management. Sutherland and Canwell (2004) argue that at times there is a need to increase rather than decrease conflict as a result. 'Constructive conflict' of this kind 'increases information and ideas, encourages innovative thinking, allows different points of view to be raised and reduces organisational stagnation'. But this is 'good' conflict. 'Dysfunctional conflict', on the other hand, needs to be reduced if not eradicated as it 'usually arises from tensions, anxieties and stresses [and] reduces trust'.

On the one hand, the change manager will need to be determined and resilient in the face of conflict situations, but on the other hand flexible, open-minded and able enough to change direction when and where it is found to be necessary. This ability to balance different and even conflicting needs includes focusing both on the task in hand and the people involved in the change so as to ensure that it is brought about. Reference has already been made to the importance of communication, involvement and training; of listening – to criticisms, concerns, suggestions and ideas – and engagement with the workforce; and of a helpful and friendly attitude to those who most need new skills. Use of appraisal schemes may be a good way of identifying needs, though re-skilling may, of course, not always be possible and, if relocations, redundancies or early retirements are necessary, they need to be made sympathetically.

In addition, there will always be a need for mechanisms to be in place to offer formal resolution of differences and conflicts if informal means fail. Procedural justice 'represents both managers' and employees' access to legitimate channels within the organisation in order to deal with problems and disputes ... The existence of procedural justice also implies that there is a standard procedure, a set of standards and ethics, which are applied to the handling of any of these situations (Sutherland and Canwell, 2004). Resistance may need to be tackled directly, especially if it is on a significant scale. It may be possible to contain differences of opinion within an organisation while still remaining sufficiently united, working for a common goal and agreed changes. But even if the change manager accepts a different and differing majority view, there will almost always be some who disagree. The involvement and persuasion of those who resist remains important in order that disagreement does not lead to destructive resistance.

Summary

This chapter has looked at all the key attributes, elements and factors that make up the building blocks of successful change management. Without a clear rationale for change, it will be difficult for the manager to persuade others that change is necessary. This is where the importance of strategic thinking and organisational development need to be stressed, while environmental knowledge is the prerequisite of good strategic change management, not least because it makes the organisation face up to the realities of its position and what needs to change or stay the same. This all leads to the development of a framework within which the change management project can take place. Timing and timescales are key aspects of the project and there are no easy answers, but rather a series of areas and issues that need to be addressed in order to determine when to change and how long to take over it. Change often fails because of inappropriate timing or unrealistic timescales; inadequate or ineffective resourcing is another key reason. The ability to recognise potential or actual failure and the need to change direction or even backtrack is an essential skill for the change manager, though iterative planning and evaluation processes will minimise the risk of significant error.

The chapter elucidated a number of 'softer' personnel-centric attributes that need to be present within both the organisation and the main leaders – at least – of the change management process. These included a clear commitment to the changes and the change process and a consistent approach to managing all aspects of the project, including a strong sense of integrity and an open, ethical and truthful approach, all engendering a feeling of trust within the organisation at a time when it is most needed. Effective communication is even more important at times of major – or even minor – change. This will ensure clarity of expectation across the organisation and help to ensure that there are no significant misunderstandings. Staff motivation – enabled through involvement, engagement and empowerment – was also discussed as a key way of ensuring that change is truly embedded within the organisation on an ongoing basis. Both 'top-down' and 'bottom-up' approaches are seen as having their merits, but for long-term success, maximum involvement at all levels of the organisation will be essential. The change manager will need to balance change and continuity within the organisation, though at times change will be necessary, paradoxically, in order for the status quo to be maintained. All change will meet with some resistance, and responding to it, managing and even engendering (good) conflict will be important factors in long-term success.

Note

1. Taken from (2005) *In Practice*, 5.

References

Abrahamson, E. (2000) 'Change without pain'. *Harvard Business Review*, 78(4): 75–9.

Advisory, Conciliation and Arbitration Service (1999) *Towards Better Employment Relations: Using the ACAS Advisory Service*. London: ACAS.

Aupperle, K. and Karimalis, G. (2001) 'Using metaphors to facilitate co-operation and resolve conflict: examining the case of Disneyland Paris'. *Journal of Change Management*, 2(1): 23–32.

Axelrod, R.H. (2003) *Terms of Engagement: Changing the Way We Change Our Organisations*. San Francisco, CA: Berrett-Koehler.

Boddy, D. and Paton, R. (2004) 'Responding to competing narratives: lessons for project managers'. *International Journal of Project Management*, 22(3): 225–33.

Bruch, H. and Sattelberger, T. (2001) 'The turnaround at Lufthansa: learning from the change process'. *Journal of Change Management*, 1(4): 244–363.

Buckingham, M. and Coffman, C. (2001) *First, Break All the Rules*. New York: Simon & Schuster.

Chreim, S. (2005) 'The continuity-change duality in narrative texts of organisational identity'. *Journal of Management Studies*, 42 (3): 567–93.

Clegg, C. and Walsh, S. (2004) 'Change management: time for a change!' *European Journal of Work and Organisational Psychology*, 13(2): 217–39.

Department of Health (2003) *Staff Involvement: Better Decisions, Better Care. A resources pack for staff involvement through partnership working*. London: Department of Health.

Donaldson, A., Lank, E. and Maher, J. (2005b) 'Making the invisible visible: how a voluntary organisation is learning from its work with groups and communities'. *Journal of Change Management* 5(2): 191–206.

Duke, C. (2002) *Managing the Learning University*. Buckingham: Society for Research into Higher Education and Open University.

Eason, K.D. (1984) 'The process of introducing information technology'. In *Organisations: cases, issues and concepts*, ed. R. Paton. New York: Harper Row.

Eccles, T. (1996) *Succeeding With Change: Implementing Action-Driven Strategies*. Berkshire: McGraw-Hill.

Hales, C. (2005) 'Rooted in supervision, branching into management: continuity and change in the role of first-line manager'. *Journal of Management Studies*, 42(3): 471–506.

Huy, Q N and Mintzberg, H. (2003) 'The rhythm of change'. *MIT Sloan Management Review*, 4(4): 79–84.

Iles, V. and Sutherland, K. (2001b) 'Changing times'. *Health Management*, 5(6): 10–12.

Jones, R.A., Jimmieson, N.L. and Griffiths, A. (2005) 'The impact of organisational culture and reshaping capabilities on change implementation success: the mediating role of readiness for change'. *Journal of Management Studies*, 42(2): 361–86.

Lowry, L. and Lewis, V. (2004) 'Redesigning an orthopaedic pre-assessment clinic'. *Journal of Orthopaedic Nursing*, 8(2): 77–82.

McCalman, J. and Paton, R. (1992) *Change Management: a Guide to Effective Implementation*. London: Paul Chapman.

Muratbekova-Touron, M. (2005) 'Permanence and change: case study of changes in organisational culture at a multinational company'. *Journal of Change Management*, 5(2): 207–19.

Neathey, F., Regan, J. and Newton, L. (2005) *Working in Partnership in Higher Education: Final Report* (a report for JNCHES by the Institute for Employment Studies). London: Universities and Colleges Employers' Association.

Newton, J. (2003) 'Implementing an institution-wide learning and teaching strategy: lessons in managing change'. *Studies in Higher Education*, 28(4): 427–41.

Oxenbridge, S. and Brown, W. (2004) 'Achieving a new equilibrium? Stability of co-operative employer-union relationships'. *Industrial Relations Journal*, 35(5): 388–402.

Sutherland, J, and Canwell, D. (2004) *Key Concepts in Strategic Management*. Basingstoke: Palgrave Macmillan.

Whetherly, J. (1998) *Achieving Change Through Training and Development*. London: Library Association Publishing.

Case study 3.1 Departmental convergence at Sheffield Hallam University

Keywords: *consultation, managerial support, resources, momentum, universities.*

Over the last few years, Sheffield Hallam University has undergone a number of structural changes. One of these was the convergence of the Communications and IT Services Department and the Learning Centre into the new Learning and IT Services. The approach taken resulted in some excellent examples of good practice that now inform University practice.

The convergence was neither easy nor straightforward to implement. Firstly, both existing departments were successful and thriving entities in their own right, and their employees did not necessarily see either the need for amalgamation or how it could be done successfully. Secondly, the Learning Centre was already made up of two distinct areas – library and media services and the Learning and Teaching Institute – which further complicated the picture. Finally, one of the two departments had only recently undergone restructuring at the time of the proposed convergence, which had the potential for making staff less willing to participate enthusiastically.

However, there were a number of driving forces that pushed the change process forward. The University's corporate strategy sought to make Sheffield Hallam more streamlined and more able to penetrate into new markets. Part of this was a reorganisation of the 10 Academic Schools into four Faculties; following this the Management Team started to look at how the central services, including IT and the Library, could also be re-ordered to fit in with the new approach. The convergence of the two was not forcibly pursued until the Director of Library Services resigned, when senior management saw an opportunity to reassess and realign the services.

The convergence made a great deal of business sense. The work of Communications and IT Services and the Learning Centre were closely interlinked; indeed, they were only truly complete when put alongside each other. What is more, those in central management knew that, although the departments were thriving now, without some attempt at rationalisation both were likely to suffer funding cuts in the medium to long-term future. Nonetheless, because the move was presented to employees as a *fait accompli*, and because those employees persisted in believing that the move was prompted solely by immediate financial motives, there was a crucial need for the change leaders to consult and engage all staff and stakeholders (including the Students' Union) immediately.

It was freely noted that the consultation was not about whether change should occur, but instead about what form the converged department would take. However, the University's commitment to powerful consultation quickly became apparent. Employees were consulted on what they wanted the new department to look like. Both sets of departmental staff were encouraged to think about the good and problematic parts of their existing departments, in

Case study 3.1 **Departmental convergence at Sheffield Hallam University (*Cont'd*)**

the hope that the converged departments would amalgamate the best of what already existed and develop solutions for any troublesome areas.

Initially, the tools used included wish-lists, discussion groups, workshops and the establishment of a Stakeholder Consultation Group consisting of Senior Faculty staff, senior staff from other departments and Student Union Executives. However, these did not manage to engage employees sufficiently. Nor did they overcome the difficulty of making people on the ground believe that convergence would provide benefits.

Consequently, the change managers decided upon more proactive involvement. Volunteer employee task-forces were established, and staff – either sceptical or enthusiastic – became the architects of the new department. One of these task-forces focused on communications, to ensure that everyone was kept up to date and 'in the loop'. At the same time, an external agent – a consultancy firm – was brought in to help develop the culture and values that would sit at the heart of the new structure. Each department did a culture and value assessment, on departmental and individual levels, and sought to answer what values were personally important to them, what their current departments were like, and what types of values they would like to see at the centre of a department in which they worked. The findings were both interesting and useful: employees realised that, although current cultures were different, individual values and wishes for the future were almost identical. This realisation and the specific data collected became a powerful change tool – the values had been identified and developed by the employees and were then used to help develop the new department, while employees had also proven to themselves how many similarities lay between the two departments.

The change project was a relentless one that spanned two years and became integral to the management of the department during that time. Although not easy, the timescale was structured enough to allow employees the comfort of knowing what was coming next, swift enough to maintain momentum, and yet flexible enough to enable consultation, analysis and considered decision-making. As the converged department only became fully operational on 1 September 2005, local commentators feel that it is still too early to see how successful the change has been. Even so, the initial indicators are encouraging, and according to the Equality and Diversity Impact Assessment there have been no harmful effects on student or staff experiences as a result of the change. The project won excellent feedback, both from those within and those outside its immediate circle, and has been held up as a model of good practice for other initiatives at the university.

One key factor in this success was the role of Sheffield Hallam's Chief Information Officer. From the beginning, he used good foresight and provided direct and open communications. He was the project's sponsor, providing the initiative with ready senior managerial support. He neither tricked nor placated people but told them the truth, and was able to fight

Case study 3.1 **Departmental convergence at Sheffield Hallam University (*Cont'd*)**

for the best results for staff, students and the university whilst also balancing any potentially conflicting interests between these different groups. He was passionate about getting the best results for the staff and the University, and he won people over even when they did not originally agree with his views. What is more, he established a dedicated and formal change project team to lead and manage the change actively and openly, rather than expecting staff to deal with all the issues as additions to existing work. This played a crucial role in the project's success. Alongside this, change agents used three key tools very well: communication – involving as many people as possible throughout, implementing regular 'reality checks' on potential policies and ensuring communications were meaningful; consultation – covering multiple angles and approaches to reach different groups of people in ways meaningful to them, and answering all feedback even if negatively; and collaboration – turning employees from resistors to architects and drawing on their skills to improve the quality of the process and end result. These were all critical to the final success.

Nevertheless, even in the midst of this apparent success, there are lessons to be learnt. Those involved on the ground felt that open discussion about options before convergence was decided upon would have helped staff to buy-in to its benefits much more quickly. In other words, the consultation that did occur later was successful, but having some before the decision to converge had been made would have helped ease the way. Similarly, a longer gap between the repositioning of one of the old departments and the start of the convergence process would have enabled new or uprooted staff time to settle before being confused again, and would have prevented some of their anxieties from being unearthed. Also, it was felt by managers that in this case it would have been very useful for someone to have spelt out what the future would look like if change were not to occur, in order to help convince employees who could only see what was good about the current set-up.

As those involved have stressed, important factors in ensuring successful outcomes include:

1. The ability of employees to exercise collective bargaining – this could happen through trade unions or elsewhere, but is crucial; if employees have no-one neutral to speak for them, the result is always one based on power and hierarchy rather than real involvement. The constructive role played by unions in this process is a good example of how co-operative the employee-employer relationship can be.

2. The existence of a dedicated Project Management Team, to deal with all the difficult and intricate organisational details; to bring clarity, order and a sense of importance; to involve the right mix of staff in the delivery of promised changes; and to ensure that strategic thinkers can focus on overall objectives without causing the minutiae of the project to stutter.

Case study 3.1   **Departmental convergence at Sheffield Hallam University (*Cont'd*)**

3. The need for committed employees on the ground.

4. The benefits of an excellent and visionary leader, to hold a clear vision of how to achieve change, and who has the experience and respect with which to back it up.

5. The need for adequate resources throughout the process (especially people, time and money).

6. The ability to provide compelling reasons for any change, and also evidence to support those reasons.

7. The use of the 'Three C's' – communication, consultation and collaboration.

8. The need to get senior staff on board first: without them there is no organisation-wide motivation: once other employees see that the senior executives have bought in to the process they are more likely to follow suit.

4

Roles and responsibilities, partners and players

Introduction

This chapter looks at the roles and responsibilities of those involved in change management. The initial focus is on the management of the organisation, for managers are necessary even in the smallest and flattest structures. The larger the organisation, the more different management levels there will be; managers at these different levels will all have a role to play in change. The chapter then concentrates on the idea of the change manager – a person or group specifically tasked with leading and managing, especially in the context of change projects and processes. The key attributes, skills and roles of change managers are discussed.

Change embraces all parts of an organisation though, and the workforce at large has a role in change and its management, especially when the change is radical and discontinuous. A number of ways in which engagement can be maximised are discussed. Foremost among these is the use of change agents, whether from within or outside the organisation. There are advantages and disadvantages to such an approach, as discussed here. As important a 'player' in change management projects is the Human Resources (HR) manager, not least as an expert adviser who, while internal to the organisation, can also provide a degree of objectivity and independence. External stakeholders also play important roles, especially in public sector organisations, with both leadership and governance responsibilities.

Ultimately, leadership is crucial to the success of an organisation and how it manages and implements change effectively. The role, nature and prerequisites of good leadership and the attributes of successful leaders are explored. Leaders in most circumstances also have to be managers, and the relationship between the two roles is discussed. Style of leadership (and management) is important, and a range of options is discussed, from the single 'heroic' leader to the increasingly prevalent team leadership approach. Team working is then considered: what it is and how it best works. The chapter concludes with a consideration of partnership working and how to achieve it most effectively.

Managers

Management takes many forms within an organisation. There will always be a need for managers who, regardless of their formal title, understand what needs to be done and have the skills to ensure that the organisation delivers to its objectives and targets. Managers will be the most crucial group in terms of helping to bring about successful change, whether or not they are directly involved in specific change management projects.

Each and every level of management should have a role to play in managing change. Managers will have different roles and responsibilities, requiring the exercising of particular skills whether in relation to people, resources or strategy. All will have an intermediary role between their area of the organisation and other parts of it, both in terms of horizontal and vertical communication; all will need to have a good knowledge of the organisation, its aims and objectives, its strategic direction and its major policies and programmes for change.

Senior managers are separate and distinct from other managers and management levels within the organisation. Ultimately, they will be responsible for formulating strategy and policy and for leading implementation. Without the direction, encouragement, support and involvement of the top levels of management within the organisation, major change will simply not happen. At the head of the organisation is the Chief Executive Officer (CEO), who will ultimately take responsibility for strategic direction and major change. An effective CEO is obviously one of the most important ingredients in success, but that person will not be able to manage alone and will need to create a management team that can help him/her to lead the organisation. But however effective the senior management team, they cannot even begin to tackle the most fundamental of organisational problems without a broader base of support and involvement from all parts of the organisation.

Middle managers have a crucial role to play in organisational effectiveness. They have an important role as a 'conduit' between the senior management and the workforce at large. In a dysfunctional organisation, middle managers may work in line with their own beliefs rather than the needs of the organisation; top management decisions and communications may therefore get 'stuck' and workforce communication also does not move further upwards; top management is therefore seen as aloof, uncaring and unapproachable.

'First line' managers are typically focused on some kind of supervisory role; they will have a major impact upon any change management programme in terms of the effectiveness of two-way communication between management and managed and hence the extent to which the changes can be implemented successfully.

The change manager

If the organisation deems it necessary to have a change programme, then it must recognise that it needs a strong yet flexible change manager to lead and implement such a programme. 'The task of the manager ... is to manage the tension between continuity and change, to combine opportunism with vision, future with past, ideas with action' (Duke, 2002). This is no simple matter! The change manager has to be capable of dealing with a wide range of changes such as personnel, budgets, technologies, competitive environments, individual mindsets, wider socio-economic contexts and competing organisational and sectoral priorities. It is therefore essential that those leading and managing change know how to adapt both their organisation and themselves, not only getting people behind the required changes, but also knowing how and when to resist what may be turning into an inappropriate or poor change that needs to be stopped, altered or otherwise re-oriented. At times, the change manager will need an ability to recognise or even create a crisis environment, where change has to be embraced in order for the organisation to survive. In such cases, it will be crucial to ensure that the crisis is presented as an opportunity rather than a threat in order to ensure that the workforce is supportive of the changes proposed.

Those in charge of the change management must also themselves be prepared to change. 'Management must transform the way it is evolved, shaped, and sustained. Managers who can change both cognitively and behaviourally can also adjust quickly and learn to cope with change and deal with stress while helping others do the same' (Belasen, 2000). Those who can demonstrate such a commitment through an open, original, wide and even adventurous approach to change will aim to ensure that they are not 'preaching' change while continuing to practise an embedded or outmoded style themselves. Change managers must be able to give the proper drive and direction to a programme, while adapting as and when necessary through the whole of the change process, for it is happening and involving them too: they are not simply observing and directing it from 'outside' the organisation (Miller, 2002).

The change manager should possess several key skills, competences or attributes and be willing and, indeed, eager to use them in order for the process to stand a good chance of success: 'management competence has a greater influence on performance in dynamic environments than in static environments, thus implying that effective management and leadership are more necessary in times of change than in periods of stability. (Bolden, 2004). The senior management within the organisation must ensure that those most closely involved in bringing about change are both properly trained to do this effectively, and helped and supported in their decision-making, ensuring that they understand in particular the impact of changes on those at 'ground level' within the organisation and empathise with those who will be most affected. Miller (2002) argues that the change manager requires a mixture of inherent skills such as optimism, self-assurance, collaborative ability, purpose, proactivity and structure, alongside more technical skills. In addition, they should have beliefs about change that are themselves conducive to the change management process, for example a rejection of forced compliance and sanctions as a means of making changes.

The change manager is also a project manager. But whereas the traditional project manager is concerned with delivering the 'iron triangle' of time, budget and quality specification, the change project manager will be more people-focused and therefore may need to develop a wider selection of skills beyond those of straight project planning and implementation, including 'softer' ones such as the ability to facilitate and empower as well as to analyse and understand complex situations. The point is that the change manager is working with intangibles – environment, culture, atmosphere – and will need to have more options, more necessary information and knowledge and a greater degree of flexibility of approach than in a 'harder', more 'technical' project. As with any programme or project, the manager will need to be someone who can focus on the task in hand, retain interest and momentum, and prioritise on the essential as well as the immediate, ensuring the best fit with what the organisation requires on the one hand and what the workforce is able to absorb and assimilate on the other. Above all, they need to be someone ambitious for the change project to succeed, not least because they are well aware of the cost of failure.

The change manager will need to have, or gain, intelligence; experience; good methods to gain and process information; skills at establishing, managing, using and detecting existing and potential networks; and, above almost all else, an ability to deal with ambiguity. Change management in this context is about looking beyond the immediate situation and prevailing views, while understanding the environment in which the change project manager is working and in particular recognising what is necessary to gain the requisite authority in order to be successful. The authority of the change project manager will be multi-faceted, and will involve the development of a series of relationships with staff and stakeholders in a whole range of contexts and hierarchies, especially given that the change manager may not be the most senior person in the organisation. A strong 'political' sense will be important, in order to establish a subtle authority over even the most senior members of the organisation, even if it is not possible to have complete control over the political or the cultural dimensions of the organisation. Without sufficient control and authority, the change manager will have an impossible task: 'the whole purpose of developing authority is to have our will prevail over others in an environment where we have little clout' (Davidson Frame, 2002).

Table 4.1   **Key attributes of successful change managers**

Skill	Rationale
Political	To deal with people within organisations.
Analytical	To provide an argument that cannot be factually contested.
People	To be communicatory, empathetic and interpersonal and able to deal with vast variety.
System	To understand both closed and open systems and how to deal with them.
Business	To understand how the sector, competitors and more specifically the specific organisation works.

The workforce

What role should the 'workforce' – otherwise known as the employees – play in the change management process? There are differing views:

The employee does not have a responsibility to manage change ... responsibility for managing change is with management and executives of the organisation – they must manage the change in a way that employees can cope with it.[1]

Though it is often perceived that change should be inspired and led by management, ideally an organisation will be able to embrace the creativity and initiative of everyone. (Whetherly, 1998)

It can be argued that when the organisation is running smoothly, different people and groups within the organisation have different roles and concerns:

- top managers ask 'why';
- operational departments ask 'how';
- middle managers ask 'what';
- marketing and service departments ask 'what' and how'.

However when major change is evident, everyone needs to be involved.

Organisational change processes often fail to look properly at the workforce and what the organisation can do to persuade employees to get 'onside' and therefore help those processes really have a positive effect. This is especially true of public sector organisations as they become more 'corporate' in their approach and outlook. Given that it is important to ensure that there is ownership by employees of any change, and that the skills, knowledge and understanding of the workforce in its entirety are required to effect real and meaningful change, it cannot just be the top management or the change project managers who are responsible for implementation. As was already noted in relation to the first level of management responsibility, the 'front line' is where significant change can happen, and where, in user or customer-oriented organisations, it may need to happen most. Much of this front-line delivery will be undertaken by 'the workers', and without their involvement in, and support for, change, the hoped-for service or process improvements are unlikely to happen.

Change agents

'[The change agent is] a person who translates the strategic change vision of leaders into pragmatic change behaviour...a positive virus infecting their host company' (Dover, 2002). In practice, a change agent could be an individual or a group of people, acting as a team with a specific brief for change within the organisation. The change agent may have various roles, including that of initiator, facilitator and co-ordinator, and may have a high profile during the early stages of the change project at least, if not throughout its entirety. Whatever position they hold, whether or not it is a managerial one, these 'agents' become lynchpins of change. They may be internal or external to the organisation.

At times, external facilitation will be important as a way of bringing to the surface sensitive issues that would otherwise not emerge. This is likely to be especially the case when major culture change is being attempted. External change agents are typically people, groups or institutions from outside the organisation that provide expertise of some kind, including analysis and diagnosis, facilitation, and/or a new or more objective perspective on the change management project, including new approaches to resistance or other problems, benchmarks and experience of how change has been undertaken successfully elsewhere. Such expertise might include those with particular technical knowledge of the sector or particular systems and technologies, and allow the organisation to solve technical difficulties or to advance to the current, and/or prepare for the future, state of the art.

Box 4.1   **Possible roles of external change agents**

- provision of expertise and experience;
- facilitation of change;
- diagnosis of problems;
- analysis of issues, environments and requirements;
- provision of benchmarks;
- identification of approaches to change.

Involving people from outside the organisation can bring a new and refreshing dynamic to the change management process and may enable difficult discussions to take place and tough decisions to be made (that might not have been possible with only internal parties) to the changes involved. Any use of outside agencies needs to be handled with care, however. The involvement of change agents not otherwise members of the organisation needs to be seen as a partnership by all involved and not just by those who have invited the agent 'in' to the organisation – typically the senior management. The agent will need to become sufficiently involved and immersed in the organisation to understand it, and those directly liaising with them will need to ensure that enough information has been given.

Those 'on the receiving end' of a change agent's work and recommendations will also need to feel that they are sufficiently involved to believe that they have at least a joint say in the project and have got 'buy-in' to it. The change agent will need to be respected by all parties as someone who really can help the organisation and all the people working within it. The change agent will need to pass on skills, experience and knowledge, helping others to solve the problems of the organisation themselves. At the same time, the change agent will need to remain at a distance from the organisation and the people with whom s/he is engaging in order to maintain the necessary objectivity to be truly useful as an agent for change: 'the effective change agent also has to remain on an unstable borderline ... between being in the organisation and remaining aloof' (McCalman and Paton, 1992).

Care must be taken to avoid the organisation relying too much on external agents to set the change agenda or the outcome measurements of the change process, not least because of their potential over-objectivity: do they really know the specifics of the organisation well enough or are they actually recommending generic solutions without sufficient fit with the particular environment in which change is required? Consultants may often present a 'package' that suggests that the actions required for change are more straightforward and less controversial than the reality of the situation dictates. Any change agent will need to be honest with the organisation undergoing change in order to ensure that the necessary actions are taken. In particular, the external change agent must make sure that they allow the organisation to take control of the change and to reduce and eventually obviate the need for any external dependency. Major change processes are long, probably complex and possibly continuous, and a deep reliance on external consultants is both expensive and burdensome (particularly in terms of management time with the agents) and may stifle continuous improvement within the organisation by the organisation itself. A senior manager appointed from outside the organisation may be brought in to lead it as a change agent, though it will be important to ensure that their fit with the organisation's future needs and present culture is an appropriate one based on proper research into what is required. There will be a particular challenge for this particular type of change agent as s/he spends time in the organisation, becomes acclimatised to it and perhaps even 'goes native'.

| Box 4.2 | Aspects of use of external change agents |

- brings a new dynamic to the organisation;
- facilitates difficult discussions and decisions;
- needs to be a partnership by all involved;
- involvement needs to be deep and wide across the organisation;
- external solutions need to be internally valid and appropriate;
- possible perception of change agent as a tool of senior management;
- change agent needs to know enough, but not too much about the organisation;
- change agent needs to be respected by all;
- change agent needs to be involved, but distant;
- change agent needs to help people help themselves;
- over-reliance on a change agent builds a dependency culture that will not solve problems internally longer term.

At least in larger organisations it may be possible to use internal change agents from a different department who can bring the necessary objectivity to the change management process, even though they are not outsiders. On the one hand, the costs of such an internal approach will be lower than use of an external change agent and the people involved are likely to know more about the organisation without needing significant briefing before beginning work. Certainly, some form of project champion or champions amongst the workforce at large is useful, helping the leadership of the organisation and the change manager in particular to 'sell' change to others and help to take the change management project forward even if the atmosphere within the organisation is uncertain. 'The change agents can be seen as the early adopters or opinion leaders in the pursuit of change ... But these efforts must be positioned within a broader change context that has clearly articulated vision, goals, strategy and desired cultural values that are continuously communicated and updated for all employees' (Dover, 2002).

On the other hand, it may be harder for the internal change agent to remain objective, and departmental rivalry or power tensions may arise.

For example, care will need to be taken when some of the change agents are trades union representatives, where, because of their 'inside knowledge' – shared with the management rather than the workforce – 'there was no easy solution to the problems they faced in attempting to balance membership views with their understanding of issues gained from exposure to strategic information' (Oxenbridge and Brown, 2004). The internal agent may also have his/her own localised agenda relating to their home department or other role(s) within the organisation that precludes them from being truly objective.

Perhaps more appropriate and effective will be a situation where key members of staff – at all levels – and especially those who form or lead opinion (whether or not they are in obvious management positions) are developed as change agents, not least as a way of helping them to ensure ownership of the changes and the change management process. The organisation will need to have structures in place within which the change agents can receive the operational support that they will need in order to fulfil their role. They are likely to be particularly useful when embedding a more incremental (though still holistic) vision of a change programme based on a series of specific and more focused tasks, rather than either isolated changes within specific areas or a major organisation-wide drive that may easily lose momentum (Dover, 2002).

Ultimately, everyone involved in a change management process is an agent of change of some sort (Whetherly, 1998) whether or not they are labelled as such, because they are a part of not just the specific change project but wider (organisational, cultural, societal) change and are being changed themselves as they grow and develop, whether at work or outside it. Indeed, Tanner Pascale and Sternin (2005) argue that an organisation can make successful change by identifying 'indigenous sources of change' and bringing these 'isolated success stories' into the mainstream, though the amount of influence employees have at both a day-to-day operational level and at a policy level varies considerably across both public and private sectors (Involvement and Participation Association, 1997). Certainly, key opinion formers or power players within an organisation – those who have credibility with both the senior management and the workforce more generally – are likely to be a valuable conduit for communications within the organisation at times of change and also possible change agents, provided they are supportive of the changes proposed.

Whatever their origin, background and relationship with the organisation, the involvement of change agents must be seen as a voluntary and a positive process and not one where the agents are seen as allies solely of the management, unsupportive of the concerns and views of the rest of the organisation. Any project involving a change agent must from the start recognise that the members of the organisation need to take over from the agent at the earliest possible opportunity. Change agents must be sensitive to the dynamics of the organisation and be appropriately creative in their approach. This is especially true in the area of culture change, where the emphasis will need to be on the most effective practical steps in the implementation phase of any change where cultural issues may be particular problematic (Thornbury, 1999). At their best, transitional arrangements will ensure that the objectivity engendered by the (external) agent will continue long after the initial project has been completed.

The HR manager

Given the importance of a strategic approach to human resource management, as noted elsewhere, the HR department has a central role to play in the organisation and any change management projects. For this to happen to best effect, the human resources department of an organisation will have to be up to date in its practices and skills, and able to provide a supportive and facilitative and flexible service, including help in choosing and training the right people for the job – both the leaders and those under them – in order for the organisation to have the maximum ability to implement its preferred strategic options and to alter policy and practice in order to cope with all likely changes.

A good HR department that is fully integrated into the change management and strategic planning processes of the organisation will be able to think through, and advise senior management in particular on, the implications and the impact of proposed changes, and suggest either alternative approaches or ensure that the strategic and policy level is effectively translated into effective implementation where necessary. For example, the HR manager should be able to see what approach may need to be adopted with regard to recruitment or redundancy, retraining or restructuring – or all of these alternatives – and what combination will make the changes feasible – assuming that a workable implementation is possible. In ensuring that the organisation is fully committed to best HR practice during times of change, many of the basic building blocks of good change management will almost all automatically be in place, at least as they pertain to good working conditions for all staff.

HR personnel can provide an important point of contact for all staff – whether 'manager' or 'managed' – especially if the department is seen as being impartial rather than an extension of the senior management and its particular agenda, particularly where that agenda is not widely shared. This is not an easy role or position to have or develop, for in times of turbulent change the HR department will be responsible for helping the change managers and departmental management with potentially difficult staffing issues, including redundancy; at the same time, they are charged and challenged with the task of helping individuals cope with change.

However, the 'independent' HR manager can act as a 'bridge' between different individuals, groups and even cultures within the organisation, even acting as a unifying force at times of major change, even though (or perhaps especially because) they are not directly responsible for driving strategic change – the job of the senior and the change management teams. The information provider role of the HR department can also extend beyond support for change projects and the people affected by it to having a strong influence on the nature and direction of the process itself. This will particularly be the case where the HR department is well connected outside the organisation, especially within the rest of the sector, and will therefore be able to assist the change manager and others in terms of interpreting and helping people within the organisation to understand change at the sectoral as well as the institutional level and how the two interrelate.

Box 4.3 **Key attributes of the good HR manager**

- up to date in practices and skills;
- fully integrated within the organisation;
- perceived as independent by all groups within the organisation;
- able to be supportive and facilitative;
- able to assist in the correct selection and training of staff;
- able to implement the organisation's preferred strategic options;
- willing and skilled in altering policy and practice to suit both internal environments and external requirements;
- a force for good change management overall.

External stakeholders

External stakeholders have a great deal of power within public sector organisations and can have a significant impact on decision-making and the direction and implementation of change. The change manager must understand the role of key stakeholders and stay up to date with who those key stakeholders are and what their views and requirements are. There is an increasingly equal relationship between different stakeholders – for example, government, staff, students, parents and professional bodies in an educational system – and there will therefore be a need to engage and negotiate with all of them. It can be difficult for organisations with many diverse, equally demanding stakeholders or other interested parties. Meeting their needs or respecting their views can lead to uncertainty in terms of the organisation's direction, structure, and even its power base, with a consequent inability to push for change successfully in the longer term. The organisation's senior management will therefore need to resolve any tensions in relationships and the possible cultural issues that underlie them as an early part of the preparation for any major change management programme. Indeed, the interaction between stakeholders and the organisation is driven in a large part by the way in which the organisation's leadership and management view the power and position of the stakeholders relative to the organisation: 'the more legitimate the managers consider the critical change stakeholders to be, the more positive their overall assessment of the change initiatives' (Solomon, 2001).

Stakeholders, then, may initiate change, either directly through their involvement in the governance and management of the organisation, or by virtue of the organisation needing to respond to their requirements by making changes within the organisation and its operations or services. An academic library is typically 'governed' by some form of user committee, where teaching and research staff are likely to be in a majority. They can often affect the library's strategy and its implementation, whereas the students are more likely to be affected by it. In this situation, we are also looking at the presence of a *dominant* stakeholder. Another example might be the management and the workforce, though in recent times increased worker participation and flatter management structures have reduced the dominance of the one over the other. The key point to stress is that the interests of the dominant stakeholder may not necessarily be the same as the interests of the other, majority stakeholders. This is perhaps particularly true of private sector organisations, where the 'profit motive' is likely to be uppermost. It may nevertheless also be true of public sector organisations, where government is often the dominant stakeholder.

Governors and leaders

Public sector organisations are typically governed as well as managed and led.

Governance is made up of: the constitutional and legal framework regulating the relationship between the organisation and its funding bodies – including the government; the overall structure and process of internal co-ordination and control within the institution, or of an institutional activity; and the specific role and activities of an institution's most senior, strategic committee or board – 'the governing body'. Those who 'govern' the organisation provide a 'point of authority' for the system, acting as an intermediary or balancing power between parts of that system, sometimes acting as arbiter between different interests, for example between stakeholders and the institution or specialist professionals and managers. In the wake of competitive pressures, this role has become increasingly strategic and supervisory. Sutherland and Canwell (2004) list the three key aspects of governance mechanisms as being:

- ownership structure;
- monitoring and controlling mechanisms;
- management performance.

'Governance mechanisms deal with the ways in which the management structure, as determined by the ownership and overall structure of the business, both monitors and controls the business while at the same time it is monitored and controlled itself' (Monks and Minow, 2003).

| Box 4.4 | Leadership and governance |

The territories of leadership and governance lie at the interface between internal and external worlds. It is here that the accountability for 'renewal' rests, although responsibility for its achievement must be shared more widely. Leadership and governance functions are of major importance in interpreting the drivers of change, outlining potential scenarios, developing organisational responses and making change happen ... In simplistic terms, leadership and governance are concerned with overall direction and strategy within a framework determined by regulatory requirements on the one hand and purpose, values, culture, history

Box 4.4   Leadership and governance (*Cont'd*)

and mission on the other. Management and administration involved processes of implementation, control and co-ordination with particular emphasis on resource frameworks and structures; human (individual and groups), physical and technological infrastructures, finance, materials and time.

Source: Middlehurst (1999).

Scott (1996) lists the key 'steerage' mechanisms available to governors and leaders of institutions.

Table 4.2   Steerage mechanisms

'Hard' steerage mechanisms	'Soft' steerage mechanisms
Legal and constitutional frameworks	Policy statements and national inquiries
Institutional types and structures	Institutional histories and culture
Funding systems and formulae	Sources of funding and income streams
Accreditation, recognition and licensing systems	National, state and local politics/power
Quality assurance regimes	University roles and expectations of universities – culture, politics and distributions of power
Governance structures: stakeholder representation and roles	Leadership and management approaches

Middlehurst (1999) comments:

> This position at the interface offers power, responsibility and the opportunity to operate either as a buffer, protecting the internal world of the [organisation] while ensuring compliance (or fit) with relevant forms of steerage, or acting as a catalyst for internal and external change. Individuals and groups involved in leadership and governance roles can influence, through informal and formal networks, the shape of both 'hard' and 'soft' instruments of steerage.

Leadership

'The goal of ... leadership is to 'transform' people and organisations in a literal sense – to change them in mind and heart; enlarge vision, insight, and understanding; clarify purposes; make behaviour congruent with beliefs, principles, or values; and bring about changes that are permanent, self-perpetuating, and momentum building' (Bass and Avolio, 1994, as quoted in Bolden, 2004). At times, the leader will work from 'behind' the organisation and its people, allowing the staff to feel that they are in charge of the changes and that they 'did it' themselves. This requires both skill and confidence.

Box 4.5	Defining leadership

Leadership can be defined as:

- a role, carried out formally by particular post-holders (as for example Vice-Chancellor, Head of Department);
- a function that can be – and needs to be – performed at different levels in an institution, in both formal and informal contexts;
- a process of social influence that guides individuals and groups towards particular goals (organisational, professional, social, creative, etc.).

Source: Middlehurst (1999).

Because the context in which leaders operate varies from sector to sector and even organisation to organisation, the elements of leadership will also vary. The nature of leaders and their relationship with the group that they lead, their qualities, behaviours and styles, their cognitive capacities, developmental experiences and use of power will all be relative to the environment in which they operate. So too will be their 'organisational functioning' (Middlehurst, 1999), including the symbolic and cultural elements of their leadership and the dominant features of their organisational design and processes of creativity and change.

Increasingly, organisations and management theorists both argue that the presence of leadership qualities in the change manager is the crucial ingredient that makes for success (Brierley, 2005a). Public sector organisations have seen their senior staff change title, job description and remit and required them to do so in order to respond successfully and proactively to changing and challenging environments. In UK universities, for example, the Vice-Chancellor is as much of a chief executive as an academic officer; formerly part-time Pro-Vice-Chancellor roles are increasingly full-time, permanent and executive; heads of department are managerial rather than pedagogic or research-centric responsibilities; and the human resource and financial functions are a central part of both the organisation and the senior officers' responsibilities. In addition, senior staff have to be entrepreneurial and business-focused in their dealings with other key stakeholders, and notably the private sector and the government.

Leaders must be able to face and tackle the problems, weaknesses and dangers facing the organisation in the context of the many paradoxes and challenges that face public sector organisations in particular. Good leadership is about getting away from 'management by avoidance' and moving towards open acknowledgement of the need for change. Prahalad (Hamel and Prahalad, 1996) stresses that leadership is particularly important in times of major difficulty for the organisation: 'leaders must behave like emotional and intellectual anchors ... The critical issue is about faith, passion, and, most importantly, authenticity ... People can see a sham'. Coupled with this is the willingness and ability to take difficult decisions, however unpopular they may be. The most important aspect of leadership for Prahalad, however, is the ability of the leader to engage in strategy and strategic thinking.

Leadership almost inevitably focuses to a great extent on the 'people' aspects of change and management, and the HR dimension must be an integral part of the job of any leader. 'High-performance leaders generate energy from within; when it erupts, it captures the minds and hearts of employees. It is positive energy transformed into a centripetal force that pulls people together by creating a shared meaning and commitment to core values' (Belasen, 2000), an 'indirect management ... the management of the ambience, conditions and environment for work, not managing and expropriating the work of the workers themselves' (Duke, 2002).

Box 4.6   **Emotional intelligence required of leaders**

Goleman (1996), suggests that the key attributes of good leaders (summed up as 'emotional intelligence')[2] are:

- self-awareness;
- impulse control;

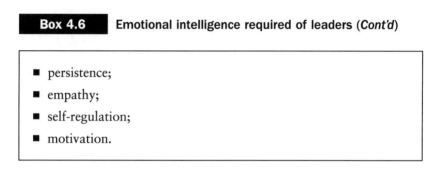

Box 4.6   **Emotional intelligence required of leaders (*Cont'd*)**

- persistence;
- empathy;
- self-regulation;
- motivation.

In general terms, leadership is about developing an environment in which the organisation can adapt and flourish. It is likely to embrace multi-disciplinary approaches and management, with a variety of leadership characteristics being required, including energy, vision, and a wide range of flexible skills – including the personal and the interpersonal – that can be used in differing contexts, including in particularly challenging situations. No single individual is likely to possess all the attributes required of present-day leaders and, even if they did, there would be concerns about the role and effect of the 'heroic' leadership style that might ensue, as noted below. A multi-disciplinary approach will identify and embrace a variety of people with different and complementary skills and expertise. 'Talent spotting' is an important element of successful management, and creating and developing a strong leadership team is likely to be a prerequisite for long-term success in change management. Different attributes and skills will be needed in different situations, however, and the senior leadership will need to ensure that the specific requirements will vary according to circumstances. Any team structure will need to be sufficiently flexible to cope with changed requirements. Once identified, expert staff need to be trusted with an appropriate level of delegated authority that the senior management is prepared to give, recognising that they should have a greater know-how than those doing the delegating.

Box 4.7   **Key characteristics of good leaders**

- vision;
- energy;
- ability to 'rise to the challenge';
- ability to face uncertainty and deal with it;
- ability to adapt;

Box 4.7 Key characteristics of good leaders (*Cont'd*)

- good and varied interpersonal communications;
- varied and flexible skills usable in different contexts and situations;
- general management and processing skills.

The best type of senior leader, then, is concerned with developing and praising others rather than taking the credit for success for him/herself, while accepting ultimate responsibility when things go wrong; working for the greater good of the organisation rather than his/her individual position; and being committed to responsible change management in all its aspects. Confident leaders will allow and encourage flexibility and freedom amongst the workforce, within overall agreed parameters, providing impartiality, proper decision-making procedures and opportunities for safe dissent. They will also lead by example, not least in terms of their own willingness to embrace change. Asking the right questions – and at the right time – is also a key element of leadership in order that appropriate action can be taken in the light of relevant information.

Box 4.8 Some key questions for leaders

- What is the appropriate structure for the organisation?
- Where should the organisation seek its partners?
- How should processes be reconfigured? Separation or integration? Strengths and weaknesses? Where is value added?
- What kind of portfolio does the organisation have and how should it be changing? Are there niche markets or potential for niche markets and is the necessary benchmark information available?
- What are the core elements of the business and its core values? Does the current mission fit?
- How will the organisation pay for or otherwise acquire the infrastructure needed – and the necessary skills? How will the current staffing profile need to change?

Source: adapted from Middlehurst (1999).

Leaders are not just those people who are the 'top' of the organisation in structural terms. Major change is at least partly about people being willing to take some responsibility and initiative right 'down' and 'across' the structure. At the same time a purely 'bottom-up' approach to change is unlikely to work, and ultimately a change process is likely to be initiated and overseen by one or more leaders who have the discipline, control and skill to set the agenda for change, albeit working with all the organisation's stakeholders to develop new visions and systems that people can and will 'buy into'. An important part of leadership, then, is getting people to follow – a good leader by definition needs support from key teams, the workforce more generally and other stakeholders. S/he must have, or develop, the ability to win and maintain that support. Those who follow will not always do so slavishly; it therefore takes skill to persuade them to do so in certain situations. However, much as people are empowered through devolved responsibility and freedom of approach within their particular working environment, they will need to be able to accept higher-level decisions. Good leaders will manage the tension between 'top down' and 'bottom up', instilling a sense of worth lower down the organisation, whilst at the same time managing tightly when necessary, in the knowledge that the rest of the organisation will follow the leader in this course of action, because the rationale for the action and approach is well understood and accepted by the workforce at large. The challenge is one of balance. While order of some kind is necessary, excessive top-down pressures will not result in successful change; rather it will cause distrust, concern, fear and resistance. It is therefore necessary to restrain 'the top-down impulse in order to create virtuous cycles of hope, collective innovation and pride of purpose' (Attwood et al., 2003).

Leadership and management

Leaders should also be managers. Leadership, focusing on dynamism, change, future strategic direction and the inspiration and motivation of the organisation and its workforce needs to be balanced by management, centred upon the technical and systematic direction of the organisation and the execution and achievement of its aims and plans through a series of activities, including resource allocation, monitoring, evaluation and revision, as necessary. Without these management aspects, the leadership dimension might become divorced from 'reality', resulting in the setting of over-idealistic and unreachable goals. Without the leadership dimension, the management element may become over-bureaucratic and lacking in imagination or momentum. Ideally, while the degree of leadership and dynamism may change over time, it is argued that organisations should seek to recruit and develop 'leader-managers capable of adopting the role in its most holistic form' (Bolden, 2004). The leadership and management elements described here should not be seen as separate or incompatible; together, they provide all the required foci for change. Leadership and management are actually part of the same job and people need to be identified and developed where they embody both parts. Leader-managers must both possess the competences and also be willing and eager to use them.

Style

Leadership style is an important component in the effectiveness and success of change management projects. There is a wide range of possible and effective leadership styles. The position is a complex one, not least in circumstances where there is an interaction between those in managerial and professional or expert roles within the same organisation, as is the case with many public services such as education or health. The most appropriate style for a given circumstance will vary depending upon the particular situation where leadership is required and be strongly driven by the current state of the organisation and its environment and where it needs to be in the future. Staff often act in similar ways to leaders, and if they have to act differently in order to secure successful change within the organisation, then it is necessary to ensure that leaders are working in ways that are in concert with the workforce at large. The approach taken will also be influenced by the background of the leader, his or her previous experience, skills and value system, and whether or not they are brought in from outside the organisation in order to lead and lead change in particular.

Whichever approach is adopted, the leadership must nevertheless stay in line with the best aspects of the prevailing culture and morality of the society in which s/he is working, with an understanding of, and sympathy with, diversity and difference in today's world. In practice, leadership is likely to be an amalgam of styles and approaches – from the strategic to the local and the influential to the directive.

The single leader

It is generally argued that the image or construct of the single visionary leader, able to drive through necessary change single-handedly, does not typically bring success, assuming that it was ever true or truly successful in the past. Charisma is an important ingredient in successful leadership, but individualistic approaches can be inappropriate. Too much charisma centred on one person is likely to be problematic for the organisation in the long run. The change process will be focused too much on one individual rather than the organisation in general. It will be hard to ensure proper dissemination and discussion with a dominant leader; and what if s/he leaves: who can easily take over the process if previous involvement in it has been limited? Collins and Porras (1994) strongly argue on the basis of their research into the most successful companies that there is no need for a single, strong dynamic leader, and that many of the organisations that they studied did not have a well known 'figurehead' in the Chief Executive Officer position; rather, most of the senior staff were too busy building the organisation through innovative and inclusive approaches to care about developing their own individual profiles. What they did have, on the other hand, was a 'cult-like' culture, where the staff of the organisation at large had a cohesive view and significant loyalty and commitment to the core values and aims; the leadership – single or otherwise – offered the workforce 'inspiration, something to believe in and a sense of purpose' (Thornbury, 1999).

Having said that the single leader is not appropriate, it may be the case, at least in extreme situations where difficult decisions have to be taken quickly, that the top-down, dominant leader approach may be necessary. In addition, the leader – in whatever context, and whatever level – must have a strong belief in the rightness of change and a confidence in the approach adopted, whether 'top-down' or 'bottom-up'. Duke (2002) says of higher education, for example: 'the leadership which manages ... a ... university must retain and project unshakeable belief in a kind of destiny, character and purpose which will bond staff as employees and students as clients into purposeful and confident collegiality'.

Teams

Some form of team leadership and, more broadly, team working, then, is likely to be the best in most circumstances, and even when major changes are being implemented. Prahalad (Hamel and Prahalad, 1996) uses the analogy of a pack of wolves for the senior team, for in hunting mode, wolves exchange roles as required, combining as leaders and team members to give the most appropriate fit for the particular challenge that they face. 'This is a lesson to be learned from nature and an organisation should not rely on a single visionary figure or an innovator to always lead the way and come up with the solution to problems' (Sutherland and Canwell, 2004).

Box 4.9   **In praise of team leadership**

The function of leadership is to assist the institution (and particular parts of the institution) to identify and evaluate emerging realities, to assess the options available and to prepare strategies for moving towards one or more scenarios ... the issues to be faced ... are complex with a range of dilemmas involved, and the organisational change required is likely to be significant. The kind of leadership called for is beyond the scope of one individual, however visionary; it requires the creative and expert input of many individuals both to identify future directions and to take forward the organisational transformation that will be necessary. A sophisticated, well-orchestrated and planned change initiative is likely to be part of institutional strategies; relying solely on the ideas of senior management teams or other levels of the ... hierarchy is not likely to be the best way forward.

Source: Middlehurst (1999).

Team leadership allows the organisation at large to identify and appreciate the problems as well as begin to offer possible solutions, rather than leaving the change management challenges in the hands of either the CEO or a small senior team only. However, there is no one mode of team working or group leadership that will fit every situation. No one person can possess all the skills and qualities necessary to lead a major change management project to a sufficient degree; and if they did, there would be a tendency for the leadership to gravitate towards an individualistic style. Good change managers at senior levels will aim to identify people who possess at least some of the required attributes at all levels and all parts of the organisation, employing and utilising complementary staff and thus spreading the expertise and experience – whether actual or potential – across the whole of the management team and beyond.

A team approach has an added advantage: the fact that a group rather than a single person is involved in developing and steering the organisation's future direction is likely to mean that little or nothing is missed and that there is no inappropriate bias in the conclusions reached and the decisions taken. As a result, when the key requirements for change managers alter, a broadly-based and complementary team will be able to respond more effectively to new and different challenges than one where all the members are similar in character and approach. The best leaders will be able, willing and confident enough in themselves to delegate tasks to others if and when they can recognise others' superior skills and abilities in a given area; even to the point at times where the leader becomes one of the team and someone else within that team takes over for a particular task. Widespread and continuous involvement in the change management process – for example through workshops, working parties and implementation groups – will give those affected by the change the opportunity to develop skills and provide leadership for themselves; as well as making them feel less threatened and more empowered, they will have identified themselves for further development within the organisation. Especially in times of major flux, those who can self-manage and develop as they lead the process are likely to be the most successful at effective change.

It will be important to work through teams and groups that accept, understand and agree with their role and that have a proper and well-understood remit not only within the team, but across the organisation more generally. Teams can, with benefit, bring together people with complementary, different, or even antagonistic views and approaches, depending how confident the change manager is about the ability of the group or the organisation to resolve any resulting conflicts. They can be large or small, or a mixture of both, depending upon what is required. They can include specialists and generalists, as appropriate to the particular task in hand. The aim of bringing a group together is to ensure that the maximum expertise and ownership is gained from the work of the team that is created, and that there is the highest possible degree of objectivity. What is crucial is that, as well as the group or team having a role, the members individually also need to be clear as to what is expected of them on the one hand and on the other that the whole team and group structure and operation is being properly managed as part of the change project overall. To this end, those setting up and monitoring groups will need also to ensure that the groups are well led and motivated, and that they are given enough time to form properly and to undertake and complete the work that they have been given to do.

| Box 4.10 | Good teamwork: key points to remember |

- choose the right mix of people – this will change depending on the circumstances and the need;
- distinguish roles, responsibilities and boundaries;
- work through strong, open, facilitative leadership and good communication;
- aim for consensus, not necessarily total agreement – a working ability to deal with disagreements constructively;
- have open and honest teams, rather than individual agendas.

Partnership working

In recent years, there has been a significant move towards partnership working – including through trades union and employee representative involvement – and this seems to be a successful approach and a welcome change in its own right compared with previous, more adversarial management–workforce relationships. 'Partnership is a way of working, but it is also a means to deal with practical issues, against the background of a changing business environment' (Neathey et al., 2005). 'A useful definition should therefore describe a set of organisational characteristics and practices that, first, do justice to the idea of managing employment relations in a 'partnership' manner and, secondly, are readily observable in order to verify a genuine example in practice' (Dietz, 2004). 'Partnership working is often neither a permanent nor a formalised way of working, and it is often the case that while an organisation takes a partnership approach to a particular issue, it may revert to a more traditional relationship at other times' (Neathey et al., 2005).

It is clear that the concept of partnership does not have one central definition, although common to all those suggested is a 'fundamental focus on the co-operative relationship between trade union or staff group representatives and management and human resources' (Neathey et al., 2005).

Box 4.11   Concepts of partnership

Partnership does not have a single definition in the workplace. The term is often used to describe anything that involves a co-operative approach to employment relations ... The emphasis of joint working is to help representatives of management and employees work together to build and develop relationships which enable the organisation to function effectively in an increasingly competitive environment (Advisory, Conciliation and Arbitration Service [ACAS], 1999).

Partnership means working together to achieve shared aims, objectives and outcomes (Cabinet Office/Council of Civil Service Unions [CCSU], 2002).

Partnership in the workplace is about employers and employees working together and creating a long-term and positive relationship that will focus on both the future of the organisation and improving the working life of the employees (UNISON, 2001).

Box 4.12   Defining partnership working

The Involvement and Participation Association [IPA] (1997) defines partnership in terms of three commitments to which all the partners should subscribe:

- the success of the enterprise;
- building trust and greater employee involvement;
- recognising the legitimate role of the partners;

plus four building blocks:

- recognition of the employees' need for employment security and the employer's need to maximise flexibility;
- sharing success with the employee;
- informing and consulting staff at the workplace and at the organisation level;
- representation of the interests of employees.

Milsome (2003) found that organisations tend to vary their approach from time to time, depending on the type of issues that were being addressed. Even with the presence of a written agreement, some organisations have also used other avenues. The IPA reported findings from ACAS research that concluded that ' ... even among organisations that adopt a partnership approach to employment relations, a considerable number rely more heavily on mechanisms that have evolved organically over time than on written arrangements' (IPA, 1997).

Partnership working of this kind still needs to recognise the basic differences between those who represent management and worker views across a whole range of areas such as (in)equalities, levels of power and empowerment, terms and conditions, basic interests and values as well as different cultural attitudes.

Box 4.13   Making partnerships work

Key elements of successful partnership working:

- mutuality – both sides recognise that there are areas of commonality/shared interest;
- plurality – areas of difference are recognised also;
- trust and respect in the intentions of the other side and for legitimate difference in interests;
- agreement without coercion – an intention to solve problems through consensus, recognising business and employee needs;
- involvement and voice – providing opportunities for employees to shape their work environment and have their opinions heard;
- individualistic and collectivist dimension through direct and indirect (ie representative) forms of employee involvement.

Source: adapted from Reilly (2001).

Prerequisites for effective partnership working

Communications:

- needs to be agreement on the status of communications between managers and unions and on release to wider organisation;

Box 4.13   Making partnerships work (*Cont'd*)

- parties need to be clear how confidential information will be treated.

Resources:

- representatives need time and skills.

Partnership relationship:

- honesty and trust are key elements of an effective partnership working;
- early engagement with all stakeholders (including trade union representatives and senior line management).

Project planning:

- effective project planning to take forward complex projects (including how long with tasks take, time for consultation, project manager).

Structures and processes:

- combination of formal and informal forums for discussion;
- clarity of status of ideas shared at different meetings.

Other:

- union representatives still need to be representing the membership;
- line management needs to be committed to the principles of partnership and will abide by decisions reached.

Source: adapted from Neathey et al. (2005).

Summary

This chapter has concentrated on the roles and responsibilities of all the key groups and individuals likely to be involved within an organisation in change and any change management project. There is a clear categorisation of the various groups involved on the one hand, but their roles and the way in which they interact with each other results in a continuum of involvement and engagement with change that the change managers, senior staff and change agents in particular will have to appreciate and facilitate to best effect.

How managers – especially in the middle levels – view the organisation and any proposed changes will be crucial to the success of any change management project. Managers (at all levels) must be willing to change themselves or their style too in order to lead and accommodate new styles of working. But the best change projects will also ensure that the workforce is involved throughout. This is where change agents of one or more of the kinds discussed in this chapter will be especially valuable. Team and partnership working are important approaches for ensuring such wholesale involvement and engagement.

In the final analysis, leadership is key to effective change management. Leadership goes beyond personal strength and ability, important though those attributes are; the leader must encourage individuals and groups working within the organisation, removing barriers to change and working towards the effectiveness of teams and the organisation as a whole rather than just the leader or the 'top' team, the goal being to create an ethos of change supported across the institution.

Notes

1. *http://www.businessballs.com/changemanagement.htm*
2. See also the Centre for Applied Emotional Intelligence: *http://www.emotionalintelligence.co.uk*

References

Advisory, Conciliation and Arbitration Service (1999) *Towards Better Employment Relations: Using the ACAS Advisory Service.* London: ACAS.

Attwood, M., Pedler, M. and Pritchard, S. (2003) *Leading Change: a Guide to Whole Systems Working.* Bristol: The Policy Press.

Belasen, A. (2000) *Leading the Learning Organisation: Communication and Competencies for Managing Change.* New York: State University of New York.

Bolden, R. (2004) *What Is Leadership?* Research Report. Exeter: The Windsor Leadership Trust, Centre for Leadership Studies, University of Exeter.

Brierley, P. (2005a) *Opportunities and Challenges for the Church of England Over the Next 15 Years: Some Statistical Trends and What They Imply for Church Leaders.* London: Christian Research.

Cabinet Office/Council of Civil Service Unions (2002) *Partnership Working Project Group: Report.* London: Cabinet Office.

Collins, J.C. and Porras, J.I. (1994) *Built to Last: Successful Habits of Visionary Companies.* New York: Harper Business.

Davidson Frame, J. (2002) *The New Project Management: Tools for an Age of Rapid Change, Complexity, and Other Business Realities,* 2nd edition. San Francisco: Jossey Bass.

Dietz, G. (2004) 'Partnership and the development of trust in British workplaces'. *Human Resource Management Journal,* 14(1): 5–24.

Dover, P. (2002) 'Change agents at work: lessons from Siemens Nixdorf'. *Journal of Change Management,* 3(3): 243–57.

Duke, C. (2002) *Managing the Learning University.* Buckingham: Society for Research into Higher Education and Open University.

Goleman, D. (1996) *Emotional Intelligence.* London: Bloomsbury.

Hamel, G. and Prahalad, C.K. (1996) *Competing for the Future.* Watertown, MA: Harvard Business School.

Involvement and Participation Association (1997) *Towards Industrial Partnership: New Ways of Working.* London: IPA.

McCalman, J. and Paton, R. (1992) *Change Management: a Guide to Effective Implementation.* London: Paul Chapman.

Middlehurst, R. (1999) 'New realities for leadership and governance in Higher Education?' *Tertiary Education and Management,* 5: 307–29.

Miller D. (2002) 'Successful change leaders: what makes them? What do they do that is different?' *Journal of Change Management,* 2(4): 359–68.

Milsome, S. (2003) 'An open relationship'. *Employment Trends/IRS Employment Review,* 779.

Monks, R. and Minow, N. (2003) *Corporate Governance.* Oxford: Blackwell.

Neathey, F., Regan, J. and Newton, L. (2005) *Working in Partnership in Higher Education: Final Report* (a report for JNCHES by the Institute for Employment Studies). London: Universities and Colleges Employers' Association.

Oxenbridge, S. and Brown, W. (2004) 'Achieving a new equilibrium? Stability of co-operative employer-union relationships'. *Industrial Relations Journal,* 35(5): 388–402.

Reilly, P. (2001) *Partnership Under Pressure: How Does It Survive?* London: Institute for Employment Studies; report 383.

Scott, P. (1996) *Governing Universities: Changing the Culture?* Buckingham: SRHE/University Press.

Solomon, E. (2001) 'The dynamics of corporate change: management's evaluation of stakeholder characteristics'. *Human Systems Management,* 20(3): 257–66.

Sutherland, J, and Canwell, D. (2004) *Key Concepts in Strategic Management.* Basingstoke: Palgrave Macmillan.

Tanner Pascale, R and Sternin, J. (2005) 'Your company's secret change agents'. *Harvard Business Review,* 83(5): 72–81.

Thornbury, J. (1999) 'KPMG: revitalising culture through values'. *Business Strategy Review,* 10(4): 1–15.

UNISON (2001) *Working Together on Health and Safety: a UNISON Guide to Partnership Agreements.* London: UNISON Communications Unit.

Whetherly, J. (1998) *Achieving Change Through Training and Development.* London: Library Association Publishing.

Case study 4.1   The merger of the Victoria University of Manchester and UMIST

Keywords: *vision, environmental change, timing, unity, leadership, universities.*

Merger explorations between the Victoria University of Manchester and the University of Manchester Institute of Science and Technology (UMIST) were under discussion for some 18 months before they were announced publicly in October 2003; until then, only senior staff knew that such a proposal was in contention. Those at the top were waiting until the chance of support from the institutions involved and from the Higher Education Funding Council for England (HEFCE) was effectively guaranteed. The merger itself made excellent business sense. From the Universities' points of view, both were in the same city and in direct competition for students, especially in the sciences, and it was difficult for the City to support either unequivocally. There was a degree of brand confusion, as UMIST had previously awarded Manchester Degrees. The existence of two research-strong institutions so closely located was inefficient and damaging, not only to themselves individually but also to Manchester's desire to develop a greater national and international reputation.

The merger only became a reality when each institution approved the proposal. They agreed to appoint designate staff to the new institution even though legal necessities were still being undertaken to dissolve the two old institutions and create the new. A clear vision of a world-class institution was established, and the new team had to spend time and energy working on methods to develop the necessary operational policies, processes and attitudes throughout the institutions. From the outset, the merger's goal was to produce more than just the sum of the two parts – adding together without improving the whole just wouldn't be good enough. This ambitious aim necessitated a stringent and wide-reaching strategy that looked beyond the immediate timeframe into the years ahead.

The University of Manchester aimed to become an internationally-recognised university for research and teaching. The merger was one stage of this, but, more importantly, it was the handling of the merger that would decide whether this overall goal was helped or hindered. Thus, the University set about integrating its vision to become one of best universities in the world into the change process: the merger became an opportunity to create a new image and style rather than simply a merged identity. The Manchester 2015 agenda, accessible via the web, established a clear strategy; key words and phrases for this new and forward looking identity include, among others, world-class, research-focused, entrepreneurship, widening participation, recognising capability, communication, innovation, rationalisation, efficiency and collaboration among stakeholders. The change was only a tool, not an end product in itself. Judgement of success or failure would come from results and outcomes measured over time, not from superficial acquiescence.

As part of this wider strategy and vision, Information and Communications Technology (ICT) systems played a crucial role in bringing about a satisfactory outcome. The managers hoped to use ICT to add value

Case study 4.1 **The merger of the Victoria University of Manchester and UMIST** *(Cont'd)*

to the University, for example to assist with research and to develop high-quality facilities such as the eGrid, data warehousing and ID Card and Swipe across the campus. They felt that installing world-class ICT systems to underpin the changes being implemented through the merger could create a significantly enhanced service. This was not an easy policy to implement. Firstly, the Victoria University and UMIST had very different ICT set-ups; secondly, it was difficult to ensure that technology was a tool of, and not the engine for, change, and that the ICT strategy stayed in line with that of the University as a whole. Business owners were stretched to support the managerial changes impacting their teams whilst adequately establishing the goals for the new systems and services. Overall, ICT strategy has been successfully aligned to the wider goals and future strategy of the merged University.

The merger and subsequent work to develop a world-class university seems to have made a very healthy start. Tools to win cultural acceptance among employees were used to good effect. These included a policy of 'healthy competition' within the ICT department, which encouraged staff to be more efficient yet also optimistic. While staff had to compete for new roles in a new structure, they were protected from redundancy. Similarly, although the merger itself was dictated 'from above', communication played a key role in winning acceptance on the ground. Workshops were held to explain why change was necessary; managers showed themselves willing to delegate, accommodate concerns and act flexibly on processes; team leaders and heads of service were drafted in to cascade thoughts and change processes downwards; and above all a strong but sensitive leader held everything together in the centre.

The changes and their repercussions are not fully complete. The Head of ICT stressed that cultural change will only really have been successful once employees stop talking about 'the merger' or 'the change', and instead accept the new realities as the only realities; he feels that about five years are needed for this process to complete fully, during which time the changes are still being lived through and tensions and issues worked out. Similarly, not everything was easy to implement, and policies and strategies were sometimes dependent on a variety of groups who were not easy to co-ordinate. Time is needed to smooth this out as the 'new' institution continues to learn and reform operational processes and refine its structural organisation, including increasing the devolution of all service areas.

Nevertheless, signs over the last two years have been encouraging. Staff seemed to accept the need for the change almost without opposition, partly because the merger was seen as being demanded from an external source, out of immediate control, and partly because consultation was used so effectively. The opportunity to 'blame' others for the need to merge made it easier for staff to get on with the changes in their own domain, while

Case study 4.1 **The merger of the Victoria University of Manchester and UMIST** *(Cont'd)*

consultation allowed them a say in the structure and future of the new environment. Arguably, it is very difficult to change people but much easier to change their operating environment, and a merger is one of the simplest ways to change the environment. What is more, the senior managers went beyond the minimum and worked hard to create a new sense of value and worth through the merger, ensuring that it had a beneficial and not merely a neutral effect on the University's mission.

When interviewed, Manchester's Head of ICT said that his top factors for the successful management of change included:

1. Having a change landscape, and knowing both where you are now and where you want to be at the end of the process.

2. Justifying the route down which you want to travel, and being able and willing to articulate this when dealing with potentially threatening human change.

3. Having a plan for operational matters, involving communications, prioritised processes, the transparent perception of fairness and equity in managerial treatment of employees, and flexibility.

4. Having a plan to deal with the winners and losers, and a mechanism to soften the inevitable effects on the losers.

5. Recognizing where change may challenge the products of human intellect, and being able to deal with the negativity this will produce.

6. Changing the environment where possible, for example through re-location or investment in infrastructure, because new surroundings help to generate feelings of deeper and more permanent progress.

5

Learning for change

Introduction

This chapter is concerned with the particular human resource (HR) management aspects of change. It introduces the concept of strategic human resource management (SHRM) – the integration of HR policies, practices and approaches with the strategic direction of the organisation and its change management aspirations and objectives. Change is ultimately about people – how they react, how they need to be prepared for change, and how they are best led, managed and involved. Taking an integrative and strategic approach to HR management is seen as a way of ensuring that change is approached holistically, with HR practices and policies as a central element of the change process, if not the actual main driver of it. Certainly, it is argued that an organisation that embraces SHRM will be more likely to be successful at long-term change than one that does not, not least because it ensures the development of staff for the future.

This strategic approach begins with the recruitment, selection and promotion of staff and their training and development. It is argued that practical experience and opportunities are an essential part of effective preparation for future changes within the organisation. Given the importance of leadership and management, this chapter considers how best to develop them. Organisation development is also crucial. At the simplest level, 'learning lessons' can ensure that change is better managed as the organisation reflects on how it handles the process and the content of change. The concept of the learning organisation – where such an approach is embedded into all that it does – is considered as a way of providing a framework for ongoing change. Ways of developing the learning organisation are then considered, including the use of action learning sets.

Strategic human resource management

In recent years, the concept of strategic human resource management (SHRM) has come to the fore (Mello, 2001), though there is no single definition of the term. It can be seen as a prescription for conducting change on the one hand or a description of how things are changing on the other. It is intended to be a broader approach than old-style HR management, and is meant to be capable of dealing with the widening demands of change that are increasingly prevalent. The aim is to ensure that HR management policies and practices are fully integrated with the workings and strategies of the rest of the organisation and not a series of activities that stand in isolation from it and, more broadly, to ensure, by using an SHRM approach, that the different aspects of that organisation link and integrate. So, for example, adopting an SHRM approach should result in the linking of individual and group performance in line with the specific goals, aims and strategies of the organisation, and foster partnership working across the organisation: 'the viability of workplace partnership is dependent upon the presence of supportive HR practices, together with the promotion of "strategic integration" between HR concerns and strategic management' (Roche and Geary, 2002; Ainscough et al., 2003).

Indeed, some writers argue that the HR function is *the* central driver for change, at least in terms of shaping the style of working. Certainly, it is important to make sure that people and organisation remain in alignment throughout any change management project, especially where

---

Box 5.1   Change and staffing

The impact of change on ... staff is no less significant an issue. For institutions (or, where relevant, the state), there is a need to reassess contractual relations, reward systems, the creation of new cadres of staff, the re-deployment and re-training of others, and the nature of training that might need to be provided or procured. For individuals, there is a need to consider the potential of 'portfolio' working, the implications of self-employment, the need for new skills or capitalisation on particular strengths in areas of knowledge and expertise; for both individuals and institutions, notions of ' ... careers' need to be re-assessed and re-conceptualised.

Source: Middlehurst (1999).

---

one element or part is driving changes in other areas. A strategic approach will help to ensure that the organisation at large keeps up with what is happening, provided that the importance of communication is emphasised and that SHRM results in widespread employee commitment to the wider policies and practices being adopted.

At its best, SHRM should result in an organisation where everyone is working in the same, concerted, agreed direction, recognising that the development of the individual is inextricably linked with the development of the organisation. Without the former, the ability of the latter to embrace, manage and succeed in and through change will be limited. Wherever the HR management dimension fits into the organisation, then, it must have a high degree of centrality to the overall aims and objectives, for good HR policies and practices have a considerable power to improve effectiveness and efficiency and have the capacity to underpin long-term, major change. Such an approach requires that there is a clear overarching strategy into which the HR strategy can both feed and from which it derives its main objectives and approaches. The latter strategy will need to be monitored, evaluated and its success measured in terms of the extent to which it enables the organisation to meet its future ambitions and aspirations in general and its ability to change as required in particular. Ultimately, SHRM needs to result in the 'systematic development of skill' (Shiba and Walden, 2001), not just as part of a one-off change management project or process, but as part of continuous improvement as an integral element of the organisation and its long-term goals and strategies. Future core competences must therefore be developed as part of the organisation's objectives, with the expectation that the organisation is collectively competent as required, with training and development structured to match longer-term needs and not just immediate requirements.

Recruitment, selection and promotion

Nowhere is the importance, and possible benefit, of a strategic approach more evident than in recruitment, selection and promotion, where the choice of the best, most appropriate people for particular roles and responsibilities – all within the generic context of what the organisation is trying to achieve – will make change – and culture change in particular – easier in the longer term. There is a view that 'who' should come before 'what'. In other words, staff should be chosen for particular roles – and particular aptitudes, for example people best equipped to deal with change or to help the organisation establish good policies or fit-for-purpose modes of thinking – before the major change management tasks are determined, resulting in a 'significant shift in the recruitment and selection process from one that traditionally focuses on matching people to specific, well defined jobs to one where emphasis is placed on finding and selecting people who have the necessary attributes to be able to adjust to changing roles' (Thornhill et al., 2000). Certainly, getting the 'right' people together at an early stage in a major project should result in the development of good relationships and a working environment that will support and facilitate major change, not least because the teams created – rather than the single leader or manager – will 'own' the problem and be more adept at working towards a solution than may be the case where the parameters of the change management challenge have already been set before the key personnel have been identified.

Training and development

Training and development needs to form part of the overall strategic approach described earlier. This will be particularly important in the context of change management, where, for example, implementing policies aimed at altering structural or cultural aspects of the organisation in order to set the stage for wider change will require a well-planned training and development programme that is monitored, evaluated and revised as necessary on the basis of set and agreed targets. Roberto and Levesque (2005), for example, argue that the seeds of effective, lasting change that is embedded within the 'architecture and fabric' of the organisation must be planted by embedding procedural and behavioural changes long before the change initiative proper is launched, and training and development will be a key way of ensuring that this happens. Take, for example, a major restructuring exercise; the (re)training and (re)development of staff will be an essential prerequisite of success; the same will be true of substantial continuous improvement programmes aimed at turning staff into thinkers as well as doers, all in the context of a 'learning organisation'.

Training, then, may be necessary in order to change or develop the knowledge, skills or attitudes – and perhaps therefore the behaviour – of the workforce. If appropriate training is not given, then people may not embrace the changes fully, as for example in the introduction of new technology – an area where there are many cases of failed change management projects as a consequence of inadequate preparation of the workforce (Baker, 2004). Mentoring and coaching staff will also be crucial once they have to start dealing with change. When altering systems, or introducing new ones, the change manager must therefore be willing to spend time with people so that they are able to work with the new systems properly; systems only work if those that run them fully understand and appreciate what is required of them. The more people are prepared for, and understand, new systems and processes before they are introduced, the more likely the changes are to be successful.

Training and development can be on a one-to-one basis and in an informal setting, to the whole workforce in more formal settings or, more likely, some combination of modes of delivery. Training as part of a change management process is likely to be an integral part of helping people to 'let go' of the past and prepare for the future, with an emphasis of the benefits of the new way of working. Those whose roles are changing will need to be prepared for their new roles, especially where either the staff are being promoted or have to work in different ways, or both. Without such preparation, the changes required are unlikely to be fully or properly embraced by those who most need to do so. Care will be needed to ensure that training is available equally and fairly to all who require it in order to avoid the creation of perceived 'inner circles with privileged access' (Terry and Smith, 2003).

A number of personal training requirements are also evident, and 'personal development' has become an increasingly important aspect of organisational and change management. In any case, individuals should take an interest in their career development and future path and be encouraged to do so by the organisation. Career ladders have changed significantly over the last twenty years and are set to change further. Outsourcing of certain activities, for example, has the potential to reduce or even completely eradicate a particular career path. On the other hand, change of all kinds can provide opportunities for individuals to progress up a career ladder, including ones that might not have previously been thought of as appropriate. In addition, given the changing nature of the workforce (with later retirement on the one hand and early retirement on the other) and a significant change in both demography and working patterns, training and re-training programmes will be essential elements of any change programme, whether aimed at the individual, the group, or the whole organisation.

At the same time, however much training and preparation is given and received, there is no substitute for practical application. Drawing on past experiences is useful, especially where this offers the change manager an opportunity to involve people in new changes. 'Each experience of successfully managed change is likely to prepare staff for constant change' (Whetherly, 1998). The importance and value of 'on-the-job' training at all levels is as important in change management projects as in other aspects of working life. The key to ensuring that such practical experience is valuable is to ensure that those involved learn – both through success and failure – in order to manage and be managed effectively through change, especially where the trainees remain in a context appropriate to their learning. This will also encourage reflection on experiences, with 'lessons learned' being put to good use in future change management situations. A reflective approach to such learning experiences will lead to analysis, synthesis and the growth of ideas, with the 'potential for the concurrent development of managers and organisations' (Gosling and Mintzberg, 2004).

Change will render some skills obsolete and demand the development of new ones. Just as technology becomes out of date, so people's skills need to be upgraded or replaced to take account of new situations. Organisations must identify present and future core competences and work to ensure that the workforce has the necessary skills for the changed position. Focusing on training and development and the creation of skills and competences that are fit for purpose is therefore an essential prerequisite of effective change management. Those who take responsibility for change – typically 'senior' management – will need to be (re)trained as their roles alter in the light of changes made. HR management is a core part of the skills base for managers, and not just in times of change. So too is the development of leadership as well as management skills and aptitudes.

Leadership development

Developing leaders and leadership capacity in an organisation has at least an implicit effect on the ability of that organisation to change, but it is also argued that such development should be explicit if change is to be achieved successfully. Indeed, leadership development could be a focus for change management and the mechanisms of change. But in order for leadership development to be successful at the organisational level, it will be necessary to ascertain where the development of the organisation in general is going and where it needs to go so that the appropriate type of leadership can be identified and then fostered.

The most effective type of leadership development in terms of helping organisational change would appear to be experiential, though much leadership training is still based on formal approaches that often involve delivery external to the organisation. There is therefore a need to achieve a shift in how development is undertaken, in particular by focusing on the role of leaders in change management rather than concentrating on the specific skills of individual leaders themselves as the main focus of the developmental process. So, for example, the organisation should look at its leaders' ability to deal with the unexpected, to respond effectively, to focus on lifelong learning, to see collaboration as good and to encourage, foster and facilitate positive interdependence, social skills and group autonomy. A mixture of results, people and project-based techniques is most likely to be successful.

There is a strong argument for making leadership development an embedded, continuous and fundamental aspect of any change management approach, assisting both leaders and led to develop as well as

Box 5.2   Key leadership capacities

- to undertake and make use of research;
- to develop scenarios, to think creatively and to build on ideas drawn from other contexts (different from strategic planning);
- to utilise the knowledge, experience and ideas developed in all parts of the organisation and in linked networks of contact (a co-ordinated technological and human 'knowledge management' infrastructure);
- use of strong external networks – optimised with purpose;
- a clear understanding of, and expertise in, change management processes, with specific experience of how those processes work in professional organisations;
- use of organisational structures and processes that will allow for existing activities to proceed, transitional arrangements to be made and new structures to evolve;
- use of operating procedures that are flexible and speedy, requiring minimum bureaucracy and maximum efficiency (personal accountability and trust are of prime importance, while committees may become increasingly anachronistic);
- development of a culture of experimentation, risk-taking and reward for innovation.

Source: adapted from Middlehurst (1999).

change. The more leadership skills are developed in a variety of contexts and situations, then the more experience leaders will have to draw on and the greater their understanding of the numerous complexities associated with change management in particular.

Management development

Management development is a crucial part of a major change management programme. Indeed, there is a 'growing complexity and interdependency that exists between management development strategies and practices and a dynamic organisational system' (Doyle, 2000) that needs to be fully recognised. Management development, then, must go beyond straightforward courses to consider and determine 'how an individual or organisation applies their ability in a confident manner to problems in new and unfamiliar circumstances as well as in familiar situations' (Townsend and Cairns, 2002). For managers, this will require the development of a strong understanding of self and one's own situation and culture and background before being able to take on board an understanding of the positions of others. It will include the development of personality traits – flexibility, adaptability, openness – alongside skills that need to be learned and developed. Programmes will also inculcate management skills that are suited to horizontal rather than vertical structures, focusing on providing leadership rather than emphasising more directive or even authoritarian management, and on developing the appropriate attitudes, approaches and beliefs rather than reinforcing a construct of the manager as the person who 'knows all the answers'. They will aim to help the manager develop different styles, approaches and understanding, depending upon the particular environment and situation in which the manager finds him/herself, including the ability to integrate, facilitate, co-ordinate, discuss, monitor, evaluate and feed back as part of the change management process.

Formal training and development needs to be integrated and balanced with practical, on-the-job experience. In the case of management development, there is much to be said for a form of 'apprenticeship' training, where new managers are linked with colleagues – senior or peer – who have been within the organisation for a longer period of time, are good 'people persons', who know the local environment, culture and politics well and can help the newer recruit or trainee to develop in-role while getting to grips with the more subtle contextual aspects of change management within the specific organisational context. Collins and

Porras (1994) take this approach further, arguing that it is important to develop senior managers from within the organisation, given that their research found that it was difficult to bring people in from outside at the key leadership levels. For them, management development processes need to encompass succession planning arrangements to ensure smooth transitions from one set of leaders to the next.

Development programmes should play a vital role in helping to equip managers for new challenges and changed circumstances and therefore help in the process of changing institutions. Management development offers an opportunity for both individuals and organisations to make sense of changes affecting the sector and subsequently to manage those changes in order to help the institution and, indeed, the sector at large, given the creation of cadres of managers who can benefit that sector within and beyond the wider organisational system. However, this will only happen if the training and development is seen as worthwhile by managers and others, and the right things are taught and then followed-up in subsequent application, both by the individual being trained and the organisation. Programmes will also need to take account of, and cope with, the potential resistance of managers, especially with regard to fundamental changes in their role. 'Some form of psychological or emotional intervention to manage frustrated expectations, a loss of esteem and identity, may become just as important as mainstream management development activity' (Doyle, 2000). Otherwise, managers – who may have as much to lose from major change as the rest of the workforce – will have mostly negative feelings towards both the change process and training and development programmes.

| Box 5.3 | Key management capacities |

- understanding of self, culture and background;
- flexibility;
- adaptability;
- openness;
- ability to work with, and in, teams;
- ability to integrate, facilitate, co-ordinate, discuss, monitor, evaluate and feed back.

Lessons learned

Very few projects will go exactly to plan; there will always be 'room for improvement'. Good project management encourages programme and project managers to identify the 'lessons learned' from completed work, whether successful or unsuccessful. The results of such reviews are likely to be of use not just in future programmes and project work, but also in relation to the development of strategy, with particular relevance to the organisational capacity to implement strategic aims and objectives. If an institution has a poor reputation for programme management, for example, it is highly unlikely to be able to turn its aspirations into reality without major organisational change. In such a case, the institutional strategy will have to concentrate on capacity building as much as change management, improvement or innovation.

In the most successful change management projects, one of the benefits of the process will be that collective as well as individual learning has taken place. At its most basic, the change manager should draw upon the relevant professional literature, research and the experiences of others, as long as this is not done in an unquestioning way. Organisations that learn from their mistakes are much more likely to be successful in their development and implementation of strategy that those that do not. In particular, negative experiences are very important, and while this will teach the organisation what not to do, it may be that a good idea was introduced at the wrong time and that, at some point in the future, the proposed change may either be possible or might come about in different ways. Even a change project that met none of its primary objectives may not itself be a complete failure because of the learning, networks, changed environments or development experiences that it engendered along the way. 'Lessons learned' reports are useful at all levels of an organisation in this respect. In terms of strategic planning, it is crucial that the underpinning techniques used allow the organisation to set an appropriate general direction, anticipating opportunities and threats, using all relevant information – information gathered effectively and efficiently.

The learning organisation

'Learning and change arise above all in human interaction' (Donaldson et al., 2005a). Change can happen in pockets, and good practice can be built on 'lessons learned' processes on a one-off basis, or reflection on what went well and what failed can be part of an ongoing 'learning' approach that pervades the whole organisation. If it is accepted that change must occur, and a culture that sees change as normal and acceptable is established, then it should be possible to take control of change agendas rather than be driven by them. Sutherland and Canwell (2004) talk of the 'absorptive capacity' of an organisation – its ability to identify, and to 'value, assimilate and then utilise, any new knowledge ... to its own ... advantage' and the importance of this learning ability to the future wellbeing of the organisation. They also refer to 'adaptive culture', where an organisation recognises 'that it is not the strength of its culture which matters but its adaptability ... [allowing] the adoption of strategies or practices which are able to respond to changing markets and new competitive situations' (Sutherland and Canwell, 2004).

In recent years, therefore, the concept of the 'learning organisation' (Chawla and Renesch, 1995; Kline and Saunders, 1998) has become popular, not least as a way of identifying and codifying the key characteristics of successful organisations that are capable of surviving and adapting well to changed circumstances and environments. Such an organisation embraces continual transformation, 'unlearning' old and outdated practices in a constructive way, bringing in new ideas and ways of working rather than reinventing a variation of the 'status quo', the basic impetus being to tackle and resolve the root cause of problems, ensuring that they either do not recur, or that if they do, there are robust processes for dealing with them as future lessons learned. Lewin (1947) suggested that learning is facilitated within a cycle of action, reflection, generalisation and testing.

A learning organisation, then, is one that regularly reviews its direction and approach in a mature, consciously self-critical way, experimenting, modifying and evaluating alternatives through feed forward as well as feedback loops or 'double-loop learning', which is about changing – and learning to change – underlying values and assumptions: learning by doing, in other words (Argyris, 1976; Argyris and Schon, 1992). Solving a particular problem, for example, allows the person doing the solving to transfer that skill and knowledge to other situations. The secondary learning will be facilitated in situations where it is possible to examine and experiment with different ways of solving problems.

Learning organisations can also be categorised as 'adaptive', where there is an assimilation of new ideas and approaches, or 'generative',

Figure 5.1 **Virtuous learning cycle**

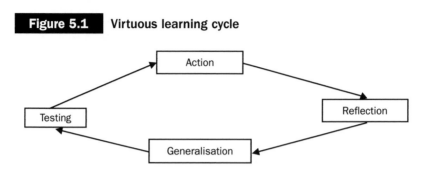

where there is a constant evaluation of objectives and approaches, its culture and structure in order to respond to changing situations.

Because the learning is meant to be organisation-wide, there has to be an underlying commitment to widespread participation in policy making involving all stakeholders and a commitment from the senior management in particular to working through differences of opinion. Communication and negotiation replace top-down control, the emphasis being rather on bottom-up initiative and empowerment, with enabling and flexible structures geared to development rather than reward. Individual parts of the organisation may be seen as customers or suppliers to each other, with appropriate agreements and understandings between them.

The learning organisation engages in 'informating' (Zuboff, 1988), using information for understanding in a holistic way; the workforce acts as information scanners, bringing back information from both inside and

Box 5.4 **Learning environments and the learning organisation**

A learning environment occurs in an organisation that is deemed to be a learning organisation. In other words, the organisation has put in place both facilities and a culture for learning. The essential encompassing concept is that the organisations learn from external stimuli and, as a result, alter or amend their internal framework to match those opportunities. This requires a re-evaluation of goals and, in extreme circumstances, a change in organisational culture, organisational structure and the patterns of work, in order to take advantage of the new opportunities.

Source: Sutherland and Canwell (2004).

| Table 5.1 | Types of learning organisation |

Type	Comment
Knowing organisation	Understands the environment, but is in a static situation.
Understanding and thinking organisations	Understands the environment, and is willing and able to adapt to a certain degree.
Learning organisations	Understands the environment and accepts change as inevitable, necessary and desirable and embraces it to the point where they are leaders of change within the sector.

outside the organisation and focusing on what is important both overall and in relation to specific groups. Learning is public, inside and outside the organisation: 'people create new meanings and insights together ... understand each other's perspectives, forge new understandings and make plans to change relationships, a collective 'making sense' takes place that acknowledges individual contributions but is shared and jointly owned' (Attwood et al., 2003). This provides common perspectives leading to everyone working in the same direction with people in the learning organisation's network being colleagues, rather than competitors.

Knowledge creation, expansion and dissemination are key, underpinned by good communications and an ability to apply knowledge as acquired and when and where it is required. The climate engendered is one where learning takes place, where help and support are provided if something goes wrong, and where the drive is towards continuous improvement, with opportunities for individual and group self-development, based on self-responsibility with external (to the group) guidance rather than direction. The role of the manager is crucial in the learning organisation, with the emphasis not so much on management as mentoring and coaching, helping staff to grow, offering feedback and moving from defensive, single-loop learning to open, double-loop approaches.

That, at least, is the ideal of the learning organisation. The reality is arguably more difficult to achieve, not least because of the need to change cultures and attitudes. Double-loop learning, for example, requires the organisation to let go of old assumptions; not everyone may welcome an analysis of the organisation that reveals poor performance and the repetition of old and avoidable mistakes. Some elements of the concept may run counter to the needs and structure of the organisation, and in particular its hierarchical and decision-making elements unless, or until, there is a significant shift in management attitudes and mindsets; and such wholesale change is likely to be difficult unless the organisation is being set up from new, in which case there is an opportunity to create attitudes, relationships, processes and working practices that will foster the learning approach from the start. But in most (pre-)existing organisations, some form of traditional bureaucracy may be required, either because of external requirements (as for example quality control mechanisms expected by validating agencies) or internal traditions and cultures.

Box 5.5	Key characteristics of the learning organisation

Iles and Sutherland (2001) identify five key elements of the learning organisation:

Structure

Managerial hierarchies enhance opportunities for all stakeholders' involvement in the organisation by empowering people to take relevant decisions. Teamwork and strong lateral (as well as vertical) networks and communications within the organisation – and externally – are well supported.

Organisational culture

Strong cultures promote openness, creativity, and experimentation; encourage the acquisition, processing and sharing of information; foster innovation and creativity; and allow experimentation through risk of failure and managed learning from mistakes.

Information systems

Information systems improve and support the organisation's activities and approaches rather than controlling them, providing rapid acquisition, processing and sharing of rich and complex information, leading to effective knowledge management.

Box 5.5 **Key characteristics of the learning organisation**
(Cont'd)

Human resource practices

People are key to the organisation's learning. Human resource management is about providing and supporting individual learning and key systems focus on long-term performance and the acquisition and sharing of new skills and knowledge.

Leadership

Leaders create an environment where an open, risk-taking and reflective approach is encouraged, as the basis for an attractive and inspiring vision of a learning organisation, providing empathy, support and personal advocacy and ensuring that the organisation in all its constituent parts has the ability and the capacity to learn, change and develop.

Breaking all this down to replace it by a 'learning organisation' may not be possible, or, indeed, even desirable. A more realistic and, in consequence, more effective approach than the wholesale abandonment of existing structures and styles may be to reorganise and reform the inherited bureaucracy, while recognising and including the best of the new ideas and understandings with those that are already 'tried and tested' and which will, in the judgement of the change manager, be just as effective in the future, if not more so, when combined with novel approaches and attitudes. So, for example, employee 'empowerment' may best be encouraged and developed not only within a set of values agreed across the organisation but also in the context of a managed approach to decentralisation that defines levels of responsibility and stresses interdependence rather than independence and the need for an overall management of the constituent parts of the organisation, with a properly, structured and equitable approach to innovation and concomitant reward.

Embracing the concept, if not every aspect, of the learning organisation may at least prevent the management – and, for that matter, the workforce – from falling into the trap of a tokenistic support that encourages people to pretend to learn, while in reality using learning experiences as a way of reinforcing existing structures, systems, approaches or cultures. Only if there is a determined approach to change – of whatever kind and approach – will aspects of the learning organisation take root. Superficial adoption of learning approaches will actually make real change – if and when it is eventually embarked on – more difficult to achieve because of increased cynicism amongst the workforce, and may even lead to organisational inertia. Open and honest approaches, as noted elsewhere in this book, may, however, lead to the long-term development and creation of an organisation that is capable of the rich learning that is meant to characterise the learning organisation.

Learning can include networking within and between organisations (likely to be within the same area) – a concept perhaps easier to implement in the public sector, though even here increased competitiveness may prove antipathetic to the open sharing of information and experience. Drawing on the experiences, realities and the ideas of others in similar positions is a proven way to develop change managers and others, whether informally or through more formal collaborative networks for discussion and support. At its most advanced, this open networking could take the form of a 'hypertext' organisation, with interlocking groups from different organisational entities working together as a single, albeit virtual, team. The members of the network group learn together, ideally feeding back into and enriching organisational learning, which in turn feeds back into the network. Networking learning goes beyond 'simple' change management, and there is no necessary or obvious relationship between specific change and network learning, because there is no single direction or particular manager of the network learning process: 'network actors are neither merely adapting to changing exogenous factors, nor managing change. Rather, they are seen here as interpretative agencies whose situated reflections, exchanges and relations cumulatively influence changes to network practices, structures and interpretations, which can be seen to feedback recursively shifting the whole network context' (Knight and Pye, 2004). 'Management' in the traditional sense cannot take place because no one person or vision is being followed, while 'change' is more complex than the difference between the start and end of a period of elapsed time.

Action learning is an increasingly common technique in management development programmes. Such an approach enables those involved to look at specific issues relating to their roles and work as managers. Learning in this way is often improved by working with people from different (rather than the same) institutions. While a facilitator may be available to start and nurture the process of action learning, the emphasis is on the action learning group itself collectively identifying and resolving the issues that the members face. A high degree of trust and confidence within the group is necessary in order for this approach to work. The process needs to be clearly defined and the protocols for working agreed from the start. Action learning appears to work best with small groups of four to six people. Some case studies that used action learning follow this chapter.

Box 5.6	Action learning

When undertaking action learning, the following are important:

- voluntary involvement/active engagement;
- real issues rather than abstract problems;
- improving current issues and situations, but also helping individuals develop, change and increase in personal understanding;
- creating a united front and aiming, through a healthy mixture of support and diversity, to find immediate and long-term solutions;
- helping participants learn from the experiences of others and widen their own knowledge to help tackle future issues.

Summary

The ability to learn, develop and adapt is crucial to the survival of any organisation. This ability can be characterised by a high degree of responsiveness, an awareness of the drivers for doing things differently, a good record at rapid and effective change, and an ability to improve on a continuous basis. A well-motivated and well-trained workforce is an essential part of any effective organisation, and especially one that is undergoing, or wishes to undergo, significant change. The changing organisation will wish to encourage both the learning and the subsequent use of newly-acquired skills.

Such a situation will best be achieved by adopting a strategic approach to HR management, ensuring the systematic development of the whole workforce, while remembering that leadership and management development will be crucial. The chapter also concentrated on the importance of developing a learning approach – an essential prerequisite of long-term change management.

References

Ainscough, M., Neailey, K. and Tennant, C. (2003) 'A self-assessment tool for implementing concurrent engineering through change management'. *International Journal of Project Management*, 21(6): 425–31.

Argyris, C. (1976) *Increasing Leadership Effectiveness*. New York: Wiley.

Argyris, C. and Schon, D. (1992) *Theory in Practice: Increasing Professional Effectiveness*. San Francisco, CA: Jossey Bass.

Attwood, M., Pedler, M. and Pritchard, S. (2003) *Leading Change: a Guide to Whole Systems Working*. Bristol: The Policy Press.

Baker, D. (2004) *The Strategic Management of Technology*. Oxford: Chandos.

Chawla, S. and Renesch, J. (eds) (1995) *Learning Organisations: Developing for Tomorrow's Workplace*. Shelton, CT: Productivity Press.

Collins, J.C. and Porras, J.I. (1994) *Built to Last: Successful Habits of Visionary Companies*. New York: Harper Business.

Donaldson, A., Lank, E. and Maher, J. (2005a) 'Connecting through communities: how a voluntary organisation is influencing healthcare policy and practice'. *Journal of Change Management*, 5(1): 71–86.

Doyle, M. (2000) 'Managing development in an era of radical change: evolving a relational perspective'. *Journal of Management Development*, 19(7): 579–601.

Gosling, J. and Mintzberg, H. (2004) *The Education of Practising Managers*. Cambridge, MA: MIT.

Iles, V. and Sutherland, K. (2001) *Managing Change in the NHS*. London: National Health Service, Service Delivery and Organisation Research and Development.

Kline, P. and Saunders, B. (1998) *Ten steps to a Learning Organisation*. Arlington, VA: Great Ocean Publishers.

Knight, L. and Pye, A. (2004) 'Exploring the relationships between network change and network learning'. *Management Learning*, 35(4): 473–90.

Lewin, K. (1947) 'Group decision and social change'. In *Readings in Social Psychology*, eds T.M. Newcomb and E.L. Hartley. New York: Henry Holt, pp. 340–4.

Mello, J. (2001) *Strategic Human Resource Management*. Mason, OH: South Western College Publishing.

Middlehurst, R. (1999) 'New realities for leadership and governance in Higher Education?' *Tertiary Education and Management*, 5: 307–29.

Roberto, M A and Levesque, L C. (2005) 'The art of making change initiatives stick'. *MIT Sloan Management Review*, 46(4): 53–60.

Roche, W.K. and Geary, J.F. (2002) 'Advocates, critics and union involvement in workplace partnership: Irish airports'. *British Journal of Industrial Relations*, 40(4): 659–88.

Shiba, S. and Walden, D. (2001) *Four Practical Revolutions in Management: Systems for Creating Unique Organisational Capability.* Portland, OR: Productivity Press/Center for Quality Management.

Sutherland, J, and Canwell, D. (2004) *Key Concepts in Strategic Management.* Basingstoke: Palgrave Macmillan.

Terry, M. and Smith, J. (2003) *Evaluation of the Partnership At Work Fund.* (Employment Relations Research Series 17). London: Department for Trade and Industry.

Thornhill, A., Lewis, P., Saunders, M. and Millmore, M. (2000) *Managing Change: a Human Resource Strategy Approach.* Harlow: Financial Times/Prentice Hall.

Townsend, P. and Cairns, L. (2003) 'Developing the global manager using a capability framework'. *Management Learning*, 34(3): 313–27.

Whetherly, J. (1998) *Achieving Change Through Training and Development.* London: Library Association Publishing.

Zuboff, S. (1988) *In The Age of the Smart Machine: The Future of Work and Power.* New York: Basic Books.

Case study 5.1 **Establishing a working group on race equality in Mytown University**

Keywords: *culture change, consultation, resources, universities, diversity, action learning.*

The decision to set up a working group on race equality in Mytown University is part of an ongoing and wider initiative at the University, which began in 2004. This initiative hopes to establish a culture where racial equality is encouraged and appreciated across the whole institution.

A mixture of external and internal pressures prompted this change initiative. The Race Relations Amendment Act (2000) stated that staff had to be consulted and communicated with on race issues, and that all organisations had to demonstrate a positive commitment and active approach towards improving race equality in the workplace. At the same time, the University was driving from within for organisation-wide and 'deep belief' in real equality and diversity.

A mechanism was needed to help bring about this culture change. The Equality and Diversity Unit at Mytown had a number of previous examples of gender and disability equality initiatives upon which to draw, but felt they needed to create a new approach to these traditional programmes in order to ensure that racial equality was properly embedded.

To date the programme has focused on establishing paths for consultation and communication. To begin with, the Head of Equality and Diversity at Mytown held conversations with some of her ethnic minority colleagues, asking for advice on how to approach racial groups in the University so as not to cause offence whilst reaching a broad range of people. She then wrote to a random selection of the total population of ethnic minority staff in the University to ask for volunteers to join an advisory group. This approach succeeded, and the Working Group on Race Equality was born.

The first meeting of the group was held in March 2004. The session was run using action learning techniques, and was designed to unearth and explore the perceptions and understandings of race equality amongst the group members. Although useful and positive, for the first year the Group had a rather reactive, ad hoc feel to it, and met only once a term. However, in February 2005 a full-time Equality Project Officer was employed by Mytown. The Group became more dynamic and proactive, looking forwards to see how it might help shape the racial perceptions and make-up of the University. As a result, an Advisory Steering Group was set up, and currently meets about once a month.

This initiative is a new one, and has so far achieved only mixed success. In the early stages, some members left the Group, and although this was partly caused by staff turnover it was also a result of a loss of initial momentum. There was a lack of resources, especially time, which was

Case study 5.1 Establishing a working group on race equality in Mytown University (*Cont'd*)

critical for the continued drive and high-level profile of the project. However, at the same time those still involved are both committed and energetic.

Local commentators feel that it is still too early to comment on how successful the Working Group will be. It is still learning 'where it is' and 'where it wants to take the University'. Even so, Mytown is now in the process of piloting a questionnaire on race, to build up widespread and inclusive consultation on race issues. This questionnaire will be sent to all staff, regardless of race; it will explore staff understanding of race issues and of racial equality in the workplace, and find out personal experiences (or the lack of them) of race equality at work in a variety of settings (for example recruitment, training and promotion). If successful, it should start to identify any race problems at the University and facilitate the provision of guidelines for working towards potential solutions, perhaps through focus groups and the recruitment of more people to the Advisory Group.

The Working Group on Race Equality is based on the idea that consultation can create an agenda for practical, positive action in the search for race equality. The Group's main remit is to make a real difference to employee experiences, and to create a situation where race equality is 'a matter of choice, not of compliance'. For the future there are further options, such as the creation of a 'network for support and brainstorming', but for now it is a case of consultation to see how employees themselves wish to see the initiative develop.

The Head of Equality and Diversity stresses that the top factors for a successful change project include:

1. Having sufficient resources: change initiators must be able to keep a change process going, and to draw on the necessary resources without delay when they are required.

2. Having knowledge and understanding of the process that you wish to undertake: not necessarily of the final destination, but of the process that will allow flexibility within desirable aims.

3. Acting in a relativistic way: being willing to change direction if necessary, to listen to the opinions of those around you, and to be sensitive to current circumstances.

4. Getting people on board: in this instance the University's Vice Chancellor, who was actively committed to equality issues, and who provided proactive, visible, practical and demonstrable leadership,

5. Using a 'pincer movement': mobilising and engaging those on the ground as well as those in power.

Case study 5.2 **Establishing a Women's Action Learning Set at King's College, London**

Keywords: *diversity, action learning, culture change, universities.*

This case study begins in 2003, when it was felt that the position of female academic and administrative employees at King's College, London was relatively weak in comparison to that of men. Those involved with equality and diversity issues wanted to look more specifically at the ability of women to progress in the higher education sector, especially within the College, in order to bring the numbers of women in senior positions to a more representative level.

The view of the Head of Equality and Diversity at King's was that action learning would be the best tool to enable women to develop techniques to assist this career progression. The first step was a set of introductory workshops; the programme was then was opened out to any women who were interested. Unlike some other examples of action learning, the women were not put into 'like-minded' groups – the initiative took a highly inclusive approach.

Funds were not unlimited, and King's therefore decided to facilitate only six sessions, after which the groups were given the option to self-facilitate if they wished to continue; this then freed up funding for new groups. The major topics at the sessions focused upon personal and general issues that arose within the context of the women's working lives – for example feelings of isolation, the desire for a network of support, and the need to cope with the 'barriers' that exist for women in the HE sector (juggling work and a family or dealing with stereotypes, to name but two).

Now in its third year, one of the strengths of the programme is its ability to develop without external management or facilitation. More recently, a Women's Network has been established to achieve practical outcomes from the ideas and issues brought up in the sets. This is in its early stages, but the Equality and Diversity Unit are already looking at ways to make the Network more self-sustainable in the future. Similarly, there is talk of extending the programme to postgraduate students as well as staff (as issues of under-representation exist in that area too), and also for structuring the groups around similar types of employees. The feedback from existing sessions is used to help frame the programme in ways that fit the needs of those it seeks to assist more closely. This has resulted in recent calls for a more explicit focus on career progression issues and on topics most relevant to Higher Education employment rather than employment in general.

This example of change management is very much one of practical activity aimed at improving the situation of one key group, rather than being based on theory. Thus, it is difficult to measure its outcomes in a tangible

| Case study 5.2 | Establishing a Women's Action Learning Set at King's College, London *(Cont'd)* |

fashion, or to distinguish them from outcomes caused by other initiatives. Most feedback on how successful the Action Learning groups have been is through anecdote or through the changed attitudes and feelings of the women involved. It is noticeable that the women have been committed to the programme, and it is very possible that those women who have left due to career progression could have been influenced, at least in part, by their experiences in the sets. Gender equality issues have definitely gained increasing interest and awareness as a result.

As the Head of Equality and Diversity said, some of her top tips for success during change management include:

1. The need for commitment from senior management in an explicit rather than merely passive way, which usually means the need to work hard with senior management and governance structures from the beginning.

2. The need to ensure that the change leaders are engaged and committed, and that they also have the right level of good quality infrastructural support to carry the changes through.

3. The need for clearly identified resources upon which the process can draw.

4. The need to plan the change, rather than rely on ad hoc measures.

Case study 5.3 The development of a Senior Women's Action Learning Set at Littledale University

Keywords: *action learning, culture change, external environment, universities.*

During 2004, Littledale University's new Staff Development Officer, Jane Gregson, became concerned about the position of women in the University. Despite the fact that Littledale had targets for numbers of academic women in senior positions, when the officer interviewed a selection of those women she discovered practical blocks that stood in the way of their promotion. For example, one factor used to decide whether or not promotion was justified was the amount of research academics published, but for women juggling families and careers it was more difficult to find time to publish work. Similarly, the atmosphere at Littledale was male-dominated and it was hard for women to speak out during management meetings.

On top of these ingrained problems, a recent restructuring at the University had placed academics of both genders in management roles even though they had little previous experience of leadership. These academics did not necessarily feel comfortable in their new positions, and many suffered from a lack of *de facto* authority.

When faced with these issues, Jane first felt rather daunted by the challenge, which didn't seem surmountable through traditional forms of training. However, on reflection she decided to focus on action learning as a technique to try to improve the position of women. This was a technique already tried and tested at other universities, and was more suited both to academics and to senior staff than other training styles because it focused on self-managed rather than imposed learning. The chance of success using action learning seemed strong, as it used tools fitted to the employees it sought to help, could be done promptly and was possible with existing resources. Nonetheless, Jane knew it would only work with active engagement from the women and if everyone stressed the need for real results.

Initial reactions were encouraging, and were not unrepresentative of future developments. More women than expected came to the pilot sessions run by the Staff Development Unit, and more than expected signed up for the programme. Once the Learning Set began attendance was over 80 per cent, a very high level for people with various demands on their time. What is more, the sessions themselves were very helpful for the attendees. On the practical side, it was interesting for the external facilitator and for the Staff Development Unit to discover that the women wanted to deal with University management issues rather than management of the work–life balance. One specific example was looking at how to balance the varying demands of academic research, teaching and management with which they were faced. Fundamental issues surrounding the lack of female promotion and support in the University were not tackled head on. Nevertheless, it was hoped that teaching such practical skills meant the women would be able to manage more effectively and would feel more confident as managers, and in so doing would force a culture change towards a more favourable view of senior women.

Case study 5.3 The development of a Senior Women's Action Learning Set at Littledale University *(Cont'd)*

The Action Learning Set has provided invaluable experience for those involved. The women have learnt that emotional support is readily available to them from others in similar positions. The project has broken down the culture of silence that previously existed, and has given women the courage to speak up in meetings without fear of being undermined. These networks of trust and support during times of difficulty are seen as highly beneficial.

Even so, it must be said that to date there has been only a limited practical effect on the University and its culture. The women did feel empowered enough to attempt to influence Littledale's policy, and wrote a paper for presentation to the Senior Management Group. This openly flagged the issues and problems they had to face, but it has not yet come onto the agenda. Clearly, work to change the present position regarding career structures for women still needs to be undertaken. What is more, the first set made too few links between academic and administrative senior women, a relationship that deserves much deeper exploration and one that could provide other important perspectives.

One reason why this lack of effect may be the case is that further and wider organisational change is under way at the University, and this has pushed other issues onto the 'back-burner'. However, the future does look good for the Action Learning Set and its successors, particularly as changes in the external environment (such as changes to the definition of academic job roles) might have a bearing and provide an opening for the women to voice their concerns. The difficulties in penetrating the University culture, though, do demonstrate that it is not easy to achieve success, even with a committed group of women.

This change initiative at Littledale University was not focused on the management of a specific change project. It was instead an attempt to bring about a change of attitudes and to alter the reality of life for women at the University. It thus demonstrates one way in which people can attempt to work around organisational blocks in order to reach practical solutions to difficult problems. Although perhaps a circuitous way of dealing with the fundamental difficulties of this case, it also represents a valid and highly feasible approach to tackling those issues. And as Jane's evaluation report said, 'This set can influence policy and culture change'.

According to the Staff Development Officer, her top factors for success in a change project included:

1. Recognising how difficult change management is, and the fact that it becomes more difficult the more it is attempted. It is not good management to pretend everything is going well if there are problems – relentless positivism isn't constructive.

2. Viewing change management as a wave rather than a curve. In other words, understanding that some people will push for change and others will pull against it, and it is much more beneficial to lean into any

| Case study 5.3 | The development of a Senior Women's Action Learning Set at Littledale University *(Cont'd)* |

resistance than to battle it. Waves can be ridden, but they cannot be forced away before they choose to disperse – trying to do so will only create a greater chance of failure.

3. Being determined not to be frustrated with people's resistance to change. Even where the change seems relatively minor to those in charge, the employees affected might hold a very different view, and it is neither fair nor sensible to shun this view. Good change managers listen to people's concerns and are careful not to disregard their worries; they have patience with the negative phase of the change process, and this makes it more likely to end quickly.

4. Being willing to admit the limits of your knowledge during the change process, which includes being honest if you don't know something or don't know what will happen next. Using integrity in this way will hopefully ensure that you keep the trust of your staff even through the difficult times.

5. Being able to handle the unknown aspects of change, either by using personal experiences or by focusing on a plan and a process for the whole project.

6

Strategy development

Introduction

This chapter is the first in a series that looks at how strategy is developed in order to determine change. It concentrates on the framing of the strategic plan that underpins the work of the organisation, its future direction and how it will achieve its longer-term goals. The chapter begins by stressing the importance of a properly worked out plan as the basis of good change management. It considers the various elements of the strategic plan and emphasises the importance of vision, mission and values. It then looks at the elements of the plan that will actually show how the high-level aims of the organisation are to be translated into action.

Strategy development

A strategy that does not drive and facilitate change and improvement is of little use. The strategy should co-ordinate the various operations that are carried out, either as ongoing activities or as finite projects, in order to ensure that they are all contributing to the organisation's overarching mission. Above all, a strategy should enable managers to make decisions within the context of risk analysis and management. A strategy document should aim to provide the route map by which an organisation, its leaders and its people can chart a course through the issues and the environment in which they will be operating over the course of the planning period. As Peter Drucker (quoted in Siess, 2002) points out:

> Strategic planning is the continuous process of making entrepreneurial – or risk-taking – decisions systematically and with

the greatest knowledge of their future consequences; systematically organising the efforts needed to carry out these decisions; and measuring the results of these decisions against the expectations through organised, systematic feedback.

The emphasis on anticipation allows the organisation to respond successfully to threats and opportunities by being better prepared. This preparedness will usually take the form of strategic decision-making in order to position the organisation to best effect within the sector and the environment.

Strategies need to be flexible in order to cope with future uncertainty and a sure knowledge that the only thing that we can predict accurately is that our predictions will be proved wrong. However, while a strategy does not of itself predict the future, it has to be based on such predictions in order to provide the necessary route map. Because strategy is so contingent upon the specifics of the environment in which it is formulated, there is no one generic model that can be identified and applied across different sectors, countries or environments. There will be a number of drivers or constraints in terms of resource availability, political and social pressure and organisational culture, amongst others.

Box 6.1   **Some key headings for strategy development**

The Royal Society's key headings for 'Tomorrow's Company' are as follows:

- company purpose and values;
- key relationships;
- success model;
- measurement;
- reward system;
- learning organisation;
- fiduciary responsibilities;
- business renewal;
- climate for success;
- raising performance standards.

Source: Royal Society of Arts Journal, March 1997. Appendix 1, 16.

The strategic plan

An organisation's future direction – where it needs to change, where it needs to stay the same, and how it is going to go about changing, and why – is typically enshrined in a strategic plan. Below is a possible summary contents page for a strategic plan. Each element of that plan is then discussed.

Box 6.2   Summary contents page for a strategic plan

Vision

A concise statement of what the organisation would like to become in the future.

Mission statement

A relatively short, clear statement of the primary purpose(s) of the organisation. It might include the reason for being, what the organisation does, how it does it, and how the organisation is different from its competitors. The mission should reflect the values or the basic beliefs to which the organisation and its stakeholders have agreed.

Aims

A list of the organisation's key strategic goals over an agreed period of time – typically five years. They should be generic and cover the whole of the planning period and even beyond it.

Objectives

Specific targets, to be achieved at various points within the planning period, with an indication of the target and the means by which it will be achieved; the objectives could be organised into a hierarchy of primary and secondary objectives.

Ways in which the vision will be achieved

This could be the 'operating statements' or 'action plans' – sets of tactics/groups of actions that will enable the strategy

---

Box 6.2   **Summary contents page for a strategic plan (*Cont'd*)**

to be implemented successfully. It might also include a Position Statement, describing the organisation's current state, its services or products and its relationship to its competitors. Such a statement might also refer to key stakeholders.

Complementary documents

A number of other documents should be referred to in the published plan. These are likely to include key policies and supporting strategies (e.g. Human Resources, Estates), as well as documents that analyse the institution's current position, strengths, weaknesses, opportunities and threats, and departmental-level plans covering the planning period.

Vision

A high-level vision is seen as a prerequisite of a good strategy. Siess (2002) defines a vision as:

> A concise statement of what [an organisation] would like to become in the future. It should be so idealistic that it is not attainable in the foreseeable future.

If an organisation has a vision, then it can start to plan the effective deployment of resources, not least against any threats that the organisation will experience within the sector. It need not be one person's vision: a whole group of different types of stakeholder might develop and share a vision. This is likely to be true where the vision is born out of the strategic planning techniques described and discussed in this book.

On the one hand, a vision that is totally unachievable is hardly worth considering. On the other hand, a vision that is too easy to achieve will neither stretch the organisation nor provide the basis for a strategy that will allow an effective response to future changes. During the 'visioning' process, therefore, it is likely that several options or scenarios will be identified that will require assessment, and one or possibly more preferred longer-term states chosen as the basis of the mission and as the underpinning of any technology choices subsequently made.

Mission

The vision is articulated in the form of a mission statement. Bart (1998) argues that the statement is a formal written document that captures 'an organisation's unique purposes and activities'. Siess (2002) defines the 'mission' as:

> A relatively short, clear statement of the primary purpose(s) of the [organisation]. It consists of the [organisation's] reason for being, what it does, how it does it, and how [it] is different from its competitors. The mission should reflect the organisation's values or the basic beliefs to which [it] and its stakeholders have agreed. It may be achievable in the medium term.

The mission statement does not in itself provide the strategy or the solutions for the institution, though it should make the thoughts of senior staff sufficiently explicit for key stakeholders to understand what the organisation is trying to achieve and what groups' and individuals' contributions to the vision and the goals are meant to be. The statement can be used as the basis for much of an organisation's external communication (Klemm et al., 1991) and provide the fundamental tool by which an organisation sums up its basic aims, objectives and core values.

Values

Values are likely to determine particular strategic choices. Adopting a 'green' policy, for example, will have a significant impact on any strategy that an organisation chooses to develop and adopt. These core values are the basic essence of the organisation and are only likely to change over a considerable period of time or in extreme circumstances, for they sum up what the organisation is 'about' (Collins and Porras, 1994). The key is not what the values are, but whether they are shared, truly believed, and put into practice by the people in the organisation: 'this should not be forgotten in any culture change programme: it is much more important to spend time engaging people's hearts and minds than it is to craft what is imagined to be a perfect 'values statement'" (Thornbury, 1999).

Box 6.3   Defining values

Values are beliefs ... [that] have a meaning to [an organisation] ... standards that the business regards highly and holds as its ideal. Values may be ethical standards, but essentially they guide the organisation as to how to carry out its business. Organisational values can derive from senior management, line management or even teams and employees ... the organisational values seek to establish role models. Typical values include ... continuous improvement, customer delight, people development, innovation, society commitment, maximum utilisation ... It is widely believed that the development, adoption and implementation of values is one of the key success factors in high-profit businesses.

Source: Sutherland and Canwell (2004).

Box 6.4   The value of values

The major restructuring and revitalisation of KPMG was driven by values – what the organisation stood for – that were 'clear and credible [and] which were not just talked about but actually embedded in the culture'. They would:

- add to the vision and help provide strategic direction and leadership;
- provide guiding principles for decisions, activities and behaviour;
- create more pride in the organisation and a sense of belonging to something bigger than the local practice.

This in turn determined how the company would work in the future by:

- harmonising and aligning activity – consistent core services;
- doing things in the same way – common internal business processes;
- common infrastructure – managed robustly from the centre.

Box 6.4   The value of values (*Cont'd*)

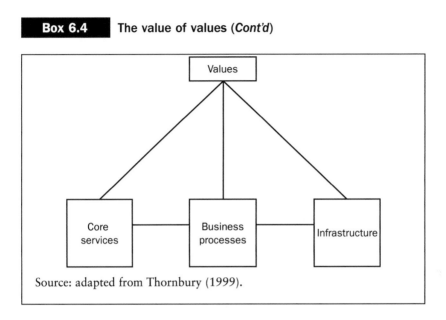

Source: adapted from Thornbury (1999).

Aims and objectives

Mission statements are normally made up of several elements. The aims of the organisation form the basis of both the statement and the strategy. Ultimately, a strategy has to support the achievement of the aims that an organisation has set itself in order to realise its vision and serve its mission. Senior managers need to outline strategic goals. They also need to check that their goals are consistent with one another and that there is organisation-wide ownership of their plans. Nobody starts with a blank sheet of paper – so they need to know what their starting point is, how far they go, and what to do to turn theoretical goals into practical reality. These aims or goals are not framed in terms of specific solutions, but are generic, covering the whole of the strategic planning period. Collins and Porras (1994) argue that goals should be 'audacious' if the organisation wishes to make a significant move – 'a paradigm shift' forward over the lifetime of the strategy.

There is often confusion between aims (or goals) and objectives. The Higher Education Funding Council for England (HEFCE) has defined an aim as being 'the high-level strategic outcome towards which [the organisation is] working throughout and beyond the life of [the strategic] plan', whereas an objective is something that the organisation seeks to achieve during the course of the plan period, with an indication of the target and the means by which it will be achieved (HEFCE, 2003). However, the term objective is often used synonymously with the word 'Aim'. Objectives are typically organised into a hierarchy. Primary Objectives are broad, visionary, fundamental and overarching. They could also easily be described as aims. They are supported by strategic objectives. These are long term, and serve the primary objectives. Operational objectives, on the other hand, are short term and serve the strategic objectives.

Position and operating statements

A position statement, describing the organisation's current state, its services or products, its relationship to its competitors, any distinctive competences – 'specific specialisms ... or abilities that mark the organisation as having a competitive edge in a specific aspect of its operations' (Sutherland and Canwell, 2004) – and, perhaps, its level of technology usage and awareness. Such a statement might also usefully include reference to the organisation's key stakeholders – those who have a particular interest in the health and future development of the organisation. Stakeholders will include staff and customers/users, but may also encompass governing bodies/shareholders, government agencies and professional bodies. Lists of stakeholders may also need to refer to other organisations – whether partners or competitors – working in the same sector. The relative importance of different objectives may be determined by the priorities of the stakeholders in general and by those of the dominant stakeholder or stakeholders in particular.

A description of the ways in which the vision will be achieved is normally included. These may be described as operating statements or as a set of tactics – a group of actions that enable the strategy to be implemented successfully. It is the operationalisation of the strategy and will include shorter-term strategies, policies and plans. At this level, some description of the options and possible solutions is likely to be included. This description may also refer to key policies that the organisation will need to adopt in order to implement the strategy. These policies will ensure consistency of application of the strategy, as for example equality of opportunity or disabled access. There might also be a commentary that gives more detailed explanations of the aims and objectives of the organisation and the principal activities through which progress will be made. This might incorporate the key elements of a 'route map', outlining where the organisation is currently on the developmental spectrum and where it needs to be.

The description should include key performance targets, by which the organisation can demonstrate, in measurable terms, progress towards the stated aims and objectives, together with the milestones by which they should be achieved and the measures by which performance will be evaluated against target. These should be complemented by a list and description of key risks and dependencies that the plan takes into account and that are specific to the key aims, with an outline of how these are to be managed. Any strategy must take account of the advantages and disadvantages of implementation and of the risks associated with undertaking the work of carrying out a strategy or, indeed, not doing so. Once a decision has been made to proceed (presumably on the grounds that the advantages of proceeding outweigh the disadvantages), then effective and efficient project management is a critical factor in success. Risks and dependencies should also include a note of constraints that are likely to limit the strategy, its key aims and their delivery.

Action plans

Can the organisation implement the strategy, once devised and agreed? Strategy implementation is typically enshrined in an Action Plan that accompanies the finally-agreed strategy document, as is the case with the case studies in this book. Sutherland and Canwell (2004) comment:

Box 6.5	The importance of action plans

Action planning is an integral part of both goal-setting and problem solving ... [and] can assist ... in planning for the future, ensuring that as future situations change they can be controlled ... Action planning is the conversion of goals or objectives into a series of steps, in order to ascertain what has to be done, by whom and when ... The action plan should describe how the business is to get from where it is now to where it wishes to be, describing in detail how it proposes to do this. There needs to be a secondary process running alongside the action plan, which checks to see whether the plan is working.

Source: Sutherland and Canwell (2004).

Many strategies fail because there is too much of a gap between conception and reality. 'It is important to avoid bland statements and rhetoric and instead make sure there are practical proposals for ensuring that they can actually deliver ... Whatever you do take a common sense approach, and avoid signing up to an agreement which says all the right things but has no practical proposals' (UNISON, 2001). Before a strategy is developed, therefore, it is important to see if the organisation is ready to meet the strategic challenges required of it. 'Because [strategic] planning is a delicate, complicated, time-consuming process, it cannot be forced on an organisation that is not prepared for self-analysis and the change that will result from the process'. (Stueart and Moran, 1998).

Box 6.6	Key blockages to effective strategy implementation

- poor definition of aims, objectives and key activities;
- implementation takes longer than was anticipated;
- major problems are overlooked;
- insufficient coordination;
- resources not properly allocated to the implementation process;
- insufficient or inappropriate capabilities or capacity amongst management and the workforce;
- lack of training;
- unforeseen changes in the external environment;
- lack of leadership from management;
- the implementation is not monitored well enough.

In order to create a meaningful and realistic action plan, it is necessary to ensure that all key stakeholders are involved in the development process. This will require not just the formulation of a plan, but also its iteration through widespread communication and feedback. A good action plan will be sufficiently detailed on the one hand to ensure that it is clear what needs to be done, how it should be done, when (and in what order or sequence) and by whom and what the measures of progress and successful completion are; on the other, it will need to encompass a contingency plan, for 'no matter how complex the creation of the action plan may have been, it is imperative that a contingency plan is created, which may need to be instituted in the event of the action planning going off track. This means that a monitoring process needs to be put in place, together with a clear idea of how to solve potential problems as they arise, in order to ensure that the goal is finally reached' (Sutherland and Canwell, 2004). Put more simply, the organisation has to answer the questions why, what, who, when, where and how in order to ensure that it has a realistic and deliverable action plan (Van Gundy, 1988).

Summary

This chapter has looked at the formal development of a strategic planning document as the basis for actions for change. It has stressed the importance of a holistic and systemic approach that brings together high-level and practical aspects of long-term change management and development. The case study at the end of this chapter shows the results of a strategic planning process. Later chapters consider the techniques associated with formulating the plan in detail.

References

Bart, C.K. (1998) 'A comparison of mission statements and their rationales in innovative and non-innovative firms'. *International Journal of Technology Management*, 16: 1–3.

Collins, J.C. and Porras, J.I. (1994) *Built to Last: Successful Habits of Visionary Companies*. New York: Harper Business.

Higher Education Funding Council for England (2003) *HEFCE Strategic Plan, 2003–08*. Bristol: HEFCE.

Klemm, M., Sanderson, S. and Luffman, G. (1991) 'Mission statements: selling corporate values to employees'. *The Service Industries Journal*, 20(1): 22–39.

Siess, J.A. (2002) *Time Management, Planning and Prioritisation for Librarians*. Lanham: Scarecrow.

Stueart, R.D. and Moran, B.B. (1998) *Library and Information Centre Management*. Englewood, CO: Libraries Unlimited.

Sutherland, J, and Canwell, D. (2004) *Key Concepts in Strategic Management*. Basingstoke: Palgrave Macmillan.

Thornbury, J. (1999), 'KPMG: revitalising culture through values'. *Business Strategy Review*, 10(4): 1–15.

UNISON (2001) *Working Together on Health and Safety: a UNISON Guide to Partnership Agreements*. London: UNISON Communications Unit.

Van Gundy, A.B. (1988) *Techniques of Structured Problem Solving*. New York: Van Nostrand Reinhold.

Case study 6.1 Learning South West: Strategy Development, 2006

The following does not aim to be a finished document, but to outline concisely what the key elements of a future strategic plan for Learning South West might be for further discussion.

1. Context

Limited public finances are being prioritised to create opportunity for all, but especially for young people, rather than lifelong learning. This is now being overlaid with a narrower focus on skills for employability and money being top-sliced for programmes aimed at improving the demand side for learning, e.g. Train to Gain.

The integration of services around children and young people continues, and is leading other efforts to integrate services around the needs of users.

Centralised planning and target setting continues to drive all sectors and has been acknowledged to have led to improved standards at the lower end, but has led to a compliance mentality combined with a management focus on financial and 'inspector' survival. In staff development, this has led to a focus on a narrow form of professionalisation associated with qualifications rather than a more holistic approach to the capacity building of people, organisations and the networks and communities of practice that sustain them.

There are new reforms planned and underway that will allow more local initiatives and softer targets for both local authorities and learning providers with a view to raising quality from adequate to good or excellent. However, centralised planning and structures set up to support planning and target setting and measurement may prevent the decentralisation required to facilitate local creativity despite the creation of national quality improvement agencies. Effective moves to 'double devolution' will require improved processes of user participation, and therefore accountability, in planning, monitoring and implementation of services.

The improved use of ICT and the development of e-learning and virtual learning environments are now fairly widespread within learning providers and local authorities but lack of ownership and understanding by most staff has meant this is yet to realise its potential.

Key regional institutions like the SWRDA, GOSW and Regional Skills Partnership are now well established but are in the process of sharpening their role and focus as strategic catalysts of change rather than key implementing or commissioning agents of change.

2. Role of Learning South West

Learning South West will build on its history and current strengths to become:

- The region's most trusted facilitator, and sometimes provider, of **regional support to workforce development and accredited professional**

| Case study 6.1 | Learning South West: Strategy Development, 2006 (*Cont'd*) |

development in the: children and young people sector; 14–19 sector; and adult learning sector.

- **The key regional agent in enabling youth participation** to be central to Children's Trusts planning and operation and also to inform Local Area Agreements, primarily through developing appropriate linkage processes between the UK Youth Parliament, voluntary and statutory youth services and other staff and departments of local authorities and other bodies. Also to use this experience to develop a similar role as an agent in enabling learners of all ages to participate more actively in the process of learning and reform of learning.

- **The largest recipient and project manager of region-wide projects** whose aim is to improve quality through workforce development or improved participation of young people and all learners in the: children and young people sector; 14–19 sector; and all levels of the adult learning sector.

- **An implementing, and sometimes managing, partner of national consortia** with other key regional and national organisations to deliver similar projects at a national level.

- An **independent**, non-statutory body that engages in **innovative and creative** work that reflects emerging trends and **catalyses new developments that reflect our values and the interests and priorities of its members, bold organisations and practitioners**.

- A body for planning, managing, implementing, monitoring and evaluating services.

- A body that offers increased levels of financial and other forms of support for members and other stakeholders.

3. Vision

Learning South West is working towards a vibrant South West region based on a diverse population and workforce who are continually learning to improve their participation in the region's sustainable development through all aspects of their lives, (not just their employment). To achieve this, we must innovate continually and challenge existing ways of working if we are to ensure learning is about creating the future society we desire rather than perpetuating the society we already have. We must also unlock the potential value offered by increasing the diversity of our organisations and society and the active lifelong participation of practitioners, young people and all learners in the process of change.

Learning South West will work in partnership with others to develop self-reinforcing and sustainable cycles of quality improvement by those individuals, organisations, communities of practice and networks who are working with young people and all learners in the South West.

Case study 6.1   **Learning South West: Strategy Development, 2006** (*Cont'd*)

The key changes this will bring about are:

- More involvement and accountability to young people and all learners by those responsible who work in partnership with Learning South West.
- Greater degrees of local flexibility and differentiation in delivery of services.
- Improved quality and relevance of services for young people and all learners.

4. Culture and values

Learning South West's culture and values remain unchanged from previous strategic plans:

- We are proactive within a rapidly-changing context.
- We work with people in a mutually respectful way.
- We understand and value difference, recognising the importance of everyone's contribution.
- We value lifelong learning.
- We value transparency, honesty and openness.
- We value our reputation and our credibility.
- We provide quality, efficiency and professionalism.
- We practice and encourage sustainability.
- We respond to change with creativity and innovation.
- We are customer-responsive.
- We give value for money, are prudent and financially viable.
- We value and support holistic thinking.

5. Goals and priorities

1. Support members and other stakeholders working with young people and all learners in the South West through facilitating, and where necessary providing, support in **planning, delivering and accrediting of innovative and holistic workforce and professional development** with the active involvement of practitioners and other stakeholders.
2. Support members and other stakeholders working with young people and all learners in the South West to **involve young people and all learners in actively planning, managing, implementing, monitoring and evaluating services.**
3. Ensure Learning South West **involves its own members and stakeholders actively** in planning, managing, implementing, monitoring

| Case study 6.1 | Learning South West: Strategy Development, 2006 (*Cont'd*) |

and evaluating its own work and **promotes individual and organisational learning** both internally and externally.

6. Strategic Implications

What does this imply Learning South West needs to start, continue and stop doing?

Start

- Improving communication and relationships with members so as to better support their workforce and professional development.

- Clearly articulating our unique approach to workforce and professional development, which is holistic in the sense that it addresses the needs and priorities of both the whole organisation and the whole person. This approach is also innovative in that it seeks to involve both practitioners and other stakeholders in the design, delivery and assessment of professional development and other learning.

- Developing and implementing a series of initiatives and projects to facilitate and, where necessary and appropriate, provide training, accreditation or other support directly to members and other stakeholders in their workforce and professional development.

- Expanding Learning South West's role in facilitating the network of Directors of Children and Young People Services to support this whole sector, i.e. not just youth services, in workforce and professional development.

- Expanding Learning South West's role in coordinating the regional UK Youth Parliament to involve facilitating young people's involvement in other areas of policy, planning and implementation. Also to use this experience to develop similar support services in relation to learners of all ages.

- Investing in improved internal processes for accountability to the Board, members and other stakeholders and to ensure Learning South West is a learning organisation.

- More proactive marketing and communications of Learning South West's role and goals, presenting our own organisational development as an inter-connected package of 'Smart Business Thinking'.

Continue

- Learning South West's role as Regional Youth Work unit, including planning for its continuation and evolution after 2008.
- Regional projects on members' interests, e.g. Crystal Chandelier, Greater Expectations, Youth projects etc.

Case study 6.1 **Learning South West: Strategy Development, 2006** (*Cont'd*)

- Support to FE Colleges and other training providers in professional development and in employer engagement.
- Providing a focal point for a multi-sector, regional coalition on learning for sustainability.
- Mainstream learning for sustainability and other approaches required to bring about sustainable development in all Learning South West's work including its own management and operation of Bishop's Hull House.
- Improving the hiring of rooms and provision of other services through at Bishop's Hull House.
- Expanding ABC Awards activity from Taunton.

Stop

- Trying to tender for research work. Learning South West should only do research when commissioned to do so directly in specific areas where Learning South West as an organisation has specific expertise, e.g. recent QCA research on Framework for Achievement.
- Trying to get involved in regeneration projects or activities unless there is a direct and clear link to work with children and young people and/or adult learning.
- Trying to get involved in projects or activities with a specific sustainable development focus, unless they offer opportunities to embed the learning within mainstream vocational provision.

6. Next steps

It is proposed to gather feedback on this potential future strategic direction from the Board, staff and other members and stakeholders over the next few months before reproducing the plan in a format for wider communication purposes.

7

Route mapping for change: techniques and tools

Introduction

This chapter looks at the major high-level strategic planning and management techniques that can be used to determine the rationale, direction and basis of change within an organisation. Many of them are common to all forms of strategic planning and management. It should be stressed that a good many techniques were excluded from this book; only those that seemed particularly relevant to change management in a public sector context were included. In any case, no single technique will solve all possible problems; there is no panacea to an area of management that becomes more difficult the more radical and discontinuous the change being proposed. However, it is argued that a sensible and appropriate combination of these methodologies in an integrated way will provide a sound basis for major change and its effective management.

There are several key benefits to the proper use of the techniques described here:

- the quality of decision-making is improved;
- opportunities and problems can be identified – and dealt with – effectively and efficiently;
- an appropriate view of the issues can be taken – a broad view in the case of strategy development, a focused one in relation to strategy implementation;
- performance indicators are created based on environmental and market factors that allow for comparison and monitoring before, during and after the change management process to ensure that the planned changes are actually working as intended and, if not, to give some indication as to what should happen.

Some of the techniques are concerned with fact finding; others with determining and planning the future; others with implementation.

Forecasting

Within the last 10 to 15 years, the concept of foresight has become increasingly important as the basis for effective strategic management. This requires an analysis of broader environmental issues so that strategic decision makers are 'informed by deep insights into trends in lifestyles, technology, demography and geopolitics' (Hamel and Prahalad, 1994). This has also been recognised by Feather (2003), who identifies four broad frameworks within which the 'Information Society' can be analysed: economic, technological, sociological and historical. Fashion may also play a part in determining future strategy. To what extent, for example, is the predominance of the iPod amongst younger members of the population in the UK the result of a market pull driven by fashion as much as innovation?

Box 7.1   **Some forecasts to 2020 for the Church of England**

While it is true the future cannot be forecast accurately, it is possible to extrapolate a series of figures from the past into the years ahead, assuming 'present trends continue'. Such effectively indicate what will be the outcome if 'nothing changes'. However, the implications of 'nothing changes' are severe, so it is assumed that actions taken by churches to combat falling numbers cause the rate of percentage decrease to slow down by half every five years.

The figures here paint a kind of 'inverse-vision', a future that is not desired, not wanted. To stop this inverse-vision happening still requires, however, ideas of how an alternative may be accomplished, and enthusiasm for making that happen.

The number of people attending church on Sunday is decreasing rapidly. In 1980 11 per cent of the population of Great Britain went to church ... this was down to under 7 per cent by 2005, and, if present trends continue, is likely to be only 4 per cent by 2020. Many have suggested it could be even lower than this.

Source: Brierley (2005a).

> **Box 7.2** Key questions in forecasting scenarios
>
> - appropriateness of the timescale for the analysis;
> - significance of trends within the sector within the given timescale;
> - effectiveness of the evaluation methodology/ies regarding the identified trends;
> - likely consequences of the trends for the structure and capabilities of the industry/sector, the shape and nature of the market and the needs of the customers/users.
>
> Source: adapted from Twiss and Goodridge (1989).

It is important to ensure that any possible environmental impact is noted; any organisation can be taken unawares. It is of paramount importance that likely future developments are foreseen in order that an effective response can be made, not least to ensure that certain scenarios do not happen (Brierley, 2005a).

Forecasting is an art as much as a science. It is necessary to stress that just because one has made predictions – on which it is then proposed to build a strategy – does not mean to say that those predictions will come true. It is important to remember that forecasting techniques are designed to create one or more scenarios – and they are no more than that until the point is reached at which they become reality, or not, as the case may be.

Delphi

Delphi is a qualitative method of forecasting that employs a team approach to decision-making. However, the team does not have to be assembled in one place, which means that the number of members can be much greater than you might normally consider possible. It is a method of developing expert consensus about a topic through a series of anonymous mailed questionnaires. The main stages are as follows:

The team may vary in size. The size of the group can be dictated partly by the type of question being asked. For technological forecasting, 15–20 specialists in the area should be sufficient. The initial questionnaire

Box 7.3 Delphi stage 1

Develop a scenario showing the problem/opportunity situation and the general reason for concern. Select the team to be questioned. Team members must:

- have a sense of involvement in the situation;
- be in possession of relevant information;
- be motivated to spend time on the Delphi process;
- have a perception of the value of the information they will obtain from the other participants.

should pose the scenario to the respondents with the general reason for concern. Then there should be two or three open-ended questions and/or requests for examples. There should also be a covering letter explaining the purpose of the questionnaire, the use of the results, instructions and a response deadline. Follow-up letters should be sent to non-respondents. The results of the first questionnaire should be analysed. The aim of the analysis is to summarise all the responses in such a way that they can be clearly understood by the respondents in the second questionnaire.

Box 7.4 Delphi stage 2

Develop a second questionnaire using the responses summarised from the first one. The questions should focus on:

- identifying areas of agreement and disagreement;
- providing an opportunity to clarify meanings;
- establishing tentative priorities for the topics or solutions.

The aim of the questionnaire is to get clear responses that could be construed as a 'vote' for one type of decision. This questionnaire should first be tested on a non-team member before being sent to the respondents, again with a clear deadline. The second questionnaire should then be analysed.

Box 7.5	Delphi stage 3 (if applicable)

You can now decide whether to terminate the exercise or continue. It really depends whether the results are clear enough to formulate a decision or whether some of the comments raise new ideas that need to be explored further. If you continue, the third and last questionnaire must pull together the entire Delphi process. Do not omit questions because they have been asked before. The results of the second questionnaire should be summarised and sent to the participants. Ask the participants to vote on or rank the items, and remember to test the questionnaire on a non-team member before mailing it. Analyse the third questionnaire and draw conclusions as to the real problem or opportunity or possible routes to your objectives. Finally, report the results of the questionnaires to all the participants. The report should review the original situation, goals or process, procedure used and final results and, if possible, any decisions made.

Environmental analysis

Organisations have to consider a large number of environmental factors when they are considering future strategy in general, and their ability to compete in particular. One set of environmental factors relates to the broad 'climate' in which the organisation is working. The other set relates to the products or services that form the organisation's output. Firstly, there may be major changes within the country at large, whether social, economic, cultural, political, commercial or technological. Take the way in which the development of the Internet has revolutionised the way in which so much of our world works. Globalisation – not least in major public sectors such as education – has increased the effect of changes elsewhere in the world on activity, demand, fashion and, hence, longer-term strategic choice. There is thus much external pressure for internal change, whether culturally or institutionally driven; either the environment forces the organisation to change, or the organisation changes in anticipation of external change; or a combination of the two. But it is important to differentiate between short-term fads and longer-term trends. The external environment can change rapidly under either heading: it is necessary to determine when the shift is a fundamental one within the environment – the society, the economy, the culture; and hence, when, where and how the organisation should alter its strategy – or develop a new one, revising or renewing its structures and policies to match.

Fahey and Narayan (1986) discuss the main aspects of environmental analysis. They define four stages: scanning, monitoring, forecasting and assessment. Scanning and monitoring the environment 'identifies surprises or strategic issues requiring action on the part of the organisation'. It is not just about an analysis of the current position but is more appropriately concerned with a study of present and future trends. There is therefore widespread agreement that the process has to be as broad as possible, as the early hints of major change may not always come from the obvious sources. STEP (or PEST), PESTLE or STEEPLE are acronyms that summarise a checklist of factors that need to be taken into account when undertaking an environmental analysis. The original four criteria are the Political, Economic, Social and Technological, the principal external determinants of the environment in which a business operates' (Sutherland and Canwell, 2004). Other criteria have since been added (Burns, 2004) to achieve the acronym STEEPLE.

Box 7.6   STEEPLE

- Socio-cultural e.g. population structure, lifestyle choices;
- Technical e.g. impact of Internet, emerging technologies, technology transfer, R&D;
- Environmental e.g. local, national and international;
- Economic e.g. stage of cycle, employment levels, income;
- Political e.g. type of government, levels of freedom, legislation;
- Legal e.g. national and international;
- Environmental e.g. 'green' legislation.

Yet more elements may need to be added to the list, for example: values or ethics; education; demography; internationalisation. The aim is to ensure that the organisation has a 'bigger picture' of the world within which people are working than just the immediate, day-to-day, localised environment, focusing on the realities of 'the world' at large and then aligning the organisation with the forces operating for change and preventing or stopping activities that will fail because of the external environment. The checklist can be a useful way to determine where the key threats and opportunities for the organisation may originate.

Stakeholder analysis

Organisational strategies typically refer to those individuals, groups, agencies or institutions that have an interest, or 'stake', in the organisation, its direction, and its future success. Some stakeholders may be able to affect the strategy, others may be affected by it. In public sector and not-for-profit organisations, stakeholders might not have the same choices as customers in the traditional sense, but it is still necessary to look at what they want, not least to prevent disillusionment, unease, unhappiness or tension because their requirements are not being taken into account and in order to ensure that they feel part of a partnership with the organisation and are more likely to work for rather than against any planned improvements.

Strategy is normally devised to take into account the requirements of all the stakeholders. Some of the stakeholders will have a direct input into the development of the strategy and/or be responsible for its implementation, monitoring and evaluation. Others will influence the strategy, but not be directly responsible for its contents. A third group will have a general interest in strategy and its implications.

Table 7.1   Key stakeholder groups

Stakeholder Group	Description
Primary	Direct interest in the strategy – typically employees, and especially senior managers and those groups and institutions that fund the programme of work that the strategy generates and that have a financial stake in the organisation to which the strategy pertains. They will have most to gain or lose from change; some of them may be defined as the key 'problem owner' in terms of the issues that are driving proposals for change.
Secondary	Indirect interest in the strategy – typically those who use the organisation whose strategy it is, or who supply goods and services to it.
Tertiary	Remote interest in the strategy – typically those who are interested in the key actions of the organisation and how those actions are performed, such as government agencies or pressure groups.

Analysing the stakeholders will take account of these three categories. Once this has been done, it is important to determine their requirements. These will naturally vary depending upon the background and priorities of each stakeholder group. There are likely to be three themes that emerge from such an analysis. Firstly, stakeholders will have demands – things that they have to do and which they will need to have satisfied if they are to be supportive. Secondly, they will have choices and will wish to exercise them. Thirdly, they will be operating under constraints – such as a limited budget or an imperfect technical knowledge or current infrastructure. These will all need to be taken into account.

Though not primarily a tool for change management, the Myers-Briggs Type Instrument (MBTI)[1] may be useful for managers because it will enable them to find out about the workforce and how they can develop and improve the way they live and work, thus helping change management to be more successful. 'Knowledge of type can help you deal with the culture of the place you work, the development of new skills, understanding your participation on team, and coping with change in the workplace'.[2] The MBTI looks at personality types and can help to show what motivates employees, how they work, how to make them work better and what would be the wrong or correct approach. It can also be used with other stakeholders to see what they need and how best to give it to them. The instrument can therefore help in the management of others, in utilising staff and in getting the best for other stakeholders or users. However, it is only one tool in the change management process, and will need to be used and blended with a whole series of other techniques in order for it to be successful in this particular context. Many organisations are also making use of staff survey tools such as those made possible by Bristol Online Surveys (BOS)[3] to support information gathering at institutional, team and even individual levels (where it is used for 360 degree feedback).

Benchmarking

Benchmarking is a technique whereby other institutions within (or possibly also outside) the sector are used as comparators against which the organisation can test itself and identify areas where it needs to improve its own performance. In order to ensure that there are appropriate comparisons not only between the organisation and its benchmark group but also that progress towards a new level of performance or achievement can be measured, a baseline is established. This summarises the current state of the organisation, using a number of measures.

At its simplest, the technique is intended to facilitate discussion between managers with regard to the key indicators on which the best-performing companies in the sector are judged as being the best, and against which the organisation that wishes to undertake a benchmarking exercise wishes to compare and contrast itself and its immediate rivals.

Box 7.7	Defining benchmarking

[Benchmarking is] ... a predetermined set of standards against which future performance or activities are measured. Usually, benchmarking involves the discovery of the best practice, either within or outside the business, in an effort to identify the ideal processes and prosecution of an activity. The purpose of benchmarking is to ensure that future performance and activities conform with the benchmarked ideal in order to improve overall performance. Increased efficiency is key to the benchmarking process as, in human resource management, improved efficiency, reliability of data, and the effectiveness of activities will lead to a more competitive edge and ultimately greater profitability.

Source: Sutherland and Canwell (2004).

Portfolio analysis

Most organisations supply or provide a range of products or services. These products or services will vary from the very profitable (as defined by the organisation's business or financial strategy) to the not-so-profitable, or loss making. Products or services in the early stages of development are likely to fall into the latter category. These may be cross-subsidised from more lucrative offerings until such time as they can stand alone financially. At the same time, an organisation cannot rely too much or for too long on its 'cash cows' – the income earners that support the activities that do not recoup their costs. They may need reinvestment, renewal or re-engineering and, at some point, will come to the end of their natural life cycle. There is therefore a balance to be struck in providing a portfolio that allows for new products or services to be developed, but not wholly at the expense of the current money earners and their future potential.

A number of techniques are available to support the analysis of current and possible future portfolios. These are typically based on a matrix approach, where the products or services are plotted against two axes. A simple model uses rate of growth and market share relative to the market leader as the two variables.

Figure 7.1 Portfolio analysis

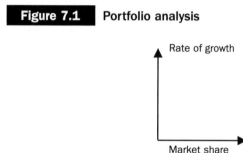

Alternatively, the axes may be the attractiveness of the product/service on the market and the competitive position of the organisation.

These portfolio matrixes are arguably more relevant to the private rather than the public sector. However, as the public sector now operates in a more competitive environment, these approaches may have their uses. Certainly it is the case that academic organisations, for example, undertake portfolio reviews that take into account the kinds of matrix headings described here. Service organisations, too, may find the approach useful in terms of analysing the present and possible future mix of services that should best be offered, though the variables are likely to stress the demand for/popularity of particular services and their cost-effectiveness relative to identified benchmarks rather than strict market share or profitability. In carrying out this analysis, of course, public sector managers will need to recognise that while a service may be unprofitable in strict financial terms, it may be academically or socially profitable, or a prerequisite of funding or constitution, regardless of any diseconomies of provision.

Market analysis

The above discussion about portfolios suggests that there is a strategic relationship between products or services and markets. Market analysis is the other side of portfolio analysis. In other words, whereas portfolio analysis looks particularly at what is provided in relation to the market, market analysis considers what the markets are and what they require, whether or not it is currently provided. The distinction is a fine one and, in reality, neither the market nor the portfolio would be looked at in isolation. In carrying out a market analysis, it is assumed that the key objective is to test out the potential for growth within the identified priority markets and/or to assess the viability of remaining within a market, whether at the present or some other level (higher and lower) of activity. Kotler (1988) talks of three kinds of market growth: intensive, integrative and diversified. Intensive growth will relate largely to existing activity and could encompass the identification and development of new markets for current products and services (such as a public library intensifying its provision of services to HE students), increasing the share of existing markets or the development of new products or services for those existing markets (as for example electronic document delivery).

Integrative growth, in Kotler's model, relates to merger, acquisition or some other form of control over businesses that are related to, but not currently part of, the organisation's activities. Three forms of integration are common. Backward integration relates to suppliers; forward integration to customers and horizontal integration to competitors. Diversified growth, on the other hand, is about acquiring or developing businesses that are unrelated to existing activities. Kotler lists three kinds of diversification. Concentric diversification is about developing new products or services that are attractive to new customers but which have strong links with existing products or services (as for example distance learning); conglomerate diversification relates to the acquisition or development of activities that are unrelated to existing activities (such as a library acquiring a restaurant); and horizontal diversification is about new developments that appeal to existing markets but that have no links with existing products and services or the technology that they use (as for example a study skills advisory service).

Balanced scorecard

Kaplan and Norton (1992, 1993) developed the balanced scorecard (BS) in the early 1990s: 'the complexity of managing an organisation today requires that managers be able to view performance in several areas simultaneously'. It is a technique that is intended to give managers a full picture of an organisation and its environment and to help in determining future vision and strategy and in formulating ways of achieving key goals. The element of 'balance' is in seeking to encourage a wider view of an organisation's progress than that derived solely from financial measures and indicators. Creating this 'complete picture' allows more comprehensive solutions to be identified and implemented, while taking into account any knock-on effects of the proposed changes; and because the focus is on aspects of organisational life that help to make up that picture, managers get what they need in terms of identifying where change is required without being bogged down in unnecessary detail, though this may become important at the implementation stage. The model suggests taking an organisational view from four perspectives: learning and growth, business process, customer, and financial; the aim is then to develop metrics, collect data and analyse it relative to each of the four perspectives.

Table 7.2   The four perspectives of a balanced scorecard

Perspective	Comment
Financial	Analysis of: cost-benefit; financial risk assessment; organisational improvement.
Internal processes	Identification of organisational performance in relation to customer/user expectations.
Learning and growth	Identification of where training and development most needs to be targeted.
Customers/users	Analysis of different types of customers/users and their satisfaction with the organisation, its products and services.

The approach combines a mixture of financial, operational (internal and external) and innovation or improvement measures to create a view of the current and a vision of the future state of the art within the sector and for the organisation. Innovation is deemed to be especially important in helping to shape vision, direction and targets. Developing a BS, then, takes the organisation beyond a short-term view, aiming to build consensus from the beginning. Indeed, it is argued that everyone within the organisation needs to be 'behind' the BS – both in terms of the rightness of the approach and the validity and relevance of the results – for the technique to work. Differences need to be acknowledged openly rather than hidden, the challenge being to find the best ways of dealing with them. Developing a consensual operational strategy is deemed to be of major importance, even if the vision that drives it is uncontroversial as a result. Actions resulting from the BS should always be pushed in the same direction, minimising wasted effort, conflict and uncertainty and, as a result, preventing – or at least reducing – problems with implementation later on.

Key stakeholder involvement in developing a BS is critical. The BS technique takes into account the views of stakeholders – both external and internal – as long as they are deemed to be important. The involvement of senior managers is crucial in developing the BS, given their role and expected ability in terms of strategic overview and planning, though organisation-wide input and involvement should also be ensured. The change manager will need to determine how many stakeholders should be involved: too many and the process is unmanageable; too few and the scorecard will be unrepresentative, with critical stakeholders cut out and therefore potentially less supportive of the results. As in all change management approaches, the 'soft' aspects – in this case 'ownership' of the process and the outputs – are of major importance.

There is no single balanced scorecard. BS is a technique that can be adapted to suit a range of circumstances. Because the scorecard approach stresses goals before means, there is an implied flexibility, provided that is accompanied in practice by a readiness to listen and change direction as required. The measures that underpin a BS are non-specific, and can be tailored to different organisations and their needs, depending on where they are and where they want and plan to be on the change spectrum. Finance, profit and productivity are seen as key measures or drivers of success within a BS. It could be argued that the scorecard approach is less relevant to public than private sector organisations, although public and not-for-profit sectors have also been under increased pressure in terms of financial sustainability and increased effectiveness and efficiency.

There is also the possibility of looking at the human resource management aspects of change along with other 'soft' factors within the internal measures, allowing the combining of the very focused and specific in line with wider organisational aims. It is even possible to establish personal scorecards that feed from and into the organisational BS, though it should be remembered that the tools selected and the way measurement is undertaken can affect employee behaviour. The individual scorecard will show how members of staff reach where they want and need to be underneath the 'umbrella' of the organisational vision. This in turn drives employment development and the measurement of achievement in the same way as an organisation's appraisal scheme, of which the BS approach may in fact form a part. On the one hand, this prevents individual aspirations or whims being over-dominant, with the organisation's aims being the key; on the other hand, there may be an over-prescription in an individual scorecard system that reduces the chances of new ideas and real change coming from the workforce at large.

A number of questions need to be answered if a BS approach is adopted. It will be important to determine who decides on the key stakeholder involvement and the extent to which the process is 'top down' or 'bottom up'. The identification of the tools that managers will be using both to measure an organisation's scores in the various parts of the BS and to settle potential conflicts revealed by the BS will also be key. Are those tools the correct ones for each category on the BS in terms of the environment and its realities and the organisation's needs? Above all, the organisation will need to determine how best to move from the results of a BS application to the realities and the challenges of change. In this context, BS is perhaps more useful allied to a change process rather than a change management technique in its own right, given that it is likely to be useful especially at identifying the current state of the organisation and where change is most required, by whom, and to what purpose. Even where change is not deemed to be essential, the BS can be a useful 'health check' for the organisation so that the management can be sure that it has a sufficiently good knowledge of the organisation and the environment in which it operates, both present and future.

Figure 7.2 **Example of a Balanced Scorecard: South West Enterprise and Skills Alliance (SWESA)**

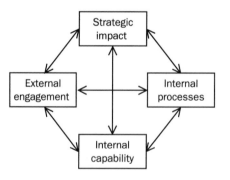

Box 7.8 **The SWESA performance measurement system**

The SWESA performance measurement system is based on a balanced scorecard approach. It has been designed both to monitor strategic impact and evaluate a set of factors that will, when linked with decision cycles, drive future performance.

Box 7.8   **The SWESA performance measurement system**
(*Cont'd*)

Whilst essential, the performance measurement data available for directly assessing strategic impact are largely embedded in the past. It can be several years before information is available on the impact of decisions and actions.

It is possible to monitor progress on key activities that underpin strategic impact within shorter time frames – so that management decisions can be more informed. This vital connection between action and measurement is reflected in the structure of the balanced scorecard, which mirrors the SWESA activity areas of external engagement, internal processes and internal capability.

Within this structure, a set of measures has been chosen that focuses on the initial goals of SWESA, including the four top priorities – business brokerage; leadership and management; literacy, language and numeracy; and joint planning.

Baseline information has been prepared for each of the four areas of focus and, in the quarters that follow, the progress of SWESA will be measured against this.

The scorecard, then, is a quarterly performance management report that monitors the performance of the Regional Skills Partnership (RSP) South West Enterprise and Skills Alliance (SWESA). The scorecard is comprised of four linked focus areas, each of which is assessed through two or more indicators. The aim is try and prevent duplication within the South West region of England and to ensure that good practice, ideas and developments can be shared and communicated amongst all the key stakeholders. Working or 'task and finish' groups and management bodies have been established to develop the strategy on which the scorecard is based. There is already evidence of joint planning at the regional level as a result of use of this tool. However, there have been a number of concerns and problems. There was a perceived lack of information and consultation in the development stages and therefore a lack of ownership in some areas. It will also take time for the effect of the scorecard to be noticed in terms of significant impact across the region, as evinced by low rating on the 'internal foci of institutional 'responsiveness to newly identified needs'

Box 7.8   The SWESA performance measurement system (*Cont'd*)

and 'effectiveness of innovation within the SWESA network'. Proposed improvements include: greater communication and involvement of stakeholders, a better link between the strategic and the operational, and the development of proper timescales and action plans. Does the scorecard, as used by the RSP/SWESA, actually have the power to improve the situation, or is it more a tool for helping discussion and enhancing other developments within the region?

Box 7.9   Balanced scorecard at Robert Gordon University (RGU)

As part of Robert Gordon University's approach to strategic planning, a balanced scorecard approach was adopted in 2003. The scorecard balances overall RGU-wide measures of progress in four areas:

- customer/stakeholder perspective;
- process perspective;
- people perspective;
- financial perspective.

For each area, critical success factors and performance indicators are set and monitored. These are reviewed as part of the overall process of moving the university forward to meet its strategic goals. The scorecard approach is used to measure strategic level progress and other organisational development (OD) approaches are integral to it, such as, for example, a leadership development programme, and an employee survey conducted every eighteen months.

Neville Browne, OD Manager at RGU, states:

As a post-92 university we seem to have a culture that is relatively happy with this approach. The balanced scorecard and its contents should be known to all employees; they can view it on the website at any time – it is a tool that is 'open' in that sense. We know, from our employee survey, how staff feel

Box 7.9   Balanced scorecard at Robert Gordon University (*Cont'd*)

> about key issues and, as a consequence, we feel that we know how our approach will 'fit'. We are a university that has some clear focus areas, so having a way of 'starting at the top' with strategic direction and measurement of progress and with enough appropriate staff engagement and involvement in the process, seems to work for us.
>
> Source: quoted in Huxley (2005).

Innovation scorecard

Innovation scorecards provide a way of assessing the extent to which an organiation is capable of innovating. They are a form of balanced scorecard that is useful for assessing the effectiveness and potential of an organisation overall (Stewart, 2001). The UK's Department of Trade and Industry (DTI)[4] produces helpful guidance and exemplars on these and other types of scorecard. The basic approach is to rate the organisation under a number of headings. A rating might look like the following:

Table 7.3   Innovation scorecard

Rating	Level
1	No real level of innovation, and no plans to innovate.
2	A basic level of innovation is evident, with a degree of motivation amongst the senior management to change.
3	Innovation is a stated and implemented key objective of the organisation
4	The organisation is 'best of breed' in innovation and innovatory performance.

This rating can then be used to score the organisation against key headings. These might be taken from the organisation's strategic plan, or be developed from the results of other analytical techniques. Once all the scores have been assigned, they are put on the complete scorecard and the areas for improvement are identified and prioritised.

What is more important in change management is not so much to identify existing gaps and fill them as to create new gaps that stretch the service, the sector, the market or all three. This is an essential part of innovation and continuous improvement. A gap might relate to competitiveness: the organisation that fills the gap first will be able to lead the market. Sometimes there is a gap in the market or sector that needs to be filled; or the gap may come from an existing product not currently being distributed to a particular market or sector.

SWOT analysis

SWOT stands for Strengths, Weaknesses, Opportunities and Threats. 'This four-fold SWOT assessment tool is regularly used to evaluate situations. Strengths and opportunities reflect positive aspects; weaknesses and threats negative ones. Strengths and weaknesses show the present position; opportunities and threats allow thinking forwards into the future' (Brierley, 2005a).

Box 7.10 SWOT analysis

A technique for analysing the environment in which the organisation operates or may operate in the future. It includes the following:

Strengths: areas in which the organisation has strong capabilities or a competitive advantage, or areas in which it may develop capabilities and advantages in the time period covered by the strategic plan.

Weaknesses: areas in which the organisation is lacking the capabilities necessary to reach its goals, or areas that can be expected to develop within the time period covered by the strategic plan.

Opportunities: situations outside of the organisation that, if capitalised on, could improve the organisation's ability to fulfil its mission. These may exist now or develop within the time period covered by the strategic plan.

Threats: situations external to the organisation that exist now or may develop in the time period covered by the strategic plan that could damage the organisation and should be avoided, minimised, or managed.

Source: Siess (2002).

An awareness of individual, group and organisational strengths and weaknesses is critical to the success of any change management project and its associated processes, for the ability to change means developing on and drawing from strengths and trying to eliminate or at least to minimise the effects of weaknesses. The analytical techniques described earlier in this chapter can all be used to provide the data that should inform a good quality SWOT analysis. The end result of the SWOT process should be that the organisation has determined either to move out of those areas where it is weak or to strengthen them in some way – as for example by creating a strategic alliance with another organisation that has the necessary strength.

The first stage will be to create an organisational profile on which the SWOT analysis can be based. The profiling process asks a number of questions about the nature of the business, the actual and potential customers, the ways in which the business is undertaken, the competition and the values that drive the business. Below is a worked example by Learning South West. It should be noted that the analysis leads to a list not just of priorities for the organisation, but also one identifying things that it may well stop doing in the future.

Box 7.11   Learning South West SWOT analysis

Strengths	Weaknesses
Longevity	No financial reserves
Dedicated staff	Reputation based on individual's performance
Bishop's Hull House	Can't expand car parking and therefore use of space
Flexible and risk taking	Board more focused on financial security than strategic role in the region
Owned by members	Membership is critical to finance and legitimacy but could be Achilles heel if that relationship breaks down due to changing climate for membership
Diversity of funding – independence	No dialogue/ownership of CPD by FE Sector
Cross sector	Our cross-sector role blurs what reputation we have and our relationship with members
ABC Awards	
Experienced in project management	Limited investment and practice of marketing
Clarity of role and clear accountability re Youth Work	Youth detached internally

A fuller working of the SWOT analysis by Learning South West is given at the end of the book.

7S model

A variant of the SWOT analysis technique is the 7S model. This was developed by Waterman, Peters and Phillips (Waterman et al., 1980). The model comprises seven aspects of the organisation that need to integrate and interlink with each other. These are:

- strategy;
- structure;
- systems;
- staff;
- style;
- shared values;
- skills.

The model can be used to identify the strengths and weaknesses of the organisation by adopting a matrix approach that matches the seven elements against each other in order to determine the degree of support that each has for the others. Where there is a strong degree of support, the organisation has strength; where the support is limited or absent, there is an organisational weakness.

Figure 7.3   7S table

	Style	Shared values	Skills	Staff	Systems	Structure	Strategy
Strategy							
Structure							
Systems							
Staff							
Skills							
Shared values							
Style							

The matrix can also be used to forecast the impact of change in one area on one or more of the others and combines the harder aspects of strategic change management (strategy, structure, systems) with the softer elements (style, skills, staff, shared values), though it underplays the more negative elements of organisational culture that can have a significant impact on performance and the ability to change. The documentation relating to Learning South West (found at the end of the book) uses elements of this approach.

Content, context and process model

Pettigrew and Whipp (1991) developed this diagnostic checklist model as a codification of the reasons why some organisations are especially able to manage strategic change and improve their performance. The model recognises that change takes place in historical, cultural, economic and political contexts, with five interconnected factors shaping the organisation's effectiveness:

- environmental assessment;
- human resources as assets or liabilities;
- linking strategic and operational change;
- leading change;
- overall coherence.

The key issue is the interaction between these five components of the model, and especially the content of change (objectives, purpose and goals), the process of change (implementation), and the organisational context of change.

Building on this model, Pettigrew et al. (1992) identified eight factors (though there were no simple cause-and-effect relationships between them) that were present in healthcare organisations that achieved a higher rate of strategic change than those that did not have the factors to the same extent, as follows:

- quality and coherence of local policy (analytic and process components);
- key people leading change (especially a multidisciplinary team);
- co-operative inter-organisational networks;
- supportive organisational culture, including the managerial subculture;
- environmental pressure, moderate, predictable and long-term;
- simplicity and clarity of goals and priorities;

- positive pattern of managerial and clinical relations;
- fit between the change agenda and the locale.

Force field analysis

A force field analysis (McCalman and Paton, 1992; Pettinger, 2004) facilitates the identification of the drivers of change and where resistance to change might come from. In particular, the analysis helps to identify which driving forces are most likely to cause which resistors and hence can help the change manager to deal with resistance, by expecting it, planning around it, or building in mechanisms and responses to combat it. The analysis is carried out by listing the forces for change on one side, and the forces against change on the other.

Figure 7.4 Force field analysis

Drivers	Present position	Resistors
>>>>>>>>		<<<<<<<<

Each force or resistor is typically scored from 1 (weak) to 5 (strong). Having done the scoring an analysis of both sides of the table will help the change manager to determine whether or not the project is viable. Looking at all the forces for and against a particular change may, of course, result in a decision not to proceed because the imbalance between force and resistance is too great. More usually, it will highlight the areas where support for the change needs to be strengthened and/or those areas where the impact of the resistors needs to be lessened.

SIPOC

SIPOC is a tool that can be used to identify all relevant elements of a process improvement project before it begins and may help to design and scope projects. 'The tool name prompts the change manager to consider the Suppliers (the 'S' in SIPOC) of the process, the Inputs (the 'I') to the process, the Process (the 'P') the team is improving, the Outputs (the 'O') of the process, and the Customers (the 'C') that receive the process outputs. In some cases, requirements of the customers can be appended to the end of the SIPOC for further detail'.[5]

Like other similar tools, the emphasis is on getting all the necessary information together before a project starts with the result that there is likely to be better planning and a higher degree of likely success in implementation.

 **Box 7.12** SIPOC

- Suppliers;
- Inputs;
- Process;
- Outputs;
- Customers.

Summary

This chapter has considered foresight and forecasting in the context of present and future environments and organisational position. It has looked at some techniques that can be employed. The Delphi method provides a future framework or set of scenarios in which a number of more specific analyses can be carried out, and can assist in the integration of different sources of data into a meaningful whole. Analysing and understanding the environment in which the organisation operates is also essential in order to determine the future strategic direction and what needs to be changed. The STEEPLE checklist can help in this context.

Other, more specific, approaches are also valuable. There will be a need to analyse all the stakeholders' needs and priorities. This is especially important when developing strategy. So too is comparing the organisation with others in the field – benchmarking – and seeing where the differences – for good or ill – are. This helps to determine priority areas. Reviewing the organisation's portfolio of products or services is one; another is the market in which that portfolio will have to be offered. These analyses can contribute usefully to a product development mapping exercise, where enhancements or other changes can be considered and prioritised.

The balanced scorecard provides a summative approach under which the organisation's position and performance can be measured, while innovation scorecards can be used to determine what the real capacity for innovation actually is. SWOT analyses are tried and tested, and still have a significant value, especially in strategic management. An important prerequisite will be the creation of a business profile that states the main aims of the organisation. The 7S model provides an integrative approach to SWOT, enabling the identification of the strong and weak linkages. The same is true of the content, context and process model, though the emphasis here is perhaps more on fitness for purpose of the organisation for strategic change. More specific aids in identifying the organisation's preparedness are the Force Field Analysis approach and the SIPOC checklist.

| Box 7.13 | Route mapping techniques at work |

- What does the future hold? **Delphi**
- What is the core environment? **STEEPLE**
- What do our stakeholders want? **Stakeholder analysis**
- How are we doing relative to others? **Benchmarking**
- Are we offering the right products or services? **Portfolio analysis**
- What do the markets want? **Market analysis**
- Where are we best and worst placed? **SWOT**
- How do we bring it all together into a plan for the future that can be measured against delivery? **Balanced scorecard**
- Is the organisation fit for purpose and well integrated? **7S**
- Is the organisation ready for change? **SIPOC**
- What is in the organisation's favour and where will the resistance come from? **Force field analysis**

Notes

1. *http://www.myersbriggs.org/*
2. *http://www.myersbriggs.org/type%2Duse% 2Dfor%2 Deveryday% 2Dlife/ mbti%2Dtype%2Dat%2Dwork/*
3. Bristol Online Survey (BOS) tool: *http://www.survey.bris.ac.uk/*
4. *http://www.dti.gov.uk*
5. *http://www.isixsigma.com/library/content/c010429a.asp*

References

Brierley, P. (2005a) *Opportunities and Challenges for the Church of England Over the Next 15 Years: Some Statistical Trends and What They Imply for Church Leaders*. London: Christian Research.

Burns, B. (2004) *Managing change*, 4th edition. Essex: Pearson Education.

Fahey, L. and Narayan, V.K. (1986) *Macroenvironmental Analysis for Strategic Management*. St Paul, MN: West Publishing.

Feather, J. (2003) 'Theoretical perspectives on the Information Society'. In *Challenge and change in the Information Society*, eds S. Hornby and Z. Clarke. London: Facet, pp. 3–17.

Hamel, G. and Prahalad, C.K. (1994) *Competing for the Future*. Boston, Harvard Business School.

Huxley, L. (2005) 'What is organisational development? *In Practice*, 6:1–4.

Kaplan, R. and Norton, D. (1992) 'The balanced scorecard – measures that drive performance'. *Harvard Business Review*, 70(1): 71–9.

Kaplan, R. and Norton, D. (1993) 'Putting the balanced scorecard to work'. *Harvard Business Review*, 71(3): 134–42.

Kotler, P. (1988) *Marketing Management*. New Jersey: Prentice Hall.

McCalman, J. and Paton, R. (1992) *Change Management: a Guide to Effective Implementation*. London: Paul Chapman.

Pettigrew, A. and Whipp, R. (1991) *Managing Change for Competitive Success*. Oxford: Blackwell.

Pettigrew, A., Ferlie, E. and McKee, L. (1992) *Shaping Strategic Change*. London: Sage.

Pettinger, R. (2004) *Contemporary Strategic Management*. Basingstoke: Palgrave Macmillan.

Siess, J.A. (2002) *Time Management, Planning and Prioritisation for Librarians*. Lanham: Scarecrow.

Stewart, W.E. (2001) 'Balanced scorecard for projects'. *Project Management Journal*, 32(1): 38–54.

Sutherland, J, and Canwell, D. (2004) *Key Concepts in Strategic Management*. Basingstoke: Palgrave Macmillan.

Twiss, B. and Goodridge, M. (1989) *Managing Technology for Competitive Advantage*. London: Pitman.

Waterman, R. Jr, Peters, T. and Phillips J.R. (1980) 'Structure is not organisation'. *Business Horizons*, 23: 14–26.

Case study 7.1 **Establishing University of Huddersfield Centres in Barnsley and Oldham**

Keywords: *consultation, flexibility, funding, staff development, universities.*

In the Autumn of 2003, the University of Huddersfield was approached by Barnsley College and the Oldham Higher Education (HE) Partnership in the hope that it would take over direct responsibility for HE in their towns. This approach came as a result of the University's 'Towns like Us' initiative, which focuses on fulfilling the Government's Widening Participation agenda. Huddersfield was to set up University Centres that would be total parts of the institution. In Barnsley's case, the move was prompted by falling HE provision in the town amidst a culture that did not really provide active support for HE among many people; in Oldham's case, some of the town's population, especially British Asian females, were capable of going to university but unable to travel away from home.

The University was enthusiastic, though the plan involved large-scale and multi-level change, and needed significant additional resource. Support and funding came from the Higher Education Funding Council for England (HEFCE), and subsequently from Regional Development Agencies and the European Regional Development Fund (ERDF)'s Objective 1. The change project itself was divided into two phases: negotiating the actual transfer of buildings, staff and students and then managing the change through the people affected by it. Both of these phases were complicated and necessitated strong yet sensitive management.

During Phase 1, complex financial and legal discussions were necessary as a result of legal and financial regulations and requirements. However, consistent determination paid off and by August 2005 the project was ready for the next phase.

During Phase 2, all the complexities of people and culture change became apparent. On the staff side, employees were able to transfer to the University of Huddersfield through the Transfer of Undertakings (Protection of Employment) Regulations [TUPE]. It was necessary to develop further their skills and knowledge base and their understanding of working in an HE rather than an FE environment. The staff employed at the new Centres had very different expectations and experiences from those who have previously worked within a University, and it was crucial to resolve those issues for the overall long-term success of the Centres. Without knowledgeable and enthusiastic staff, the scheme would have a much lower chance of survival. Consequently, formal staff development initiatives and informal contact between Centre and University staff were put in place; both integration with University counterparts and appropriate training made a significant difference. For the students – existing ones who would be transferring to the University and new ones arriving for the first year – there was good communication to ensure that they felt engaged and involved in the whole initiative. Meetings, personal

Case study 7.1   **Establishing University of Huddersfield Centres
in Barnsley and Oldham (*Cont'd*)**

letters and newsletters all played their part. Similarly, Huddersfield
allowed final year students to remain under their old degree
programmes, causing administrative difficulties for University staff but
demonstrating the sensitivity and flexibility required in such situations.

This change initiative has been well received and appears to have
been successful, although those involved have said that it is still much
too early to see clear indications of this. Firstly, the project itself was
unique, and the University of Huddersfield was almost venturing into the
unknown, yet found a way. Secondly, throughout the process the
managers have paid close attention to the needs of the towns
themselves, and to the rationale behind the project. Partnership Boards
at each Centre act in an advisory capacity to the University Council. They
include local representatives and, in a two-way dialogue, seek to ensure
that local needs and wants for HE and local academic and financial
provision are heard and taken on board, whilst gaining as much local
information as possible to help make the Centres sustainable. Thirdly,
consultation and communication have been utilised consistently and
well. Centre and University staffs' joint work on the development of the
curriculum have helped to develop links between the two, as well as
engendering a feeling of ownership by Centre staff.

The project has a long way to go, not least in establishing true HE
cultures in Barnsley and Oldham. However, the strong levels of support
from important stakeholders, especially HEFCE, regional bodies and local
populations, and the existence of a firm managerial structure to link the
two Centres with the University all bode well for the future.

When asked for his views, the Dean of the University Centres gave his
top factors for success in a change project as:

1. Being clear about what you want to achieve.

2. Ensuring that the resources you require are available from the start,
   and finding them if they aren't.

3. Finding ways to deal with the fundamental challenge of change
   management, which is to bring about change through and with the
   people affected by it, and to be able to provide skills development,
   communication, support and an ear to listen to any anxieties that may
   crop up along the way.

8

Change implementation: techniques and tools

Introduction

This chapter looks at the key planning and management techniques that can be used to facilitate an effective and appropriate change management process. It should be noted that many of the techniques and tools are relevant in two ways. Firstly, they can help to focus and codify a change in attitude, approach or vision for an organisation and its management. Secondly, they can help lead to successful change management processes and projects within the organisation.

The chapter first considers the differences and links between the strategic and operational levels of both the organisation and the change management project, emphasising the need for an holistic approach. It then introduces the concept of systems thinking as a way of dealing with problem issues – either as difficulties (likely to be more containable, with a clearer solution), or messes (that are more diffuse and are unlikely to have any easy or obvious solutions). The Hard Systems Approach is likely to be useful when the problem is definable, and a number of clear, though iterated, stages are listed and described. In the case of a mess, a 'softer' approach is likely to be required, and the Soft Systems Methodology is discussed. The Systems Intervention Strategy approach combines elements of both hard and soft methodologies. The chapter then considers two emerging approaches to change implementation: Appreciative Inquiry and Spiral Dynamics, which could be useful techniques in a larger approach to change management that needs a strong emphasis on the 'people' elements.

The second part of the chapter considers organisational development as a concept and a framework for major change and reviews major techniques or approaches such as Business Process Re-engineering,

Investors in People, Total Quality Management, Continuous Improvement, the European Foundation for Quality Management and Team Management Systems.

Strategic and operational levels

In order to formulate and then implement strategy effectively, it is necessary to have a full understanding of the situation to which the strategy pertains. Without this understanding, currently held assumptions may prevail when they need to be challenged and, indeed, overturned. It is especially tempting to think that enough is known about a situation before embarking on implementation through specific programmes of work and individual projects. Time is money and having a competitive edge is a finite state. However, 'more haste, less speed' remains a crucial adage. It is important to focus down to the operational level when considering strategy implementation. In doing this, it is assumed that the strategy itself has been properly formulated and is ready to be implemented, and that the 'bigger picture' is already well known and understood. The emphasis in strategy implementation, then, is on the operationalisation of the aims and objectives set out in the strategy. This requires the systematic reduction of the problems implicit in the strategy as formulated. The narrower the approach, the more likely that strategy planners and managers will fall into the trap of thinking that they know how to solve the challenges and problems associated with implementation on the basis of past experience without looking more broadly at the issues that really need to be taken into account before proceeding. The emphasis in much strategy implementation, then, is on holistic thinking.

Systems thinking

A system can be defined as a set of interdependent components interlinked in an organised way for a specific purpose (Checkland, 1981). Systems are typically described as closed or open. Closed systems are just that: they are independent of what is going on around them. Open systems interact with their surrounding environment, and cannot be viewed in isolation from it, as is the case with most organisations. In terms of change management, then, it is open systems that will be of most interest. Two particular points need to be borne in mind when considering change in open systems: if the system is 'in balance', then some form of positive action will have to be taken to alter it; people working within the system will have different and possibly contradictory views of that system, its nature and purpose. The components within the system interact with each other in a particular way; changing or removing one of the components from the system will alter the way in which it works. The interactions between the various components may not always be easy to identify. In human interactions, for example, unofficial channels of communication often complement – or even contradict – official ones. 'Corridor chat' is one form of communication that is often overlooked in systems implementation and the management of change. Changing the official channels without taking into account the unofficial ones may mean that the new system is ineffective.

In systems thinking, the manager has to take an overall viewpoint where the whole is greater than the sum of the parts, not least because due account needs to be taken of the interactions between the major variables. In the case of strategy formulation and even implementation, it is highly unlikely that management will have control over any of the major variables and their interactions. Using a systems approach will help to ensure that an holistic view of the strategy, its environment and its implementation pathway is adopted. It is based upon the idea of the model: a set of organised assumptions about a particular aspect of the world and the way that it works. Modelling allows managers to select from, and simplify, all the possible information that is available relating to a given problem or opportunity. The more complex the model, the more planning techniques will be required in order not only to incorporate all the required data, but to organise it in a meaningful way. The model is most useful in predicting the way that a system will behave in given circumstances, and particularly when a specific route towards set objectives is being proposed.

In systems thinking, it is usual to refer to problems (or opportunities) as being either a difficulty or a mess (Ackoff, 1974). A difficulty is relatively well defined. It is normally clear what the problem is and, when it is identified, what the correct solution is likely to be. It is possible to define (and measure) what success and failure will normally be over what time period and which people are involved. A mess, on the other hand, is poorly defined, with ill-defined problems and unclear solutions. Success and failure are also therefore difficult to define and differentiate. The desired objectives are not agreed or even known and no timescales have been identified. There is just a major problem that can no longer be tolerated. In reality, problems fall somewhere on a continuum between the two extremes. The better defined the difficulty, the more likely reductionist thinking will succeed. The more extreme the mess, the more some form of systems thinking will be required. There are two basic types of approach: Hard Systems Approach (HSA) and Soft Systems Methodology (SSM) (Stacey, 2003).

Hard Systems Approach

HSA can be used where the problem can be clearly defined and there is a reasonable degree of stability within the organisation and, arguably, its surrounding environment also. HSA takes both quantitative and qualitative issues into account. The approach involves a number of activities.

Table 8.1   Stages in a Hard Systems Approach

Stages	Questions to answer
Define the problem/analyse existing situation and relevant systems	What needs to change? Where are we now?
Identify objectives and constraints	Where would we like to be and what will stop us?
Generate ways of meeting objectives	How will we get there?
Formulate measures of performance	How will we know when we have achieved change?
Develop options	What are the options?
Test these options	Are these feasible and achievable within the timescale and budget?
Choose to implement the most relevant option	What are the key drivers of choice?
Implement option	What are the implications of the implementation? How do we ensure success?

At all stages, it is important to allow for iteration of a sequence or sequences in order to incorporate new information, not least because the completion of a later stage requires it. While the Hard Systems Approach looks like a logical, well-ordered approach on paper, it becomes more complicated in reality when iterations take place, as they often do.

The approach requires two separate roles to be identified: consultant and client. The consultant need not be someone from outside the organisation, but it is important to ensure that such a role is fulfilled. At the start of the process it is important to ensure that the client's level of awareness of the problem and their level of commitment to solving it is known and understood. The problem may well be poorly defined at this stage. It may even be nothing more than a vague sense of unease on the part of the client. The Hard Systems Approach encourages both the definition and redefinition of the problem until it is sufficiently focused for the later stages of the process. It also requires the consultant and the client to say why the problem needs to be solved and why they are involved. If there is general agreement that the problem needs to be solved or the opportunity taken, then the approach can be considered as a way of handling the situation.

Stage 1 is about identifying the opportunity or problem, describing it and the existing system, the environment in which old and new systems operate/will operate, and the systems' behaviour in given circumstances. The first stage of any project is the most crucial, and mistakes made here will affect the success of the later stages and the project overall. The project participants must therefore take care to look at all aspects of the project and the new system that will solve the problem or maximise the opportunity. This requires a holistic approach that takes account of all possible perspectives.

Stage 2 can begin once there is a clear definition of the problem or opportunity. At this point the key activity is to identify the objectives and the blockages to achieving them. In other words, those involved in the problem have to answer the question: 'where would we like to be and what is going to stop us getting there?' This articulation process is useful for several reasons:

- it makes those involved clarify their thinking about what they really hope to achieve;
- it should bring out into the open any disagreements between the participants;
- it builds ownership of the project and the solution;
- it provides a firm basis on which to build the rest of the project, provided that the process has been undertaken in a meaningful and effective way;
- objectives and constraints can be either quantitative or qualitative. The first group can form the basis of modelling exercises; the second group will assist in the determination of the overall boundaries within which the new system will have to operate.

The objectives that are identified need to be set into the broader context of the overall mission and goals of the organisation, the programme of projects or the larger system of which the project or system under consideration is a part. This hierarchy of mission – goals – objectives will be repeated at different levels, and it is important to ensure that the appropriate level is chosen for the project under consideration.

Stage 3 involves the identification of the preferred route or routes by which the objectives can best be achieved. This is the most creative part of the process, and a wide range of techniques are available, as discussed in this book.

Stage 4 is about evaluation of performance. The Hard Systems Approach stresses the need to have measures in place by which the effectiveness of the proposed way forward can be tested. Typically, measurements of effectiveness are linked to the objectives. But it is not just about knowing 'when you have arrived', but how well you have performed in getting there and whether or not your arrival is well-timed and in the appropriate place. Several measurements are likely to be required in order to measure effectiveness and efficiency to the full. Cost is an obvious one; timeliness is another. Other measures are likely to centre upon quantifiable improvements, such as turnaround time or increased productivity in a service or technical process. The achievement of this target is both a clear and a measurable goal. These latter targets need to be set realistically in the context of the overall environment in which the system will have to operate. A target of 5 per cent, for example, could be high or low depending upon the context. Evaluation of measures used in previous programmes and projects could be useful. Were they successful? If not, why not? There are always lessons to be learned from previous activity.

There will often be a tension between the different objectives: cost and quality are the obvious ones, but particularly cost and other objectives are likely to cause tensions within a project. Given the finite nature of resources available in most circumstances, the emphasis will normally be on the reduction of cost wherever possible. Wanting to get a project finished as soon as possible and to the highest quality will drive up the costs of completion. There is therefore a need to determine the best route between low cost and high performance in the achievement of the other objectives. But even an optimal route may not be possible. A decision will need to be taken as to when and where 'the best is the enemy of the good' or where a satisfactory route is preferable to the optimal one.

Stage 5 looks at the possible routes to be taken in order to ensure that the project reaches a successful conclusion, as measured by achievement of the objectives and the associated target measures. The likely outcomes from each of the proposed routes can be modelled in order that a decision can more easily be taken as to which route is preferable. This modelling process is likely to concentrate on quantitative rather than qualitative inputs and outputs.

Stage 6 is concerned with evaluation. Once a model has been constructed, the various outcomes that will result from the alternative routes need to be assessed in terms of their effectiveness in reaching the desired objectives. It is particularly important to ensure that the model does in fact reflect the real-world situation in which it is to be applied. At the end of the evaluation process a number of conclusions can be reached, but there should be one obvious one that provides the most effective solution to the problem or opportunity being faced.

Stage 7 is about validating the outcomes of the evaluation process. While one route may be the best in terms of 'hard', quantifiable data, 'soft', qualitative information also needs to be taken into account. It is rare that one single solution will in fact perform best in all circumstances and relating to all objectives, and at this point the perspectives of all the stakeholders need to be taken into account.

Stage 8 is the final implementation stage. If the Hard Systems Approach has been fully and effectively undertaken, then implementation should be relatively straightforward, though it will still require the development of a programme of work or a project plan.

Soft Systems Methodology

Soft Systems Methodology (SSM) was developed by Peter Checkland (Checkland and Scholes, 1999). Checkland found that it was not possible to apply a HSA to 'human activity systems', where people worked together to achieve a goal or objective, because:

- organisation goals were matters of controversy;
- formal methods usually begin with a problem statement, whereas the real problem might not have a clear definition, at least to begin with;
- the method itself restricted what could be discovered.

In response, the SSM is based on the following assumptions:

- problems do not have an existence that is independent of the people who perceive them;

- solutions are what people perceive to be solutions;
- people perceive problems or situations differently because they have different beliefs about what the situation is and what it should be;
- problems are often linked to 'messes';
- the analyst, researcher, consultant or manager trying to solve the problem is an integral part of it.

SSM is used when there is little or no agreement about the shape and nature of the problem and, hence, possible solutions. It is a methodology that has been used in a wide range of change management situations, including within the public sector (Iles and Sutherland, 2001), not least to gain feedback and commitment from a wide range of stakeholders. It is a holistic approach that includes the 'people' dimension and the broader environment. Its open-endedness means that it can be difficult to evaluate its success, though it can be used with other 'harder' techniques such as those underpinning Business Process Re-engineering or Total Quality Management.

Almost by definition, the opportunities and problems that are particularly susceptible to the SSM treatment are likely to be at the mess rather than the difficulty end of the systems thinking spectrum – simply because they involve people and all the different possible perspectives that they bring to the environment in which the system is likely to be operating; as with the Hard Systems approach, there is a need to identify consultant and client roles. SSM has seven distinct stages: problem expression, situation analysis, relevant systems and root definitions, conceptual model, comparisons, debate on changes and action.

Stage 1 is about looking at the problem situation. All the factors that might contribute to the problem need to be identified. At this stage, the factors are simply identified in an unstructured way. They may or may not have a causal relationship with the problem. However, it is important to determine the role that you yourself are taking in the SSM – what are your objectives and why are you involved in the problem analysis? Once you have started the process you are a participant and not an outside observer. The roles of all the other stakeholders also need to be considered at the same time. As noted earlier, they will all have potentially different perspectives on the problem.

Stage 2 sees the start of the analysis. Once sufficient information about the problem has been gathered, a 'rich picture' is drawn. A rich picture is a graphic representation of all the elements of the problem, as identified through the initial process of analysis. The picture can include hard and soft information. Hard information relates to facts, data, charts; soft information concerns things such as attitudes, fears, concerns and relationships. There is likely to be a feedback loop between the identification of the factors and the drawing of the rich picture, as drawing the picture may lead to further identification of important factors. Ideally, the picture is drawn by all those who have a stake in the problem situation. By doing this, not only should their views be taken into account but communication between the stakeholders will also be enhanced. Once the picture has been drawn, the key themes should be drawn out. The themes are then briefly described.

Stage 3 is about determining the ideal situation and the bridging of the gap between the real-world situation described in the rich picture and that ideal. Systems that meet the requirements of the themes are identified. Not all the themes and their matching systems are necessarily taken forward to the next stage – only those themes that are to form a part of the conceptual model that will form the basis of the solution to the problem. It may be that all themes need to be considered, but it is often the case that one theme stands out above all the others in the rich picture as needing attention first.

Having chosen the priority theme and its attendant system, a root definition needs to be constructed. This definition should sum up the system in one sentence. The root definition aims to identify:

- Who are the victims and the beneficiaries of the system?
- Who undertakes the activities?
- What is the transformation process?
- What 'world-view' is being used?
- Who owns the system?
- What environmental constraints need to be taken into account?

Stage 4 relates to the building of a conceptual model of the system. The model must show how the system relating to the root definition should work – what it is and what it does. The model concentrates on activities and their logical interaction with each other. It needs to take account of the six areas listed above that are incorporated into the root definition. Having identified the activities, they need to be linked, preferably through a diagram to form the conceptual model.

Stage 5 compares the models and the reality of the rich picture. The results of this gap analysis will point to where the existing system needs to be changed and where it can remain the same.

Stage 6 is where a set of changes are discussed and agreed between the stakeholders. These changes are designed to improve the situation.

Stage 7 is about taking action. Here the changes agreed are implemented. Other forms of analysis may be required and a project or programme plan and management structure will be required. Monitoring and evaluation of the plan, the changes and their effects will be important.

Systems Intervention Strategy

Systems Intervention Strategy (SIS) combines elements of hard and soft system methodologies (Mayon-White, 1986, 1993) and aims to build on the strengths of both, though SIS is usually described as being nearer the harder end of the hard–soft methodologies. The key difference between SIS and Checkland's SSM approach is the use of 'systems concepts' in the former: 'SIS uses the concept of system to impose a shared structure on the problem setting and so makes the initial analysis possible' (Mayon-White, 1986). It is based on the assumption that there are three types of basic change, relating to technical, organisational and personal elements, where organisational development is concerned with structure, roles and processes; technical development focuses on control and predictability; and personal development revolves around culture change and the development and embedding of new perspectives. The three types of change are deemed to be interdependent and interactive, but are also all influenced by the environment. SIS is intended as a way of encouraging learning and understanding with regard to change within the organisation. The methodology is cyclical and iterative, and is based on a team of 'inquirers' looking at all major aspects of a situation and producing appropriate models to act as an intervention strategy for change. It focuses on stakeholders, as their 'vested interests' may create resistance to change.

SIS has three phases:

- diagnosis;
- design;
- implementation.

The first phase is concerned with developing a particular view or perspective from which to address a set of problems. The design stage identifies and explores alternative methods and options for achieving the desired change. Implementation is the committing to change through a plan for making change happen. The stages are broadly chronological, though there can be a return to the earlier stages if there is a need to re-visit and reiterate the initial approaches, discussions, decisions and actions.

The SIS process begins with a determination as to whether or not the problem is a mess or a difficulty, and hence whether or not the approach is appropriate. The next stage is to undertake the diagnosis, by describing the problem in detail and establishing appropriate boundaries around it. The initial aim of the methodology is to reduce the possible options to one or two manageable ones, the point being that exploring a problem in its wider context is antipathetic to determining specific changes. Objectives are then set and constraints identified, the emphasis being on prioritising any lists that are formulated at this stage, especially in terms of importance or seriousness. Options should then be generated, modelled and evaluated until the preferred ones emerge as the best for the particular situation. Implementation strategies are then developed, though at all times there should be feedback to earlier stages or development into new iterative cycles that formulate new interventions for change, the emphasis being on continuous learning.

Appreciative Inquiry

'Appreciative Inquiry is not so much about new knowledge but new knowing. Indeed people frequently talk, as they move through the

---

Box 8.1　　Defining Appreciative Inquiry

Appreciative Inquiry is about the co-evolutionary search for the best in people, their organisations, and the relevant world around them ... AI involves, in a central way, the art and practice of asking questions that strengthen a system's capacity to apprehend, anticipate, and heighten positive potential.

Source: Cooperrider, D. and Whitney, D. 'A positive revolution in change: appreciative inquiry'. Available at: *http://appreciativeinquiry.cwru.edu/ intro/whatisai.cfm*; quoted in Huxley (2005).

---

pedagogy of life-giving Discovery, Dream, and Design, that something suddenly hits home: that interpretation matters.'[1] 'The basic premise of Appreciative Inquiry (AI) is that it is better to build organisations around what works, rather than focus on what doesn't work' (Huxley, 2005), and comprises questions, dialogue and stories of 'peak experiences' that are used to support the development of a shared vision and the detailed planning for the realisation of that vision.

AI (Cooperrider and Srivastva, 2001) is a way to look at life, society and the world, helping to shape a new environment through a strong and proactive approach to change and systematic development. By understanding the world within which changes are taking place, those involved in change are helped to clarify the type of changes needed and the best ways to implement them. AI can thus help to make culture change more successful by ensuring that change management projects and processes are embedded within the organisation in a deep, sustained and more complete way than might otherwise be the case. AI provides a vision, though still based in realities, going beyond present thinking and aiming to keep the change management process going by providing a proper direction and more 'moral' worth.

AI is about having a lack of preconception – though execution of an AI-based project still has to be methodical – with a 'clean slate' approach to the challenges of change that could allow a better view of the issues and the potential solutions. AI is about taking a positive stance towards change management, asking and identifying what is good and how it can be improved rather than engendering a 'blame culture' by looking for problems and how they can be removed. AI stresses a continuous and potentially innovative and improving approach rather than one that is short-term, defined and limited in its approach to problem solving. It aims to get down to the core reasons for change rather than focusing on the surface problems and the immediate need for solutions. Asking key questions itself means changing, and changing causes more questions to be asked. The theory of change that emerges from the inquiry can be the bedrock of the change management process, especially during periods of turbulence, for it generates language and dialogue that can help to create new 'cures' for challenging issues, thus leading to successful change.

The process of dialogue in AI is a never-ending one; the quest is for better understanding and a way to live and work. Language and communication are therefore key components of AI, stimulating new ideas, language and developments. How you ask is as important as the asking itself in AI; a personal approach and direction matters. Discussion helps to create common feelings, ideas and a collective strength for action. The emphasis is on collaboration not coercion and on ownership not enforcement, with individuals all working towards a common view, their different ideas helping to provide a more complete picture.

An internal approach is deemed to be best, with employees themselves involved from the start in the data-gathering exercise, for example through interviewing other colleagues. This helps staff to feel involved and worthwhile, as well as helping them learn new skills. Focusing the AI within the organisation means that there are no inappropriate external influences or conflicts of interests. However, there may be a lack of objectivity: serious issues and problems that need to be identified and resolved may not be fully recognised nor the correct attitudes developed because local interests predominate.

Appreciative Inquiry does recognise the uncertainties, difficulties and potential problems of change, and this approach needs to be carried into the change management process. In addition, while AI takes a holistic view of change, because the technique is centred upon theory there is no specific structured approach to an inquiry as such, and a disjointed and ineffective result may ensue without changes proposed and made being attached to real and specific problems. Planning is therefore a very important step in the development of an AI. A methodical approach means that processes are more likely to work, with change being more focused, more prepared and more thoroughly understood. With fewer structures and processes to follow than in some approaches, there will be a need for an individual or small group to draw the inquiry results together and make them coherent at key stages in the change management timetable. AI is therefore likely to be more successful when experienced change managers are leading and steering the inquiry. This will especially be the case when the programme formulated through an AI does not go to plan.

Appreciative Inquiry is about a fundamental approach to change and may therefore be inappropriate where the external environment is forcing change and there is insufficient time to adopt this technique to the full. A simpler, problem-solving based approach could be more effective in some circumstances. For example, specific forces or problems may be driving the need for change and these have to be dealt with reactively and speedily. However, once such immediate issues are resolved, an AI approach may be appropriate for the longer term. In any case, is constant change, development and new theory always a good thing? As noted earlier in this book, it may be dangerous and potentially unsettling – as well as unnecessary – to rely on theory and new ideas all the time. Much depends upon what kind of change is required or desired: radical or limited; 'clean slate' or incremental. If much of the current organisational structure, culture and approach is sound, then AI may not be the best way forward.

Spiral Dynamics[2]

The underlying idea behind Spiral Dynamics is that human nature is not fixed: humans are able, when forced by circumstances, to adapt to their environment by constructing new, more complex, conceptual models of the world that allow them to handle new problems. These conceptual models are organised around memes, systems of core values or collective intelligences, applicable both to individuals and entire cultures. The model appears to offer an approach to understanding the state and nature of value systems and cultures through a range of levels that are colour-coded. Its application in 'how do we go from here ...' is less clear. Spiral Dynamics is a way of looking at the underlying nature of what happens and why, so that it can be understood more deeply as part of a change management process, for example. This understanding helps people to work out how to cope with changes and how to shape their process. The technique looks at the integration of various factors underlying actions, and hopes to integrate the actions too.

Organisational Development

Sutherland and Canwell (2004) describe Organisational Development (OD) as 'a planned process of change ... [that is] about performance improvement in which a business will seek to align more closely to the environment and markets in which it operates in order to achieve strategies efficiently and effectively. OD can involve development in the areas of culture, values, people, structures, processes and resources'.

The overriding aim of OD is to identify and harness the collective talents of the organisation – and at all levels – in order to ensure its continued success. The key benefit of an OD approach is an increased organisational capacity to learn and change, particularly through an

| Box 8.2 | Defining Organisational Development |

Huxley (2005) describes OD as focusing on:

> ... how an organisation currently functions and may be helped to function (more) effectively. An initial approach often involves organisational audits of some kind that aim to capture and diagnose the organisational culture(s), processes and practice. Analysis of outcomes compared to objectives is followed by design, development, delivery and evaluation of change programmes and related learning and development actions with the aim of enhancing capacity and capability at the individual, team/unit and institutional levels. In the abstract all this sounds neat and tidy, even naïve, but in practice, and over time, it can result in a rich and complex set of activities that in the multi-faceted [organisation] helps to prompt a fuller understanding of the organisational context(s) and the management of successful change ... The usefulness of most OD approaches lies in the differing perspectives they offer on how an organisation operates, leading to the engagement of a wider group of people in focused conversations, questioning how the organisation might move forward. A portfolio approach ... is common ... with a number of methods being used flexibly, and in tailored form, to suit [different] contexts ... Key to the appropriate selection and use of any of the approaches ... is an understanding of the organisational context ... and of the aims of any OD activity.

integration of the various 'people processes' with strategic management more generally (HESDA and SSDA, 2004). 'It is clear that OD should not be in any way separate from the business of leading and managing – indeed knowing the climate of an organisation and selecting the most appropriate ways in which to apply that knowledge is at the core of sensitive and effective leadership' (Huxley, 2005).

In using an OD approach, it is typically assumed that the likely solutions to an organisation's change problems cannot be formulated or implemented in a wholly objective, rational or technical way, and that the change manager must spend time understanding:

- the nature of the individual and the organisation and the various responses to change that may be encountered;
- how culture and attitudes might impact on the changes proposed;
- how the resulting prejudices need to be prevented so that they do not get in the way of real change.

Because OD is focused more on process rather than goals, it is envisaged that a good base of trust across the organisation will be established that minimises resistance to change and so makes changes easier to implement when they are actually needed. Changing culture rather than structure or process is an area where it is often hard to quantify success, because when changing behaviour, attitudes or culture it may be impossible to measure progress. Certainly, while there are a number of techniques that are available to help gather data and information (including with regard to the feelings of the staff), every organisation is unique and will require its own particular mix of techniques.

Sutherland and Canwell (2004) stress the importance of 'research into the current situation to assess all the issues [and involving]:

- clarifying the impact of obligations that have to be honoured;
- the availability of appropriate resources such as skills, facilities and finances;
- the desires and career aspirations of those who will be affected;
- the proposed plan's overall fit with futures business strategy.'

Box 8.3   **Key actions in an Organisational Development project**

- agree the mission;
- assess present contexts (internal and external);
- gather data (including the views and feelings of the staff);
- gain involvement;
- set change targets – how much change is needed to get the organisation where it wants/needs to be and where in the organisation does change need to be implemented?
- implement change activities;
- evaluate/reinforce changes and see if/how far successful.

Undertaking research in this way will enable the organisation to have a good view of how the change programme should be undertaken. The programme may 'involve the design of [a] new organisational structure, job descriptions and evaluation, salary and benefits provision, physical resources, the phasing in of the overall project, and the management of impacts on existing employees' (Sutherland and Canwell, 2004). As with all change management projects and processes, communication, development, mentoring and counselling of staff will be important.

Some specific frameworks and techniques relating to organisational development are now discussed.

Business Process Re-engineering

Significant change may require an organisation to have a radical re-think of the way that works, the products that it offers, or the services that it provides. It may therefore require a re-engineering of the business processes that underpin the work of the organisation and, as a result, will need a significant and appropriate change management process to be in place if it is to be truly successful. Business Process Re-engineering (BPR) is a concept that was fashionable in the 1990s. Hammer and Stanton (1995) define it as 'the fundamental rethinking and radical redesign of business processes to bring about dramatic improvements in performance', while Hamel and Prahalad (1994) stress that 're-engineering aims to root out needless work and get every process in the [organisation] pointed in the direction of customer satisfaction, reduced cycle time and total quality'. While not written about so widely in recent years, BPR is still an approach that is often adopted when there is a wish or a need to promote discontinuity as a part of a fundamental, innovative approach to the renewal of an organisation in order to accommodate major change – often brought about by technological development and implementation.

In order to implement BPR, a number of stages must be completed. The process starts with the identification of the 'process vision' (Davenport, 1993). This defines the process to be re-engineered, its objectives and its key attributes. Following on from this the main characteristics are identified: how will the process work? Performance measures and objectives are then formulated: what does the process have

Box 8.4   BPR and radical change

> BPR, by radically altering business processes and their accompanying organisational structures, fulfils ... [the] need [to] ... make substantial 'discontinuous' leaps in organisational performance ... Basically, BPR is taken to be an approach for generating radical improvements in the major dimensions that an organisation uses to compete in existing markets ... [it] provides radical improvements across a number of, if not all, competitive priorities.
>
> Source: Burgess (1995).

to achieve? Perhaps the most fundamental stages are then reached: what are the critical success factors (CSFs) and what are the potential barriers to implementation?

Discussions about BPR in a public sector context have concentrated on 're-engineering for value' (Wreden, 1995), though, as noted by Halachmi and Bovaird (1997), it is often difficult to concentrate on either core business or core users when powerful stakeholders may insist on the continuation of marginal business at marginal value, not least because of political considerations. BPR is perhaps especially useful as a technique when a major new technology is being adopted within an organisation, whether in the public or private sector. Combining a technology application and a BPR exercise may therefore yield particularly impressive results if properly integrated. Experience of BPR has shown that it is difficult, if not impossible, to achieve the 'clean slate' that was thought necessary to achieve a full re-engineering, unless the organisation is being founded from new rather than being reorganised from existing structures and activities. The effective discontinuation of an organisation can rarely be contemplated, and fundamental organisation change is arguably not helped by a complete restart of processes and procedures – though BPR may be valuable as a technique to be used in specific areas where radical change really is necessary.

Investors in People

Investors in People (IiP)[3] is an established organisational development tool in the UK. The standard is now widely and well used in the public and voluntary sectors (including educational and religious institutions) and experience of organisations that adopt IiP suggests that employees are better motivated, more willing to take personal responsibility for their development, and hence more willing to embrace change. IiP provides a standard that seeks to make sure that employees perform well within an overall framework encompassing:

- strategies (business, learning and development, people management, leadership and management, work–life balance);
- actions (effective management, recruitment and selection, learning and development, recognition and reward, involvement and empowerment);
- evaluation (measuring performance and working for continuous improvement).

This in turn helps to improve the performance of the organisation, bringing benefits for employees, employers and other key stakeholders, improving communications and understanding in order to increase effectiveness. IiP focuses on the workforce, in order to ensure that an organisation's most important asset is in the best position to perform to greatest effect and to their highest potential. The standard is centred on knowledge – about systems, roles and skills, and about what is expected, particularly in relation to the objectives of the organisation.

Adopting the standard is a change itself for an organisation, but it is also a tool that can help change management to be successful more broadly, for without high-achieving staff no organisation will be truly

Box 8.5	Use of Investors in People

As government-initiated frameworks go, IiP has been remarkably resilient. One of its strengths has been its simplicity; another its flexibility. It is built on a conceptual framework that has its origins in Kurt Lewin's notion of action research, in which the first step is to define intentions and shape them into outcomes developed through a sequence composed of a circle of planning, executing, and reconnaissance or fact-finding for the purpose of evaluating the results of the second step, and preparing the rational basis for planning the third step, and for perhaps modifying again the overall plan.

Source: Huxley (2005).

successful, and during times of change and stress the performance and willingness of employees to work hard is crucial. It can stimulate change, for as the organisation looks at the way in which it treats its workforce, it may also look at its structures, processes and approaches and make other improvements. An organisation that successfully adopts the standard, then, is also likely to be better organised, not least because it will have thought carefully about the people, skills and leaders that it needs to be successful and will work harder at communication with the workforce at large. The key test will be the extent to which staff actually feel involved, empowered and drawn in to the development and improvement of the organisation and have themselves embraced the IiP philosophy. The emphasis needs to be on *investment* in staff, including through training and development and a range of human resource management approaches – including appraisal and performance management mechanisms, together with increased empowerment of staff.

Box 8.6   Two adopters of IiP

Robert Gordon University

RGU has been an IiP-accredited institution since 1995 ... [their] Organisational Development approach is subsequently shaped, to some degree, by the IiP standard, and its Organisational Development strategy, developed in late 2004 and updated in early 2005, encapsulates how the organisation intends to develop in terms of people development, team development and leadership development.

University of Teesside

'We see the Standard as a framework of best practice in people development which ultimately makes things better for everyone who works here by providing the support people need to do their jobs effectively and develop as individuals. There is also evidence from new staff that they were attracted to our University because it has Investors in People recognition.'

Source: quoted in Huxley (2005).

Total Quality Management

In competitive environments, organisations need to improve in order to maintain and increase their competitiveness. In the public sector, this drive to increase competitiveness is typically translated into targets for increased efficiency and effectiveness. Continuous Improvement (CI) is now a well-established concept and the concept of Total Quality Management (TQM) 'has been stimulated by the need for organisations to conform with regard to quality levels ... [as a result of] an increased demand ... for higher-quality products, parts and components. The fundamental principle ... is that the management of quality is addressed at all levels of an organisation, from the top to the bottom. Improvements are made on a continuous basis ... in an attempt to improve quality and decrease organisational costs. The emphasis, primarily on quality, is also very much on people and their involvement ...' (Sutherland and Canwell, 2004).

Ultimately, the level of quality to be pursued and achieved is a strategic management decision. Once this is known, then the organisation has to work out ways of ensuring conformance to that quality specification. These policies should be supported by benchmarking, as discussed elsewhere in this book. The important point to stress is that quality costs and that an understanding of this 'is essential for any business. The costs associated with the mismanagement of quality (the costs of non-conformance) are often large; are non-productive; and are avoidable through the implementation of TQM ... In most [organisations], the majority of quality related costs are incurred putting things right after they have gone wrong – the costs of non-conformance ... the objective of TQM is to continuously improve quality by eliminating non-conformance in every activity ... total quality involves everyone and influences the performance of the whole business' (Munro-Faure, 1993).

There are many techniques for the management of CI, and the ways in which systems can be developed in order to ensure that products and services conform to the quality standards set. It is outside the scope of this book to look at them in any detail, hence only one is discussed here as an example (Crosby, 1979). Its main characteristics (that are similar to most quality management and improvement approaches) are:

- an emphasis on 'conformance to requirements';
- a target of zero defects – perfection is possible;
- top management responsibility and attitude is crucial to success;

- an organisation's current quality management 'maturity' and therefore its desired position regarding its approach to quality must be assessed;
- the cost of quality is used to measure the size of the quality problem;
- there is an emphasis on prevention rather than detection;
- there is a strong focus on changing corporate culture to ensure quality actually does improve.

This approach is set out in the diagram below:

Figure 8.1   **Continuous improvement**

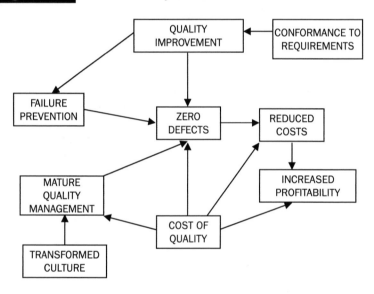

One important element of quality management, as noted in the diagram above, is the prevention of failure. This is an important aspect of strategic management of all kinds, especially in terms of anticipating success or, perhaps more appropriately, possible blockages to it. Indeed, TQM approaches emphasise the need to remove barriers to effective working through a focus both on external and internal (different departments and activities) customers or users of the organisation, with everyone working to deliver a good service or product, whether to the next part of the organisation or those outside it. Dialogue and interaction with both types of users will therefore be a prerequisite of any successful TQM process, especially in terms of identifying the key requirements and success factors that can then be drawn together to establish a route map that shows what outputs need to be changed, and traces back to the inputs that created them to show what needs to be improved in the organisation's processes. Shigeo Shingo developed the idea of Poka Yoke (or mistake proofing), as a way of anticipating those things that will create difficulties in order to move towards the ideal situation of 'zero defects'. While this approach is perhaps more pertinent to a production-line approach and less to the 'soft' side of change management, the concept is worth remembering in that it encourages the manager to make sure that all aspects of the change management project and the associated processes are covered before the project is initiated, in order to ensure that failure is minimised and challenges to the project are anticipated as far as possible.

EFQM

The European Foundation for Quality Management (EFQM) Excellence Model is based on a set of principles (Sullivan, 2002) that 'largely revolve around those areas common to all or most organisations – managing and developing staff, organisation of work, clarity of policy and practice, effective communication, efficient management of financial and non financial resources. In essence, it suggests that if core aspects of the organisation are efficient and effective there is a significant knock-on effect, releasing resources to focus on main aspects of the "business"' (Huxley, 2005).

The technique is concerned with improving an organisation after a period and a process of self assessment. The aim is to establish a purpose that reflects needs and wider environment: '[this] reflects the requirements of all stakeholders, but especially customers. Central to achieving purpose is getting clarity about key delivery and support processes' (Sandbrook, 2001). Putting things another way: getting things done for the user or customer will help the organisation to work backwards from the desired results (customer satisfaction) to identifying how these can be achieved, thus identifying what processes are needed and what changes should therefore be made.

One advantage of the approach is that it can be made specific to a particular organisation. It relies on (but can also create) a desire to improve the situation, fostering the use of good mechanisms for both discovery and evaluation, for identifying where improvement is required is also the first step on the way to finding a solution. The questions asked are initially high-level ones, underpinned by further, detailed sub-categories to help the organisation delve more deeply into the issues and challenges that it faces, the aim being to maintain a focus on the overarching aims and change requirements while at the same time homing in on the specific areas where improvement is needed.

| Box 8.7 | Report from a practitioner of EFQM |

We have been piloting the use of EFQM in one service area and hope to do more, but the existing internal and external Q[uality] A[ssurance] processes make more of this sort of 'additional' activity hard to sell, especially as the current culture is to paint as good a picture as possible for both internal and external audiences. EFQM tells it like it is and whilst this is great for a culture that embraces continuous improvement, it is hard for a prevalent culture ... that assumes excellence as a starting point!

Source: quoted in Huxley (2005).

| Box 8.8 | Key elements of Team Management Systems |

- team management – understanding where employees' work preferences lie, and working with these;
- types of work – what employees are expected to do (critical aspects of job) – particularly important where roles are altering within the organisation;
- linking skills – how to create a truly coherent and integrated workforce;
- team performance – assessing performance, helping to maintain momentum and motivation;
- opportunities-obstacles – who sees the risks and who the opportunities, to what extent and with what reactions?
- influencing skills – how to build a collaborative, motivated, hard-working, engaged workforce even in times of change;
- window on work values – finding out what motivates people and how they view the organisation;
- strategic team development – how to work as an effective team, all pulling in same direction with a common purpose, communication and trust, getting added value from all.

Team Management Systems

A Team Management Systems approach (TMS)[4] looks to explain why some organisations and their people are able to work effectively and successfully while others are not, and includes reference to staff motivation, working together, present and required skills.

All these elements are important aspects of change and change management, and being aware of the organisation's particular internal environment using these headings will help to ensure that the change manager knows how to:

- ensure that all staff are adding value;
- ensure that staff feel involved, integrated and worthwhile;
- build a group all working for the same purpose;
- ensure that managers have the correct management and people skills to create a successful organisation;
- find the right balance between risk and sense;
- improve the reputation of the organisation internally, which then improves how it performs externally.

Summary

This chapter has considered a number of approaches to change management. Each have their merits and drawbacks, for they all have different foci, levels of fluidity, levels of involvement and spheres of interest. In reality, therefore, while the techniques are useful in different situations, they are likely to be best used in an appropriate combination, depending upon the circumstances. Deciding upon which approaches to use and when will be assisted by the results of the tools described in Chapter 7. Some mixture of 'soft' (people and culture management) and hard tools is likely to be best, underpinned by one or more of the change management or development frameworks discussed in the second part of this chapter. While the softer tools are important, they cannot be used effectively if the groundwork of change has been undertaken by using the harder tools. The 'hard' approaches will enable projects to be started and evaluated more easily than the 'softer' ones but, on the other hand, 'soft' tools will increase the chances of really successful change that is embedded in the organisation as a group or groups of people and cultures.

Notes

1. Cooperrider, D. and Whitney, D. 'A positive revolution in change: appreciative inquiry'. *http://appreciativeinquiry.cwru.edu/intro/whatisai.cfm*
2. Spiral Dynamics. *http://www.spiraldynamics.com*
3. Investors in People UK. *http://www.investorsinpeople.co.uk/*
4. Margerison McCann Team Management System (TMS). *http://www.tms.com.au/*

References

Ackoff, R.L. (1974) *Redesigning the Future: a Systems Approach to Societal Problems*. Chichester: Wiley.

Burgess, T.F. (1995) 'Systems and re-engineering: relating the re-engineering paradigm to systems methodologies'. *Systems Practice*, 8(6): 591–603.

Checkland, P. (1981) *Systems Thinking, Systems Practice*. New York: Wiley.

Checkland, P. and Scholes, J. (1999) *Soft Systems Methodology in Action*. Chichester: Wiley.

Cooperrider, D. and Srivastva, S. (2001) 'Appreciative inquiry in organisational life'. *Research in Organisational Change and Development*, 1: 129–69.

Crosby, P.B. (1979) *Quality is Free*. New York: McGraw-Hill.

Davenport, T.H. (1993) *Process Innovation: Re-Engineering Work Through Information*. Boston, MA: Harvard Business School.

Halachmi, A. and Bovaird, T. (1997) 'Process re-engineering in the public sector: learning some private sector lessons'. *Technovation*, 17(5): 227–35.

Hamel, G. and Prahalad, C.K. (1994) *Competing for the Future*. Boston, MA: Harvard Business School.

Hammer, M. and Stanton, S.A. (1995) *The Re-Engineering Revolution*. London: Harper Collins.

HESDA and SSDA (2004) *Organisational Development in HE Project Materials*. Available at: *http://www.hesda.org.uk/activities/projects/ssda/odhe.html*

Huxley, L. (2005) 'What is organisational development? *In Practice*, 6: 1–4.

Iles, V. and Sutherland, K. (2001) *Managing Change in the NHS*. London: National Health Service, Service Delivery and Organisation Research and Development Unit. Available at: *http://www.sdo.lshtm.ac.uk*

Mayon-White, B. (1986) *Planning and Managing Change*. London: Paul Chapman.

Mayon-White, B. (1993) 'Problem-solving in small groups: team members as agents of change'. In *Managing change*, eds C. Mabey and B. Mayon-White. London: Paul Chapman.

Munro-Faure, L. and Munro-Faure, M. (1993) *Implementing Total Quality Management*. London: Pitman.

Sandbrook, M. (2001) 'Using the EFQM Excellence Model as a framework for improvement and change'. *Journal of Change Management*, 2(1): 83–90.

Stacey, R.D. (2003) *Strategic Management of Organisational Dynamics: the Challenge of Complexity*. London: Prentice Hall.

Sullivan, P. (2002) *EFQM Excellence Model: a Great Way to Manage and Develop a University*. Sheffield: Higher Education Staff Development Agency Briefing paper 101.

Sutherland, J, and Canwell, D. (2004) *Key Concepts in Strategic Management*. Basingstoke: Palgrave Macmillan.

Wreden, N. (1995) 'Re-engineering for revenue'. *Beyond Computing*, 4(7): 30–6.

Case study 8.1   **Managing with Emotional Intelligence at Cityroad University**

Keywords: *flexibility, personal development, Emotional Intelligence, universities.*

In 2005, the Staff Development Unit at Cityroad University decided that a course for managers focused on the mechanics of Emotional Intelligence would provide significant benefit both to staff and to the institution as a whole. A course for administrators on personal effectiveness was already in existence, but it was felt that a course for the managerial tier would be both useful and informative.

Originally, the Staff Development officers hoped to base this new course around the faculty structure, including academics as well as administrative managers. However, initial publicity did not bring forth any academics, and so the course was re-modelled around 'managers'. Its title, and its emphasis on interpersonal rather than technical skills, made it appealing, and the structure of the sessions aimed to get managers to think more deeply about their own role in relation to the wider success and quality of their departments.

The circumstances in which the programme took place were an important factor from the outset. The University had recently announced that it was facing financial difficulties, and this caused uncertainty and fear among managers both over their own job security and that of their staff. The original intention of making managers scrutinise their own position in order to manage more effectively now took on a new angle – that of learning how to manage during times of stress and anxiety, and whilst dealing with crises out of their own control.

The course itself seems to have been a great success. It has become a regular feature at Cityroad, with many of the places filled on the recommendations of those who have already taken it. What is more, despite time and work pressures, made worse by the financial difficulties, course members have been committed participants. The feedback from participants mentioned that the skills learnt regarding Emotional Intelligence were especially useful when dealing with the consequences of the difficulties, for they helped the managers to develop their ability to listen and respond well to staff negativity. The fact that 6 out of 10 from the original programme formed an Action Learning Set to draw up concrete objectives and actions is a sign of how worthwhile it was viewed to be.

Emotional Intelligence as a tool is highly relative and dependent on specific circumstances and environments, but is also flexible to individual needs. Its success in helping managers at Cityroad University highlights this.

Programme and project management

Introduction

This chapter considers programme and project management. Programmes and projects are the ways in which strategy is turned into reality; it is the main way of actually 'making things happen'. However, while programmes and project management relate largely to practical matters, they are also about making changes to existing products, services, structures or ways of working. This requires programme and project managers to interact with other parts of an organisation, and for senior managers – typically the people who sponsor programmes and projects – to ensure that the work that they have commissioned is well integrated with the organisation both operationally and strategically.

Effective strategy formulation must ensure that when the strategy is implemented, the three key objectives of the classic project management triangle are met in order to produce a result that is:

- on time;
- to budget;
- of the required quality.

These three criteria are the fundamental building blocks of the techniques discussed here. They underpin all implementation programmes and activities. The challenge is to balance the conflicts between the three variables. A project that is on time and to budget, for example, may not be of the required quality; only the injection of resources additional to the original budget or the extension of the project beyond the original deadline may actually produce the required quality once work has actually started and the true requirements have been assessed.

Defining project and programme

A project can be defined as 'a group of connected activities with a defined starting point, a defined finish and need for a central intelligence to direct it' (Taylor and Watling, 1973). The 'central intelligence' is the 'glue' that binds the various elements of the project together. It is typically supplied by a project manager, backed up by a project management structure appropriate to the requirements of the project. The project manager's role is a challenging one. It requires the postholder to plan, schedule, direct and control a wide range of resources not only within constraints that are set by the project sponsors (the three basic criteria noted above) but also in the context of external environments that present an additional, and often uncertain, set of challenges.

A programme is typically a cluster of projects that together are intended to meet the aims of the organisation that is commissioning the programme. The projects within the programme will need to be integrated with each other and the overarching needs of the parent body that is controlling and resourcing them. Programmes, like individual projects, must be led and managed. This is normally done by a programme manager, backed up by some form of programme management board.

The rationale for undertaking programmes and projects

A project, or a programme of projects, is typically undertaken in order to carry out the aims and objectives of a given strategy. A change or transformation will have occurred at the end of a project or a programme. This could be the introduction of a new product or service, or the implementation of a next-generation technology or some other improvement that is designed to improve efficiency or effectiveness within the parent organisation and to make it more competitive. It is the finite nature of programmes and projects, together with their fundamental aim of bringing about change, that makes them different from the normal ways of working – ways that are designed to cope with routine and predictable situations. Because the environment in which any institution operates is constantly changing – and not least through the continual upward spiral of technology advancement – the benchmarks by which projects and programmes will be judged will vary over time and in the context of the generic or sectoral environment in which they are being carried out (Clarke, 1999). It is thus crucial that programmes and projects are 'fit for purpose' with the overarching strategies that they are intended to support. This requires the development of intermediate level aims and objectives that on the one hand link with the higher strategic levels, and on the other hand give those who are implementing and managing the programmes and projects sufficiently concrete aims and objectives with which to work and on which they and others can judge the effectiveness of the projects being carried out.

Organising programmes and projects to best effect

There is no single way of organising a programme or a project to best advantage. A number of factors will influence the ways in which a project or programme is managed. Context, culture, external environment and organisational priorities are some of these. There is one element of programme and project management that tends to be common to most activities of this kind, regardless of the particular context. It is highly likely that the management will be organised as some kind of matrix, with the programme or project manager managing, or at least interacting with, a wide range of staff from different areas of, and levels within, the organisation.

In order for programmes and projects to work successfully, it is essential not only that there is a highly competent manager in charge of all aspects of this matrix, but also that this person has the authority to act and has the support of the senior management within the organisation, especially where the desired changes that form the output of the programme or project are controversial and not universally welcomed by all the stakeholders.

The main stages of a project

Almost inevitably, and in all but the smallest of change management projects, there is likely to be more than one stage in the process. Breaking a change management project down into stages will be helpful

Box 9.1   Project organisation

Because of the uncertainties and changing aims and environments that surround most programmes and projects, they

> ... must be actively managed in order to allocate resources and instil a sense of urgency. It demands a person who understands the totality of the project in relation to its business objectives, who is dedicated to its success, and who is in control of the resources needed to achieve the end result. Whilst a good planning and control system is essential, it can only provide a framework for decision-making and supply the information required for managerial intervention. The greater the degree of change from normal practice, the greater the number of variations from the plan and the greater the demand upon management.
>
> Because there is an urgent need for remedial action it cannot be left to the deliberations of a committee. This is the rationale for a system of project management that enables one person to take timely decisions with the minimum of interference. This person's position is analogous with that of the champion, but whereas the champion assumes the role him or herself, the project manager is appointed to implement a change that has already received the support of management.

Source: Twiss and Goodridge (1989).

in any case. Change begun in one part of the organisation or on a pilot basis can be adopted organisation-wide at a later stage without the need for a repetition of the early initiation stages, provided that the organisation at large has been fully informed and involved with regard to the change project and the experience of the 'early adopters' of the new approach. Major change approaches – such as Learning Organisation, TQM, or BPR – are in any case continuous and continuing processes where a momentum needs to be maintained and even increased as the project progresses in order to 'keep up the good work'. Every project, then, will have a number of stages or phases. Typically, these will be delineated by key milestones or objectives that

Figure 9.1   Project stages

CONCEPTION

Development of initial broad objectives, scope, constraints, needs, feasibility. May be underpinned by a stakeholder and/or environmental analysis as well as a financial assessment – likely budgets and return on investment. There will also be a need to estimate the time required to complete the project.

DEFINITION

If the output from the conception stage is approved, then the project is defined in full. The main stages of the project are identified and broken down into manageable elements or work packages, each of which has a set of deliverables, tasks and dependencies. Resource requirements and timescales are also identified.

ORGANISATION AND START-UP

Once approval is obtained from senior management, the project can begin. At this stage, all the necessary 'housekeeping' activities that are required before the project can begin must be undertaken. These will include issues such as staff recruitment and training, and organisational structure. There will be a need to determine both quality standards and performance indicators and the means by which these can be achieved.

EXECUTION

This is the phase during which the project is actually carried out, as far as possible according to the full project plan and, ideally, it ends with the delivery of the product, service, improvement or other desired change. The extent to which the project is successful during this phase will depend in large measure on the effectiveness of the management, both in day-to-day aspects of the project and in the management of the 'exceptions' that may cause the project to run behind time or below standard or over cost.

PHASE-OUT

The project is wound up at this stage. All deliverables should have been completed and handed to the project sponsors. Formal project review should take place and any lessons learned summarised. There may be follow-up projects that are identified also at this stage.

need to be met at various critical points in the project's phasing. The chances of completing a programme or project successfully will be increased significantly if milestones are clearly specified so that there is no room for doubt or dispute as to when and whether they have been completed.

In reality, most projects will be much more complex that the basic five-stage model suggests, and a number of iterations may be required at various stages of the project and in relation to particular aspects of the desired aims and objectives. In addition, it will be important to ensure that the key risks to successful completion have been minimised and that there are back-up plans in place in the event of the programme or project under-achieving at any point.

Programmes and projects in context

It is important to ensure that programmes and projects fit into the overall institutional aims, objectives and management structures and into the routine operations of the organisation while they are in progress and, once completed, that their results can be integrated into the future workings of that organisation. There are many examples of projects that were successful in terms of delivering their objectives, but unsuccessful in terms of the actual take up or 'embedding' of their outputs. In addition, programmes and projects have the capacity to unbalance an organisation in terms of day-to-day operations, especially where staff are seconded to the special work, with perhaps a responsibility additional to that of their colleagues. This requires careful handling if the project output is not to be prejudiced because of local enmities. More fundamentally, it is essential that programme and project work is complementary to current activities rather than detrimental to them, both in terms of resource allocation and management time devoted to what may be perceived as non-core business. Much will depend on the particular environment in which the organisation is operating and the extent to which project and programme activity is crucial to future viability. Good project management cannot make up for a poorly-designed project; conversely, a good project is unlikely to be made better by good project management (Munns and Bjeirmi, 1996). Strategic viewpoints are crucial if success is to be achieved (Artto et al., 2001).

Defining success

The 'strategic trap is embarking on a project without first assessing the full consequences of its success' (Roussel et al., 1991); any approach to the strategic management of change needs to take account of previous success or failure in the area. However, there is no widely accepted definition of 'failure' or 'success', and it is not always easy to forecast, manage or determine the extent to which a given programme or project has succeeded or is likely to succeed. Data and knowledge extracted from past practice, successes and failures is one of the most important resources available to the change manager: what did and did not work? What is likely to work in the future, in a particular environment?

Different stakeholders have different perspectives of success, failure and process that all need to be taken into account (Gray, 2001). There is a need to be clear about what constitutes success and to understand how and why a project is successful or unsuccessful in order to reduce failure rates and maximise the considerable investment now being made. Traditionally, 'success' is the completion of a project on time, to budget and to agreed quality (Zwikael et al. 2000). It is the delivery of what was promised, expected and hoped for – what the project instigators said would happen, with the attendant benefits that justified the change in the first place. Cooper and Kleinschmidt (1987) looked at the criteria for success, and found that success (or failure) is governed by the nature of the interaction between the environment and the appropriateness of the new strategy and its implementation.

Critical success factors

Critical success factors (CSFs) need to be taken into account as a means of achieving the organisation's key strategic objectives (Sashkin and Sashkin, 2003). CSFs will be linked to particular objectives and these factors will be an integral part of any change project, determining the particular milestones and performance indicators. If the key CSFs for a given project have been recognised and are catered for at the beginning of the project, then there is likely to be a greater correlation between inputs and successful outputs. CSFs can be categorised on the basis of experience across a number of sectors and used to improve success rates (Johnson et al., 2001). The CSFs drawn from other sectors include: leadership style

(Thite, 2000), team communications (Thomas, 1999), ability to iterate and be flexible (Ambler, 2001) and ability to spot trouble early and take decisive action, including project closure if necessary (Feldman, 2001).

Management of resources available to the project is a key part of the process. There are generic skills to do with managing resources that are essential to the success of a project (Johnson et al., 2001). These consist of political nous (Pinto, 2000), good 'timing' (Thoms and Pinto, 1999) and business process re-engineering, where it is especially important that resources are deployed as flexibly as possible (Dey, 1999).

Project manager workloads need to be optimised if resources are to be managed effectively and project outcomes are to be as desired (Kuprenas, 2000). As importantly, clients, project teams and functional managers should be involved at all stages (Jiang, 2000). This needs to be handled carefully if it is to be effective. It might best be done through the use of Total Quality Management (TQM) techniques (Orwig and Brennan, 2000).

Box 9.2	Reasons for failure in change management projects

- lack of consistent leadership;
- demotivated, unknowing staff;
- lack of capacity;
- lack of initiative;
- recycled mistakes;
- lack of proper planning;
- lack of ownership;
- lack of measurements or data;
- limited dissemination;
- unrealistic promises or plans;
- false discussion or pretend dialectics;
- self-centred, egotistic attitudes;
- exclusive approaches;
- threatening style of implementation;
- lack of urgency;
- no acknowledge of past failures or successes;
- lack of embeddedness of changes.

Risk management

Risk management is fundamental to the success of any project (Chapman, 1997; Jaafari, 2001). The model postulates that the effectiveness of risk management techniques and of development and usage of performance indicators is fundamental to forecasting success. Together, risk management and performance management underpin the correlation process. The more effective the risk management process and the more correlated it is with desired outcomes, the greater the chance of success. In managing risk, an organisation can then apply the four 'T's: terminate or stop the activity; treat or control the risk; transfer (e.g. insure) the risk; or take (accept) the level of risk identified.

Risk management should begin at the conceptual stage in order to maximise the chances of success (Uher and Toakley, 1999). But it has to be integrated with the rest of the project (Jaafari, 2001). Nor is risk management an exact science. It needs to take account of specific contexts (Ward, 1999). The literature is divided on what is most appropriate (Raz and Michael, 2001; Stewart, 2001). Risk management processes need to be expanded and enhanced, not least to include risk associated with the nature and composition of the project team (Williams, 1997).

Risk registers

Some form of risk register should be kept in any major change project. The aim is to:

- anticipate the main problems;
- identify where those problems are most likely to happen;
- analyse and assess the effects of the problems identified;
- facilitate the development of a plan to prevent the problems identified actually happening and/or to mimimise their effects if they do.

The register can relate to a specific programme, or parts of it, or in relation to one specific element, albeit as one tool in a whole collection of tools. The risk assessment might best be commissioned by senior management as part of an overall change management or quality improvement programme. Maintaining a register is particularly useful for activities where risk, and the effect of the proposed responses to that risk, need to be identified in particular. High-risk results will point the way both to 'breakthrough' projects and priority objectives for control. Scores can also be used to assess the effectiveness of the teams involved ('How quickly do they identify key risks and reduce them? How accurate are their analyses?).

A register typically uses an analysis sheet. This can be adapted to suit local conditions and specific projects. A significant advantage of the technique is that it can be used in a wide range of diverse situations. The key disadvantage is that it relies on both subjectivity (the scores and rankings are a matter of opinion rather than hard scientific fact) and historic experience ('this happened last time').

The main elements are as follows:

1. **Project stage:** This should be a concise description of the stage of the project.
2. **Potential failure mode:** There are likely to be many ways in which the project fails to meets its aims. Each likely cause of failure is described as a 'failure mode'. Each of these modes should be listed.
3. **Potential effects of failure:** It is then necessary to describe the potential effects of the failure mode on the project – including the next stages rather than the project overall – and the project's desired outcomes.
4. **Severity ranking:** The SR (severity ranking) measures the seriousness of the effect of the failure mode on the user. The level of severity is

Level	Severity	Ranking
Minor	The user is unlikely to notice any problems. The failure can be rectified easily and without any real impact on either cost or quality.	1–2
Low	The user will notice the effect but is unlikely to be more than a little irritated by the change to expected outcomes. The project will be delayed, but only by a little and additional costs will be minimal.	3–4
Moderate	The user will be noticeably dissatisfied with the results of the project. Quality will be lower than expected and the original timetable for completion will be exceeded. Some aspects of the project may have to be re-done, causing extra expense.	5–6
High	The user will be severely dissatisfied with the results of the project. The introduction of the project as a working service or product may have to be deferred. It is highly likely that the project will be unsuccessful in terms of its original stated objectives and outcomes.	7–8

Level	Severity	Ranking
Very high	The user will be almost wholly dissatisfied with the results of the project. In fact, they may not get any of the desired outcomes and benefits that were promised at the outset of the project. The project is likely to be deemed a failure and may be cancelled before the end of the allotted time period.	9–10

typically measured through a ranking process such as the one described in the table below:

5. **Potential reasons for failure:** The main reasons why projects fail include: lack of skills, poor project management, insufficient resources allocated, fragility of systems or approaches being adopted, or unreliability of the technology (where new technology is at the heart of the project).

6. **Likelihood ranking:** The LR (likelihood ranking) measures the extent to which a potential cause of failure will actually happen. The assessment of likelihood should be carried out before any preventive action is carried out. As with the severity ranking, a 10-point scale is recommended.

Level	Likelihood	Ranking
Certain	Has occurred or will definitely occur.	10
Very high	Will almost certainly occur as an 'odds-on favourite'.	8–9
High	Likely to occur (50% chance).	6–7
Moderate	Could occur (Less than 50% but more than 10% chance)	4–5
Unlikely	Unlikely to occur (1 in 10 to 1 in 100)	2–3
Extremely unlikely	Highly unlikely to occur (well over 1 in 100)	1

7. **Priority risk factor:** The PRN (priority risk factor) is expressed as a number. It is calculated by multiplying the SR and LR numbers. It provides a good indication of relative priorities in terms of managing risk.

8. **Prevention plan:** The prevention plan (PP) should include a description of all the actions that need to be undertaken in order to minimise the failure modes identified.

9. **PEN**: The PEN (plan effectiveness number) is a rating of the likely effectiveness of the preventive actions. The PEN is calculated using a ranking grid similar to the following:

Level	Degree	Ranking
Certain	The PP will be certain to prevent failure in the areas identified.	0
Extremely unlikely	If the PP is undertaken successfully, then the failure will not occur.	0.1–0.2
Unlikely	It is unlikely that the failure will occur if the PP is carried out successfully.	0.3–0.4
Moderate	Even if the PP is undertaken successfully, the failure may still occur.	0.5–0.6
Likely	Even if the PP is undertaken successfully, the failure is likely to occur.	0.7–0.8
Extremely likely	The failure is almost certain to occur regardless of the PP.	0.9.–1.0

10. **Residual Risk Factor**: The RRF (Residual risk factor) is the final and most important calculation. It is obtained by multiplying the PRN by the PEN. The result provides managers with a numeric value that sums up the level of risk that remains after all the preventive measures have been put in place. If the RRF is too high, then further ways will have to be found of minimising risk or an alternative strategy will have to be devised. In projects with a large research and development component, the high level of residual risk is justifiable, provided that lessons can be learned from the project, even if it fails.

Figure 9.2 is an extract from the Risk Register for the College of St Mark and St John, Plymouth, using the technique of risk analysis and assessment described here.

Summary

This chapter has considered the programme and project aspects of change management. A programme and project approach will ensure that there is a clear and systematic framework in place when any major change is undertaken within the organisation. There will need to be clear

Figure 9.2 An example of a risk register entry

10	**Risk – Failure to expand and enhance our strategic human resource management.** The College is proud of its record of developing its staff and can offer its continued accreditation as an Investor in People, being one of the first HEIs to be awarded full HRS Stage 1 compliance status and of having achieved full implementation of HERA and working hours harmonisation (ahead of national timescales). Further developments are planned **as part of the ambitious** HRS 2 plan.					
	The College does face some issues in staff management and support relating to outcomes from the Academic Portfolio Review and faces competition in recruiting and retaining high calibre staff (academic and support). **HRS 2 is addressing** many of these issues although some factors, such as salary comparators with other sectors and competitors, pose potential risks particularly in education and health staffing	5	6	30 Medium	Loss of high calibre staff impacts on quality and, ultimately, funding. The exact position is, however, impossible to calculate	No	Principal with Deputy Principal (Business and Administration), Personnel Manager and all line managers	Consider further market supplement payments to key staff and seek to develop younger staff to address demographic trends within the College

linkages between the agreed strategy and the programme of projects that are designed to implement it. The prerequisites of good programme and project management were then discussed. While there is no single prescription for success, it is crucial that there is a competent project manager in charge, supported by both senior management and adequate resourcing.

The second part of the chapter looked at the stages of a project. In theory, there are a relatively small number of phases of a project, though in reality there are typically several iterations of one or more of those stages before a project is complete, and especially where the overall objectives relate to the 'softer' people aspects of change management. The chapter therefore looked at both definitions of success and ways of measuring it, and the critical factors that are likely to help achieve it. Any change involves risk, and a key aspect of good change management projects is not the avoidance of risk but the identification and mitigation of it. The risk register is a valuable tool in this regard.

References

Ambler, S.W. (2001) 'Planning modern day software projects'. *Computing Canada*, 27(4): 11–16.

Artto, K.A., Lehtonen, J.-M. and Saranen, J. (2001) 'Managing projects front-end: incorporating a strategic early view to project management with simulation'. *International Journal of Project Management*, 19(5): 255–65.

Chapman, C. (1997) 'Project risk analysis and management – PRAM the generic process'. *International Journal of Project Management*, 15(5): 273–81.

Clarke, A. (1999) 'A practical use of key success factors to improve the effectiveness of project management'. *International Journal of Project Management*, 17(3): 139–45.

Cooper, R.G. and Kleinschmidt, E.J. (1987) 'New products; what separates winners from losers?' *Journal of Production Innovation Management*, 4: 169–84.

Dey, P.K. (1999) 'Process re-engineering for effective implementation of projects'. *International Journal of Project Management*, 17(3): 147–59.

Feldman, J.I. (2001) 'Project recovery: saving troubled projects'. *Information Strategy: the Executive's Journal*, 17(2), 6–12.

Gray, R. (2001) 'Organisational climate and project success'. *International Journal of Project Management*, 19(2): 103–10.

Jaafari, A. (2001) 'Management of risks, uncertainties and opportunities on projects: time for a fundamental shift'. *International Journal of Project Management*, 19: 89–101.

Jiang, J.J. (2000) 'Project risk impact on software development team performance'. *Project Management Journal*, 31(4): 19–27.

Johnson, J., Boucher, K.D., Connors, K. and Robinson, J. (2001) 'The criteria for success'. *Software Magazine*, 21(1): 1–8.

Kuprenas, J.A. (2000) 'Project manager workload – assessment of values and influences'. *Project Management Journal*, 31(4): 44–52.

Munns, A.K. and Bjeirmi, B.F. (1996) 'The role of project management in achieving success'. International Journal of Project Management, 14(2): 81–87.

Orwig, R.A. and Brennan, L.L. (2000) 'An integrated view of project and quality management for project-based organisations'. *International Journal of Quality and Reliability Management*, 17(4): 351–63.

Pinto, J.K. (2000) 'Understanding the role of politics in successful project management'. *International Journal of Project Management* 18: 85–91.

Raz, T and Michael, E. (2001) 'Use and benefits of tools for project risk management'. *International Journal of Project Management*, 19: 9–17.

Roussel, P.A. et al. (1991) *Third Generation R&D: Managing the Link to Corporate Strategy*. Boston, MA: Harvard Business School.

Sashkin, M. and Sashkin, M.G. (2003) *Leadership That Matters: the Critical Factors for Making a Difference in People's Lives and Organisations' Success*. San Francisco, CA: Berrett-Koehler.

Stewart, W.E. (2001) 'Balanced Scorecard for projects'. *Project Management Journal*, 32(1): 38–54.

Taylor, W.J. And Watling, T.F. (1973) *Practical Project Management*. London: Business Books.

Thite, M. (2000) 'Leadership styles in information technology projects'. *International Journal of Project Management*, 18: 235–41.

Thomas, S.R. (1999) 'Compass: an assessment tool for improving project team communications'. *Project Management Journal*, 30(4): 15–25.

Thoms, P. and Pinto, J.K. (1999) 'Project leadership: a question of timing'. *Project Management Journal*, 30(1): 19–27.

Twiss, B. and Goodridge, M. (1989) *Managing Technology for Competitive Advantage*. London: Pitman.

Uher, T.E. and Toakley, A.R. (1999) 'Risk management in the conceptual phase of a project'. *International Journal of Project Management*, 17(3): 161–9.

Ward, S. (1999) 'Requirements for an effective project risk management process'. *Project Management Journal*, 30(3): 37–44.

Williams, T.M. (1997) 'Empowerment vs risk management?' *International Journal of Project Management*, 15(4): 219–22.

Zwikael, O., Globerson, S. and Raz, T. (2000) 'Evaluation of models for forecasting the final cost of a project'. *Project Management Journal*, 31(1): 53–8.

Case study 9.1 **Performance management in Littlefield's Healthcare Library**

Keywords: *workforce, commitment, buy-in, culture, healthcare, libraries.*

In 2003, a new manager was appointed to run Littlefield's Healthcare Library. There were some change management challenges from the beginning. The library was both about to relocate and to amalgamate with another library. The manager did not have enough time to put in any processes to help with the changes or to get to know the staff involved, and had to continue to run a functioning library even though everything was about to alter. What is more, she did not receive specific management training or an induction, but was expected to get straight to work in the complex atmosphere.

The manager's predecessor had been organised, and had made many plans for the new library. Consequently, because there was no reason for the present manager to believe differently, she assumed that the library team was thus reconciled to the changes, and that all that remained to be done was to deal with the practicalities and logistics. As a result, no specific 'change management' procedures or concepts were introduced. Team-building sessions were not attempted; the changes simply happened.

Once the relocation and amalgamation had taken place, staff continued to go about their business. However, underneath the surface there were a number of tensions and clashes between individuals. Finally, after two years, a team-building exercise with an external facilitator was considered imperative. At the session, the manager and Library staff went back to basics, and had to answer questions such as 'what is a team?', 'what is a team for?', and 'what do you expect from yourself and from others in the workplace?'. These simple questions unearthed many differences of opinion among the staff members, which had to be tackled if the problems at the Library were to be resolved. The session seemed positive and successful, and the team returned to work with a set of practical targets and keywords to use as a starting point for developing team spirit and stronger working relationships.

Nevertheless, since the team-building session things have only partially improved. One member of staff in particular failed to co-operate in team activities or in the initiatives put in place to tackle the problems, and this manifested itself in a failure to accept or carry forward the targets adopted at the session by the others. For Littlefield, there is a lot of work that still needs to be done to bring about fully accepted change.

Littlefield Healthcare Library brings out some interesting points. It provides an example of change being waylaid by one person, and this is not something that can be resolved easily. Attempts to manage change, in whatever sense, can only do so much; trying to get people to buy into those changes can be an almost insurmountable task unless those

Case study 9.1 **Performance management in Littlefield's Healthcare Library (Cont'd)**

involved want to listen and compromise. The management of specific people and expectations will not necessarily be successful, however much effort is used.

When interviewed, Littlefield's manager stressed the following factors as being necessary for successful change initiatives:

1. Making use of a team-building day, especially if staff have never worked together before.

2. Being careful not to assume that the process of change is in itself enough to resolve all issues and build a team, but that change needs to be managed actively and openly.

3. Communicating the changes.

4. Getting Human Resources staff on board as soon as possible, as these are the people best qualified to help with difficult staff members, staff concerns or any 'losers' in the changes.

5. Talking to employees, listening to their concerns and ensuring that even apparently well-planned and unopposed change situations are and remain that way.

10

Summary

The necessity for change

Change is a very necessary part of the future for an organisation. The drive to invent, innovate or improve is driven by a whole range of reasons. Above all, however, the ability and capacity to innovate is fundamental to maintaining and developing competitive advantage (Collins and Porras, 1994). The need to improve efficiency and effectiveness is also an important driver. Feather (2003), stresses, however, that 'it is, by and large, users who determine ... success or failure'. This is especially true in service industries, where 'fashions' or client preferences can make a considerable difference to the success of an innovation or improvement (Baker, 2004). Innovation and improvement should not happen separately from 'normal' work but integrate with it. There is no single way to innovate or improve. Organisations will need to determine their approach and to assess and, as necessary, develop their capacity and capability. However, innovation and change can be harder in service than in manufacturing sectors, for the 'product' is often less easy to define and therefore to improve. Even an innovative change in an otherwise successful organisation cannot, and should not, be made in isolation: 'innovation is rarely a source of competitive advantage on its own ... [success also depends on an organisation's] distribution capability, their depth of technical expertise, their marketing skills' (Henry and Mayle, 2002).

The ways in which change is embraced and managed can significantly affect the position of that organisation and its long-term strength. In particular, it will be necessary to ensure that there is development rather than stagnation, and that fundamental failings are tackled. The greater and broader the involvement of all concerned, the more there will be an understanding of what needs to happen and why at core levels and the better the organisation will be at facing relevant issues with more interest. Such involvement will ensure that the loss of particular individuals – even if regarded as 'key players' – will not be crucial to continued success. If the change manager can develop and maintain a momentum, new attitudes and approaches can feed off continuation projects and the initial changes. Initiatives will thus keep on appearing, though this is likely to require continual support and leadership from senior management. But maintaining momentum requires enthusiasm and determination, especially when the change management process gets into difficulty or does not yield the desired results.

In each situation, different skills and approaches and possibly different scales of change will be required. The choice depends on the level of unrest, dissatisfaction or difficulty with the current state. The key challenge is to decide what to do, when to do it, and how. Continuing change may run the risk of building up resistance within the organisation if it is thought to be too much, too frequent or unnecessary by those who will have to live through the change. Change must never be 'for the sake of it', though it can be tempting to make changes because other organisations are doing so, or it is the latest 'fashion' to operate in a particular way. Making changes on a cyclical basis, with approaches or initiatives following one after the other in a less than coherent way, may disrupt and destabilise the organisation without any real gain. In an age when dynamism is seen as a key organisational virtue, there is a danger that the senior manager in particular will create or subscribe to a belief that the best ideas and solutions are always the newest ones and that progress can only be achieved through constant change.

So what is good change management?

Good change management uses a broad range of techniques, including systems thinking, to develop a shared vision – led by management but involving everybody – with a focus on encouraging, engendering and utilising team and organisational learning. This will result in an organisation that 'moves as one', recognising trends in complexity and encompassing breadth, flexibility and interdisciplinarity. Change management may include changing managerial behaviour and organisational structure. It is inseparable from good management more generally, given the pervasiveness within and outside the organisation and the ongoing need for managers to respond to pressures for change. But it is management and not control: full control is both impossible and undesirable. The key environmental aspect of change is its uncertainty and complexity, and the change manager must try to appreciate this almost as a given, to make sense of it, and to work with it. There is thus no 'one' change situation requiring management; additionally, and perhaps especially, in the public sector, there will typically be so many groups involved in any major change project that it will be impossible to provide the 'correct' solution easily or quickly. Therefore any and all theories and theoretical approaches are just that: they can never be definitive or defining, though they should be considered seriously as part of the necessary in-depth analysis of the particular situation that requires a change management approach or project to be introduced or implemented.

Good change management is concerned with dynamism and proactivity: 'dynamic environments ... require dynamic processes, people, systems and culture'[1]. It means: building in time to plan change and possible changes to the original plans, deal with resistance and ensure effective communication and dissemination at all stages; communicating in anticipation of gossip or before discontent arises, or in response to undercurrents of tension; dealing with specific situations at the time rather than leaving them to deteriorate beyond a retrievable point; boosting morale at times when it is less than good, but only by making promises that can be kept and by remaining confident and truthful at all times; not letting the organisation feel isolated during major change and when it is therefore vulnerable, by bringing in external points of reference and sending people out to understand and compare with the rest of the sector and the relevant environment more generally (as for example through conferences or inter-organisational discussions and meetings).

Good change management is also about balancing continuity with change. Wherever possible change projects should aim to find an area of stability or continuation – some kind of holding framework – on which the organisation can focus in times of otherwise rapid destabilisation. This framework could be the values and overarching vision, aims or objectives of the organisation: for example, the drive for quality or the principles of access in education. Such an approach will provide the underlying rationale for the changes themselves – a central and solid point that people have supported in the past and are likely to support into the future. Stabilising change may also be facilitated by running pilot changes first, where this is feasible; wider change could then follow on from successful prototyping. Managing stability in the context of change is also about recognising the importance of structures; changing structure will need to be undertaken with care when other changes are also planned, for restructuring could undermine the organisation at a time when it is least safe to do so: structural change has to be thought through like any other change and it must be integrated fully with other key changes proposed. Stability of a kind is also engendered through consistency – especially from senior management – in communication, approach, and action, and helps staff to feel more secure and trusting with regard to what is going on around them, even if there is vast upheaval across the organisation.

The 'balancing act' that is change management is about not only solving immediate problems but also about working to remove the cause of those problems in the first place so that they do not occur again in the future, ideally by putting in place mechanisms to ensure that the organisation really does learn not just from its mistakes but in addition from the way that it changes and will change in the future. Good change management, then, is preventative as much as it is curative. It questions mindsets, going beyond incremental learning and system or process correction to a deeper, more embedded, fundamental change. Such a root-and-branch approach can be a major risk to the organisation and may be of serious concern to the workforce, but such an approach is necessary if true change is to be effected and effective, with its almost inevitable break away from the old constraints towards a new stability for the future. This will require implicit as well as open change management and, as already noted, the building of an ability to change into all aspects of the organisation's work.

Throughout this book, there has been an emphasis on communication, information generation and dissemination that is free flowing, open, two-way, and horizontal as well as vertical; not top-down, detached, distant or controlling. Not everything has to demonstrate either an instant or a permanent change; some ideas can be open to debate and criticism, but merely stating them openly can establish a process of iteration and discussion, a climate of change and an atmosphere of action. Bringing ideas and issues – especially radical or controversial ones – into the open will raise awareness and initiate discussion. Healthy scepticism of both new and old should be encouraged as part of the drive to open dialogue and interchange.

Critical thinking is crucial to good change management. The organisation, its managers and its workforce needs to move away from biased or narrow-minded thoughts and approaches towards clear, rational, fair and level-headed thinking. This will result in an ability to see all points of view on the one hand, but with a clearer picture of what needs to be done on the other. Without such an approach, there is a risk of small, specific or minority groups within the organisation getting an unfair hearing. Being objective can be difficult, but it is vital.

Key skills

This book has argued that there are several key skills that need to be possessed (or acquired) and used in order to manage change successfully:

- political skills, to deal with people and cultures;
- analytical skills, to provide logical and rational arguments that cannot be contested factually;
- people skills, to ensure appropriate communication and empathy – hence an ability to deal with the vast variety of interpersonal interactions;
- system skills, to understand organisational systems and how to deal with them;
- business skills, to understand how a business – and specifically the organisation undergoing change – actually works.

The change manager needs to move away from and beyond organisational politics and the problems that it can cause with regard to a whole range of topics, including co-operation, relationships, dissemination and communication, and the formulation and implementation of common objectives. Going beyond the constraints of the organisation means recognising the generic factors that cause change, identifying and engendering the equivalent attitudes needed to ensure that change happens properly, developing the key skills needed for change management in the particular context and fostering the necessary culture changes required to fit in with the new environment.

Cook et al. (2004) sum up the key requirements of good change management as the four 'intelligences', listed as business, political, spiritual and emotional. Business intelligence is concerned with the external environment and user demands, as related to the areas in which the organisation is working, for it is highly likely that other organisations within the same sector will also be changing, or at least be under pressure to change. The organisation therefore needs to ensure that it is aware of and understands where new ideas and attitudes are coming from, and to gain a range of knowledge from as broad a range of experience and know-how as possible. The more knowledgeable the organisation, the better able it will be to draw on its information base to determine when, where and how it should be changing. Business intelligence, then, informs, initiates and drives the necessary changes through an understanding of what stakeholders are demanding and/or what is required in a new or changing environment; identifies where and how the organisation should be dissatisfied with its current state; anticipates and provides a map of where the organisation needs to be to reduce or eradicate the dissatisfaction; aims to ensure the choice of a model of change that is most likely to fit in with the current and forecast future business situation. Business intelligence needs to ensure that the situation is read carefully and properly, with an emphasis on the long term, the buy-in of key groups and the effective delivery of what is proposed or promised, the whole underpinned by a continuous, truthful and comprehensive risk assessment.

Political intelligence is concerned with the situation within the organisation itself, its power bases and the key influences on the people who work in the organisation or are otherwise associated with it in some key way. It aims to prevent personal gain getting in the way of the good of the organisation by identifying and using the key motivators that will get people 'on board'. This will happen best by accepting that resistance and vested interests cannot be ignored, but if they are understood, they are more likely to be dealt with effectively. The agreements and solutions that will work best in the context of organisational politics will be those where all parties have gained: so-called win-win outcomes, achieved through partnership rather than adversarial working and negotiation as discussion, not conflict, with differences of opinion being recognised openly and as a positive rather than a negative element of the change management process. Political intelligence recognises that employees cannot be 'lumped together' as a single group, but rather they may comprise a number of different sets of stakeholders in their own right, with the need to take account of their needs and to anticipate how they each will react to proposed changes and the ways in which they might be implemented. There will be an understanding of who has power within the organisation, where it comes from and to what extent it will affect – whether positively or negatively – the change management process and its outcomes. It will also be about using a variety of the best, most appropriate techniques for a given situation, with subtle judgement as to when and how to negotiate and when to be assertive: a mixture of 'push and pull' that uses incentives and threats wisely. Political intelligence will identify or create, use and capitalise on roles and make the most of all the staff by spotting their talents and using them to best effect in the better management of change within the organisation.

Spiritual intelligence focuses on 'the organisational vision and values' (Cook et al., 2004), for even in times of change, the vision and values of the organisation are something for the stakeholders to hold onto. It centres upon the manager and their level of self-evaluation and self-awareness. It relates to their integrity, sense of purpose and moral worth; their encouragement of diversity and creativity and their willingness to share power with others in the organisation. It can be especially helpful in this context if the people who are managing change have also been on the 'other side of the table' as employees who have experienced change as followers rather than leaders, for example managers in an academic institution who have been academic members of staff themselves. They are then able, as a result, to understand why academics defend their autonomy, even if to the detriment of change overall, and can persuade such people to change nevertheless because as leaders they have credibility as well as empathy and understanding within the community that is undergoing the changes. A high degree of self awareness and self belief amongst change managers will allow them to encourage interest and instil belief and enthusiasm in others through dealing with resistance and fear on the one hand and helping employees to feel better about themselves on the other, through developing confidence, giving people roles and ensuring buy-in to the changes.

Emotional intelligence is concerned with people's ability to understand and empathise with the feelings of others, by understanding and trusting one's own feelings and reading and appreciating others. Effective interpersonal skills are crucial in terms of effective communication and interaction with both staff and other stakeholders: 'despite the growth of e-mail, the Internet and other technologies, there is no substitute for developing strong interpersonal relationships. This is particularly important in truly understanding other people's perspectives' (Cook et al., 2004). Nowhere is emotional intelligence more necessary than in the area of leadership within the organisation, for transformational leadership is more necessary than transactional management at times of change. So the leader must be self confident and independent in order to lead effectively, but s/he must also possess empathy, be socially aware and responsible and be sensitive to the needs and feelings of others, able to build relationships on the basis of an ability to use emotions wisely, pragmatically and optimistically.

Complexity of change

There are no 'easy fixes' in change management. It is wrong and even naïve to assume that there are simple solutions to complex problems or, even worse, 'off-the-shelf' answers to localised questions. It is important to avoid using a preset rulebook: such an approach will simply not work, for the change manager needs to expect unexpected consequences of, or reactions to, policy implementation. The search will be to find the real problems and the true solutions to them; but sometimes there are no real solutions, in which case it will be hard to develop a successful change management approach in order to prevent further problems arising. Hard work does not guarantee success, even though it is an essential ingredient in change management. Other essential prerequisites are: a sound vision and strategy, adequate resources, working collectively in the right way and direction. Many change managers focus on the 'soft' factors, such as culture and leadership. However important though these are, the 'hard' aspects and approaches that are a key part of any good project – such as timescales and staffing requirements – will also need to be central to any major change management process (Sirkin et al., 2005).

Vision and opportunity

A clear vision of the future is essential: something to work towards, to frame what is changed and how, and something that can be used in communications with those affected. The good change manager treats change as an opportunity rather than a threat, and where impact will be long- rather than short-term. Almost irrespective of the specific environment, the given situation or the possible future challenges, the change manager will seee many opportunities through which the organisation can adapt – opportunities from which it should be possible to choose those options that will make the most (positive) difference. The change manager needs to engender a feeling of change as something that is embedded within the institution and a relatively safe exercise (even if it is an ongoing and drastic process) rather than a feeling of stepping into the unknown for an indeterminate period of time and without any real sense of direction. Continued momentum through a major change management project is vital, but can be difficult to achieve. Collins and

Porras (1994) argue that it is not enough to develop vision and mission statements; they need to be understood and supported by everyone within the organisation, with all the workforce knowing what the 'core ideology' is and then working towards the basic values that it embodies. But it is also necessary to ensure that the organisation can focus on those values and not be distracted by other, albeit pressing, shorter-term problems and challenges, for example immediate financial difficulties that run counter to the more aspirational and idealistic values. As noted elsewhere, this relates back to the timing of change.

The organisation

The type of organisational culture will be a crucial determinant in the way that change is implemented. Indeed, it may be that the culture of the organisation must be tackled before changes that are actually wanted by top management can be put in place. If a fundamental shift is required within the organisation, then it is almost inevitable that culture change will be required. The change manager – and the organisation more broadly – will need to combine an ability to confront all the facts, however unpalatable, with one that enables all the key players to 'hold faith' that a solution will be found to even the more intractable problems. The organisation must believe in, rather than delude, itself and be prepared to take necessary action, however unpopular that might be, both outside and inside. It is essential that the organisation has a holistic approach to change, without there being a disjunction between the top-down and bottom-up views of change management.

It is important to work as your organisation requires, knowing current drivers both within the field and within the organisation, and having a flexible policy for dealing with them or reacting to them where necessary while still seeking to reach the desired goal. To do this, the change manager must ensure that the change project will fit with the future – if not the present – organisational culture, standing and position and that it is not based on fashion or outmoded or inappropriate policies or theories. The organisation needs to be focused on the real problems; otherwise there will be a vicious rather than a virtuous circle of problems arising because the underlying issues have not been tackled. Tackling embedded, 'root-and-branch' difficulties 'head on' is usually the best way of attempting to prevent overt resistance or merely superficial change. If there are no real problems, then the organisation needs to think very carefully about whether or not any changes should be made.

The people dimension

In an ideal situation, the majority of employees will want and are ready for any changes before implementation begins. But this really is an ideal. Recognising and dealing with the people issues and finding the most effective way of managing employees during change is often the difference between success and failure in the use of change management techniques and ideas, almost regardless of whether those ideas or techniques are good ones (Plant, 1987). The people dimension of change management is part of everyone's responsibility, whether a senior manager or a member of the 'front-line' workforce. The human resource aspect will not take care of itself: it needs to be planned, managed and integrated with the overall approach to change. Without due regard for employee concerns, the wider picture will be blurred, the project disjointed and the whole change process made more difficult and a successful outcome put at risk. As may be evident from some of the case studies that have been included throughout this book, it is important to ensure that people are used in ways that suit their strengths rather than expose their weaknesses and which allow them to focus on what they need to concentrate on, for example senior management and their particular responsibility for strategy. 'Middle management' in any organisation is always a key group of workers, for they can affect the success – or otherwise – of the change management process, and need to be fully involved with true roles rather than bypassed or disempowered.

Communication, iteration, evaluation

Communication is key in dealing with people and change, ensuring that links up, down and across the organisation are strong and that understanding between various groups within – and even outside – the organisation is good. Organisations – and even sectors – are rarely structured simply, and communication networks must be established that aim to tackle the complexity of the organisation and the environment in which it is functioning. Developing a common language through regular meetings and forums (Boddy and Paton, 2004) as well as other, standardised forms of communication – including the sharing of reports, documents and even the creation of written materials as well as their distribution – will help to ensure that work based on informal conversation and sharing of experience – important though that is – will not be lost but rather become visible to others outside the immediate circle in order to 'surface and legitimate learning processes that may otherwise go under-recognised' (Donaldson et al., 2005b).

Iteration of success, lessons learned and failure within a learning framework will help people involved in change – however peripherally – to see what has been done and how it has had an impact as well as helping to change and refine the impact and outcome of the change management project and improve the engagement and embeddedness of the changes across the organisation. Similarly, constant and continuous evaluation of the processes and the direction of changes – based on research that is focused on action and outcomes that can demonstrate (or not as the case may be) that the expenditure of resources has been effective and worthwhile – should lead to quicker, more continuous and easier to implement improvement in the longer term.

Stakeholders

Throughout this book, much has been said about stakeholders, whether they be staff or users, external agents or funding bodies. Change management, its rationale and its meaning is increasingly seen as being about the stakeholders, what they need from the organisation and what the organisation must do to satisfy them, albeit in the context of the overall external environment. Determining who the stakeholders are, then, must be a top priority: 'think of your stakeholders as any individual or group that has the resources you need to deliver an initiative successfully; or even more widely, a group or individual that has a stake in that initiative' (Dewhurst and Fitzpatrick, 2006).

Donaldson (2005b) has shown how, working within a particular part of a sector, making improvements for one's own stakeholders can result in a broader influence over the sector in general: by doing things well 'in house', it is possible to help other organisations if the opportunity arises, at least where the changing organisation is strong, directed, cohesive and committed and, as a result, ahead of others within the sector who may be languishing at a resistant stage in their change management processes.

The change manager must know who the key stakeholders are well before the project is proposed, let alone started. It will be necessary to work out which stakeholders – whether as types, groups or individuals – are most likely to offer dangerous opposition and wreck the chances of success in change, and where they stand in relation to proposed changes. It should be noted that those who provide the support for change may not always be the most powerful or the ones who can most easily help to deliver change successfully. Where key stakeholders have radically different views from those proposing change, or present serious opposition, then there may need to be compromise, something best achieved where there is a mutual understanding of the different perspectives and ideas about what is required and how it should be implemented.

New ideas and attitudes

Collins and Porras (1994) stress the need to evolve as an organisation, trying new things and using what works as a way of adapting successfully. Visionary organisations 'keep abreast of upcoming changes, anticipate them, or make them themselves, or else the company's products will become obsolete. You try different things and see how they work, quickly getting rid of the things that don't work', often metamorphosing as an organisation in the process. It is important to ensure that new ideas and attitudes have an opportunity to be heard, considered and implemented. Many organisations do this by employing new (to the organisation) people, mixing their 'freshness' and 'external' objectivity with the retention of good, longer-serving staff, whose knowledge of the organisation and mature skills and experience is irreplaceable. Longevity in the managerial role – or other key roles for that matter, such as trades union representation (Cabinet Office/CCSU, 2002) – can be helpful, for it makes it easier to act intuitively and with initiative as change progresses, and to draw more carefully on people within the organisation, knowing how to manipulate the politics and culture, because the longer-serving manager will be well aware of the organisational environment and how to negotiate their way through it. However, a manager brought in from outside will also have attractions and advantages, not least because they come fresh and objectively to the situation – especially important, perhaps, when a good deal of change is required and/or the organisation is currently stagnating.

Targets, timescale, timing

Change must take place at the right time and, as far as possible, in the most appropriate environment for it to flourish. It is important not to focus on short-term or tangible targets at the expense and to the detriment of real, long-term significant change, the ideal being true, sustainable, sustained implementation. The change manager, then, must look both to the immediate and to the long-term future. If possible, there should be no 'leaping in', but rather planning, discussion, engagement and understanding, in order to ensure that all processes are in place. Too much emphasis on finding immediate solutions may inhibit sustained and sustainable change and learning; taking longer over the earlier planning stages will almost always help implementation. Developing overarching vision and nesting stepped changes within one overall framework and integrated policies will prevent disjointedness or 'quick fixes' and enable the management to build a culture where change is seen as a positive force for success. Where initial change is urgent, and there is insufficient time for consultation, it is essential that it does take place once the initial urgency has passed, otherwise change will not be embedded sufficiently, however pressing the initial need for it actually was.

Change as project

Any change management project should establish timescales, milestones and points at which to review progress, reassess direction and approach and give praise where praise is due. The more comprehensive the pre-implementation phase, the more likely it will be that the conditions have been created for the change project proper to have the best possible chance of success. But change management projects must go beyond solely implementation, with the post-implementation phase being crucial in enabling changes to become embedded, problems to be ironed out and new changes to be established on top of a first group.

While any project should be broken down into its constituent parts, it is important in managing change to ensure that there is an overview of the whole project from the start. This is because different stages are often not discrete entities, given the complexities and subtleties of change, but rather parallel or overlapping layers of activity and transition or transformation, not least because individual elements of a project may change as new things happen or lessons are learnt. Projects must be tailored to the specific needs of the organisation: it is inappropriate to superimpose a ready-made plan; every institution is an individual, living organism with its own unique structure, background, issues and history and context of change. At the same time, change management projects are likely to have a number of stages, and will almost certainly include the following, though not necessarily in a single, chronological sequence:

- developing a shared understanding;
- getting commitment from the top;
- setting objectives;
- agreeing an action plan;
- involving the workforce;
- developing (partnership) agreements;
- investing in training;
- making it happen;
- evaluating the outcomes.

(Source: adapted from the TUC Partnership Institute: *http://www. partnership-institute.org.uk*).

The processes used in managing change can be as important as the content of the change project, in that they provide the 'glue' by which the change manager helps to create common values, a sense of direction and organisation-wide support for the change. However, in the final analysis, the content is required as well, or the changes will not be embedded because they are not real in the sense that they will not truly re-form or improve the organisation as it needs to be in order to meet future challenges. The process must begin with the rationale for change and work out from that. Is it a reinvention of the organisation out of choice or necessity; does the change require small-scale adjustments or a fundamental directional shake-up? The level and depth of change and the reasoning behind it will determine who needs to be involved and to what extent. Some changes can be done almost overnight or subconsciously, while others will need months of planning, in-depth analysis and even soul-searching before implementation can even begin. The rationale will set the stage for incremental or fundamental change, though the two are not mutually exclusive.

There are some useful checklists for assessing change as project, for example the DICE model (Sirkin et al., 2005), which asks the manager to assess: the likely Duration of the project, the performance Integrity or capabilities of the organisation, the Commitment levels of the senior management and the amount of (additional) Effort required of the workforce in order for the change to be successful.

Table 10.1 The DICE model

D	Duration
I	Integrity of performance
C	Commitment
E	Effort

McCalman and Paton (1992) suggest a longer list.

Table 10.2 The TROPICS test

Timescale
Resources
Objectives
Perceptions
Interest
Control
Source

The change manager/leader

There needs to be someone to 'direct' discussions, make final choices and ensure that things get done. Without leadership and direction, there is a risk of procrastination and lack of impetus and initiative. After due data collection, analysis, consultation, discussion and agreement, a range of appropriate techniques should be employed to draw all the ideas together and choose the final direction. In doing this, it is crucial to keep 'on side' those who had different ideas and approaches, including by explaining the rationale for the preferred strategy and direction and why they were chosen above others. The strength to persevere with, and adhere to, the chosen path needs to be matched by a willingness to change direction or approach if the original plan is not working, once it is clear that this is the case. It is important that the change manager has the ability to step back as well as to manage, aiming to ensure that 'managerialism' and overly tight controls are avoided, while still demonstrating accountability and a strong structure and managerial rigour within the organisation.

How can trust be married with necessary control? The change manager will need to avoid being seen to be manipulative. At the same time, s/he must define the overall direction of change projects sufficiently so that employees know the frame in which they are working. The ability to anticipate is a key requirement of the change manager. The change manager needs knowledge in advance: what they want to change, what they want to keep, the specific needs and direction of the organisation, where to anticipate resistance, where to be flexible and where to have a 'bottom line'. The best chance of success in change management will come if the change manager knows, understands and is at one with the organisation and, according to Milsome (2003), can base a change management project on solid foundations of trust and commitment from all parties, with sufficient time for implementation, supported by good lines of communication.

Impact, balance, integration

The change manager must accept the full potential impact of the changes that are to be made and remain proactive at all times, engaging all people who will shape and influence the change management process rather than becoming reactive or even unable to control what is going on. The change manager will need to live with teething problems and even a possible drop in standards, efficiency and effectiveness while change is occurring, by being confident that change will eventually bring improvement. It may be necessary to engender change by restructuring: some form of 'shake-up' regarding roles, responsibilities and positions. There may be a need to persuade some staff to take early retirement or otherwise to encourage some staff to move on to roles elsewhere if they are not happy with the new environment or atmosphere.

The change manager must learn how to balance what can be ambivalent or even contradictory forces, whether social, economic, cultural or institutional. There needs to be a balance between an open, adventurous, original and wide approach to change, but within a strategic framework that is as precise as possible in order to provide a stable environment within which change can be managed. The clearer the strategy, the easier it will be to allocate resources effectively to it and the more likely it is to be managed to successful implementation. It is crucial that the change management policies are not only produced but directed by the team responsible for them. It is not just about establishing the 'bigger picture', but also about providing resources and being operationally involved throughout the process.

Tools and techniques

This book has explored a number of different tools and techniques. These are means to an end: the determination of what needs doing, how, when and by whom: with what impact, where and when; what the organisation does or does not have that will help or hinder the change management process; and the drawing up and implementation of strategies and plans that will take into account all the relevant environmental or market forces and their underlying meanings and which select the most appropriate processes for successful completion of the change management project and its associated processes. Is change and improvement to be on a continuous scale or is it more a case of radical re-engineering? Much depends on the starting point for the change and the needs of the organisation: what is the level of dissatisfaction with the current state of affairs, especially when measured against both the current and likely future states of the art in the given sector and external environment within which the organisation is located? Answering this question objectively will determine how drastic the change needs to be.

The choice of which change management tools and techniques to use should always be based on an assessment of what is appropriate and what is most likely to work, bearing in mind that each situation is dynamic and different from previous ones. Given the complexity of significant change, most projects will adopt a multi-faceted approach, rather than trying to use one or two techniques in isolation. Nor is it possible to 'cut and paste' from previous experience, even from within the same organisation, important thought the dissemination of good practice or lessons learned is. Tools and techniques should therefore embrace the complexities of the project, including the internal, external and politic realities of the environment. As far as possible they should be safe for the particular context in which the organisation is working and the changes that are proposed, balancing the culture change and human resource issues with the more specific project aspects.

Tools should be used to gather enough, rather than too much, information, so that the picture – and the different options – can be seen clearly: information overload will only lead to the organisation and the change manager in particular being bogged down by data, theory and options. It will be necessary to take into account the fact that different people using the same analysis techniques will come up with different results and proposals. Some may also view the ideas and attitudes of their colleagues differently depending upon a whole range of factors, including age, gender, race and experience. The change manager will need to develop some mechanism for dealing with this in order to minimise any potentially adverse effects and get the best options agreed across the organisation.

Unless the change project is a very simple one, it is likely that a combination of 'hard' and 'soft' approaches will give the best chances of success. Neither will work on their own: the harder techniques may yield a superficial success, but the soft, more people-oriented tools are those that will bring real culture and attitudinal change among the human dimension. It may be that a change project best begins with the harder techniques and approaches in order to identify the strategic and business imperatives, with the soft approaches being used to involve and empower all those who will be affected by the changes and who therefore need to own them.

The new change management

The process of managing change is itself changing. A number of writers argue that it is time to develop a 'whole new language about the subject and the areas in which change management is working', for 'we are using metaphors that are restricting the way we think about change' (Baloguna and Jenkins, 2003). Future rhetoric, then, it is suggested, is more about knowledge generation and knowledge management than change management as such. This relates to changing ideas about work itself, with an emphasis on, firstly, the 'component knowledge' necessary to do the work, and, secondly, the 'architectural knowledge' of function and change across the organisation that it needs to develop and grow properly.

This new language of change also requires an acceptance of how change must be done, how people must be involved and in what ways: 'it is never simply a question of relabelling ... rather the use of language reflects another way of looking at the world, it points to a change of perception, a change of consciousness' (Bassnett, 2005). But, it is argued, shifting perceptions through changed language could well signal real underlying change, for change will almost inevitably involve dialogue as part of the process of absorbing and assimilating new ways of working as old views – especially if deeply, but quietly, held – are brought into the open and then properly and fully replaced by the new approach; it will assist in the amalgamation of old and new groups within a workforce and back up changes in structures through the support of mechanisms that are designed to change attitudes and cultures.

The organisation that wishes to change will need to put the development and management of knowledge at the top of its agenda for change, passing on best practice and learning from worst practice and developing ways of dealing with challenge and difficulty to best effect as a collective, rather than through force or dictation from the top. This should result in 'intelligent change', where there is a 'weighing [of] problems against opportunities, deliberative changes against insightful initiatives, organisation-wide change against focused adjustments, and widely accepted change against the more innovative' (Springer, 2005); all this is underpinned by an understanding of internal and external atmospheres and how both impact on the specific issues that need resolution through changes, and results in the best way forward for the organisation, in context.

Endnote

This book has been concerned with strategic change management. Ultimately, for effective change to take place within a well-planned and managed framework there needs to be a tension and a balance between dissatisfaction with the present position and a vision of, and aspiration towards, a better future. Without the first, there is no desire to change; without the second, there is unlikely to be the resolve to continue with the changes and the likelihood of disillusionment or even despair at the first sign of major problems or early hardships when the change management plan is not working as intended. This can be summed up in the 'change equation' of Gleicher (Beckhard, 1969) where, for change to work:

$$D x V x M > R$$

Where D = level of dissatisfaction with status quo; V = attractive ideas/vision for better future; M = method; R = resistance to change. (Note that M is sometimes expressed as F = achievable first steps towards the future, and R is sometimes expressed as P – pain or C – cost to the people involved.)

Change will not work if the resistance (or pain or cost) involved is greater than the other three elements of the equation. If it is, then either the resistance has to be reduced or the other three increased. Nor will change work effectively if any of the level of dissatisfaction, the vision or the method to be used have a low or zero value.

To ensure successful change, it is necessary to 'use influence and strategic thinking in order to create a vision and identify those crucial, early steps towards it. In addition, the organisation must recognise and accept the dissatisfaction that exists by communicating [sector] trends, leadership ideas, best practice and competitive analysis to identify the necessary change'.[2] Having done the identification, then there are a whole series of processes, approaches and styles that need to be used selectively, according to the particular environment and summed up, according to Palmer and Dunford (2002), by a subtle mix of the art and science of change management that encompasses: directing, navigating, caretaking, coaching, interpreting and nurturing. Above all, the organisation that looks to the future must develop processes for the strategic management of change, in the knowledge that change will bring continuity (Pfeifer et al., 2005).

Box 10.1   Aide memoire for change managers

- Know what you want to change, and what you want to retain.
- Know your organisation – where is it now and where does it need to be?
- Know your people – listen and learn.
- Anticipate – be prepared for resistance, conflict, 'noise'.
- Be flexible **but** have a 'bottom line'.
- Know as much as possible about the organisation.
- Encourage open team working.
- Involve senior management.
- Build in feedback, stages; clear, sensible timescales; flexible priorities.
- Separate the urgent from the important.
- Be open to as much data as possible; collect data on the detailed impact of any changes – especially on staff.
- Engage in action research, and don't pre-empt any findings.
- Create networks to glean ideas, advice, support, advance warning of difficulties.
- Develop loyalty to the change process rather than trying to buy it.
- Document the process.
- Be optimistic and resolute.
- Be ready to play different roles within the project.
- Be ready for failure and learn from it.
- Remember that 'the best is the enemy of the good'; no-one ever has 100 per cent support for change.
- Celebrate successes on the way, however small.
- Finish what you start.

Notes

1. *http://www.businessballs.com*
2. *http://en.wikipedia.org/wiki/Formula_for_Change*

References

Baker, D. (2004) *The Strategic Management of Technology*. Oxford: Chandos.

Baloguna, J. and Jenkins, M. (2003) 'Re-conceiving change management: a knowledge-based perspective'. *European Management Journal*, 21(2): 247–57.

Bassnett, S. (2005) 'The importance of professional university administration: a perspective from a senior university manager'. *Perspectives*, 9(4): 98–102.

Beckhard, R. (1969) *Organisation Development: Strategies and Models*. Reading, MA: Addison-Wesley.

Boddy, D. and Paton, R. (2004) 'Responding to competing narratives: lessons for project managers'. *International Journal of Project Management*, 22(3): 225–33.

Cabinet Office/Council of Civil Service Unions (2002) *Partnership Working Project Group: Report*. London: Cabinet Office

Collins, J.C. and Porras, J.I. (1994) *Built to Last: Successful Habits of Visionary Companies*. New York: Harper Business.

Cook, S. and Macauley, S. (2004) *Change Management Excellence – Using the Four Intelligences for Successful Organisational Change*. London: Sterling.

Dewhurst, S. and Fitzpatrick, L. (2006) 'Ideas at work: turning stakeholders into advocates'. *Strategic Communication Management*, 9(3): 6–7.

Donaldson, A., Lank, E. amd Maher, J. (2005b) 'Making the invisible visible: how a voluntary organisation is learning from its work with groups and communities'. *Journal of Change Management*, 5(2):191–206.

Feather, J. (2003) 'Theoretical perspectives on the Information Society'. In *Challenge and Change in the Information Society*, eds S. Hornby and Z. Clarke. London: Facet, pp. 3–17.

Henry, J. and Mayle, D. (eds) (2002) *Managing Innovation and Change*. 2nd edition. London: Open University Business School in association with SAGE.

McCalman, J. and Paton, R. (1992) *Change Management: a Guide to Effective Implementation*. London: Paul Chapman.

Milsome, S. (2003) 'An open relationship'. *Employment Trends/IRS Employment Review*, 779.

Palmer, I. and Dunford, R. (2002) 'Who says change can be managed? Positions, perspectives and problematics'. *Strategic Change*, 11(5): 243–51.

Pfeifer, T., Schmidt, R. and Voight, T. (2005) 'Managing change: quality oriented design of strategic change processes'. *TQM Magazine*, 17(4): 297–308.

Plant, R. (1987) *Managing Change and Making it Stick*. London: Fontana Collins.

Sirkin, H.L., Keenan, P. and Jackson, A. (2005) 'The hard side of change management'. *Harvard Business Review*, 83(10): 108–18.

Springer, C. (2005) 'Keys to Strategy Implementation'. *PA Times*, 9.

Appendix 1

The SWESA performance management system

The SWESA performance measurement system

The SWESA performance measurement system is based on a Balanced Scorecard approach. It has been designed both to monitor strategic impact and evaluate a set of factors that will, when linked with decision cycles, drive future performance.

Whilst essential, the performance measurement data available for directly assessing strategic impact are largely embedded in the past. It can be several years before information is available on the impact of decisions and actions.

It is possible to monitor progress on key activities that underpin strategic impact within shorter time frames – so that management decisions can be more informed. This vital connection between action and measurement is reflected in the structure of the Balanced Scorecard, that mirrors the SWESA activity areas of external engagement, internal processes and internal capability.

Within this structure, a set of measures has been chosen that focuses on the initial goals of SWESA, including the four top priorities – business brokerage; leadership and management; literacy, language and numeracy; joint planning.

Baseline information has been prepared for each of the four areas of focus and, in the quarters that follow, the progress of SWESA will be measured against this.

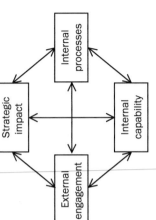

Strategic impact focus

Strategic impact will primarily be reported annually, based on the evaluation that concludes in the spring of each year. However, some updates will be included in the quarterly reports – so that information can be reported as soon as it is available.

The Healthy Labour Market Review uses a system that differentiates 'close to policy indicators' from 'broad outcome measures', allowing a stronger focus on the impact of SWESA interventions. While close to policy issues have an impact on performance in the broad outcome category, the latter is influenced by a very wide range of factors that are outside the control of SWESA – for example the global economy. The logic is that any impact SWESA can have on, say, productivity must be indirect and channelled through close to policy actions – so the focus of attention needs to be on outcomes that reflect SWESA activities. Of course, the close to policy indicators are also influenced by external factors but less so than broad outcomes.

As a baseline assessment for strategic impact, a summary analysis of the key indicators is shown on the next page. As well as providing updates to this in the future, there will be in-depth evaluation on specific issues that have been identified as important but lacking a sound evidence base. An academic panel supports this process and also provides strategic level interpretations of the indicators and insights on labour market health. For the spring 2005 report, the focus of additional investigation will be on labour market dynamism,[1] sector productivity analysis, under-utilisation of skills and the causes of differences in inactivity rates within the region.

GOALS

Skills: *'By encouraging aspirations and developing skills, the dynamics of the economy in the South West will change to provide a high quality of life and sustainable prosperity for everyone.'*

Enterprise: *'To build a region where the potential of our enterprising businesses and people is unlocked and encouraged to flourish so we can create the growth and wealth that a healthy, balanced and diverse South West England economy depends on.'*

The SWESA working vision statements

The South West Labour Market: an summary analysis of key indicators[2]

Broad outcome indicators	Closer to policy indicators
Employment: There is a self-contained labour market with high employment rate – 78.7 per cent in June to August 2004, compared with 75.1 per cent for England. **Balance and quality of employment:** The sector balance of employment is similar to England but with more in distribution, tourism and public services and less in financial and business services. **Work patterns and job types:** There are very high levels of self-employment and part-time employment. During the year ending August 2004: ■ 360,000 people were self-employed, 9.1 per cent of all people aged 16+. This was well above the 7.8 per cent average for England. ■ 30.1 per cent of the workforce was employed part-time, compared to a national average of 26.2 per cent. **Output and productivity:** Output (GVA) per head was £13,900 in 2002, which was 91.4 per cent of the £15,300 UK average. In 2001 labour productivity, in terms of GVA per hour worked, stood at 90.2 per cent of the UK average – which is worrying when set against the extent to which the USA (39 per cent), France (22 per cent) and Germany (19 per cent) lead the UK.[3]	**Business generation and survival:** The region has a relatively high rate of business generation but also a high level of deregistration. Compared with the UK, it performs well on survival rates for VAT-registered businesses. **Research and development:** In 2002, total research and development expenditure by business, government and higher education in the South West was £1.7 billion – compared with a figure of £4.5 billion for the South East. The total expenditure for England was £17.2 billion. **Labour market turnover:** There is a high labour market turnover relative to other regions, which can be interpreted positively as flexibility or seen as indicative of a negative hire and fire culture. The Healthy Labour Market Review Group is researching this in more detail for 2005. **Vacancies and skills:** The 2003 National Employer Skills Survey (NESS) found that hard to fill vacancies in the South West represented 1.7 per cent of total employment, compared with the national average of 1.2 per cent. However, at only one in six, a lower proportion of these vacancies relate to skills shortages than in other parts of the country.

Population and migration: about 5 million people live in the region, 3 million of them of working age. There is a larger proportion of older people than nationally, with less young adults. Worryingly, there is a net outflow of graduates from the region of over 2,000 every year.

Labour supply: Overall a high proportion of the working age population is active in the labour market – 81.9 per cent compared with 79.3 per cent in the UK – but there are lower economic activity rates in the south and west of the region.

Unemployment: In June to August 2004 period the unemployment rate in the South West was 3.4 percent, the lowest rate in England.

Equity in the labour market: Relative to the rest of the country, the region scores well on indicators of individual equity covering gender, disability and race.

Work-related training: according to the Labour Force Survey, 28.4 per cent of employees and self-employed undertook work-related training during the three months preceding the summer of 2003. This is identical to the UK figure.

Participation in learning: In 2003, 55.7 per cent (GB 52.3 per cent) of the region's 16-19 year olds participated in education and training. In 2002, 84 per cent of adults had participated in learning over the previous three years (GB 73.8 per cent).

Qualifications: The region has a well-qualified workforce. In the spring of 2003, 75 per cent (UK 71 per cent) of the population of working age were qualified to at least level 2, 51 per cent (UK 49 per cent) had a minimum attainment of level 3 and 26 per cent (UK 25 per cent) were qualified to level 4 and above.

Skills for Life: according to estimates made in 2003, 49 per cent of the region's 16 to 65 year olds have numeracy skills below the Skills for Life baseline[4] of level 1 – compared with a national figure of 47 per cent. In the case of literacy skills, 14 per cent are below the level 1 baseline (national figure 16 per cent).

External engagement focus

The potential for SWESA to have an impact is reliant on the participation of individuals and employers in the activities that have been identified as drivers of the strategy. Hence the customer perspective of the Balanced Scorecard will initially concentrate on individual and employer engagement in SWESA top priorities of business brokerage, leadership/management and literacy/language/numeracy.

Three measures have been developed to enable progress to be gauged:

- Engagement of Small and Medium Enterprises (SMEs) through business brokerage.
- Engagement of individuals in leadership and management programmes.
- Engagement of individuals in literacy, language and numeracy programmes.

Goal: To increase the numbers of individuals and organisations engaged in skills development and enterprise.

In the future, this part of the Balanced Scorecard will evolve alongside the external engagement priorities of SWESA. It is likely that skills utilisation by employers will be an important issue and engagement with developing intermediate skills is a logical area for future measurement. Customer satisfaction is also an area of future interest – the potential for using existing partner mechanisms for gauging employer views on the responsiveness of the training system will be investigated.

Engagement through business brokerage is being reported as the standard Business Link SME penetration measure (established and starts), with data provided by the Small Business Service. For the July to September 2004 quarter this stood at 10.8 per cent, compared with a 9.6 per cent SME penetration rate for all of England.

The numbers of individuals engaged in leadership and management programmes is being assessed through quarterly returns from Business Links (co-ordinated by the Small Business Service) and Leadership Southwest – covering specifically defined publicly funded/supported provision. The baseline assessment revealed that 1837 individuals were participating in these programmes during the period ending September 2004.

The numbers of individuals engaged in literacy, language and numeracy programmes will be reported on a sixth monthly basis, starting with the first quarterly report in February. This will include enrolments in autumn 2004 and form the baseline figure for SWESA.

External Engagement Focus	Baseline
Business brokerage: % SME market penetration.	10.8%
Numbers of individuals engaged in publicly funded/supported leadership and management programmes.[5]	1837
Numbers of individuals engaged in literacy, language and numeracy programmes.[6]	–

Internal processes focus

Working together, to achieve a greater impact, is at the heart of the SWESA strategy. Outputs will be driven by collaborative activities to make the services provided more responsive to the needs of individuals and employers – and wider social and economic priorities. Measuring the progress of the internal processes that underpin this collective action will provide management information to support both development and delivery of SWESA functions.

In the first instance, the internal processes perspective of the Balanced Scorecard will concentrate on the fourth top priority of SWESA – joint planning of training for adults by the major funding agencies in the region. Two measures have been developed to enable progress to be gauged:

Goal: To deliver a responsive, coherent and mutually supportive set of business support and learning services in the region.

■ Partner employee rating of the effectiveness of joint planning in the region.
■ The value of the publicly funded training budget aligned with SWESA planning processes.

As these initial joint planning goals are achieved and the focus of development moves on, it is anticipated that there will be an increasing focus on the integration of skills and enterprise activities. Another potential future measure is the length of development cycles between customers'needs being identified and skills/enterprise services being provided.

The rating of the effectiveness of joint planning is being assessed through a quarterly poll of one hundred strong panel of partner employees. There are five questions relating to joint planning, which participants are asked to assess on a scale of 1 to 10. The recruitment of the panel has been based on a sampling matrix that comprises 50 per cent from the major funding agencies and 50 per cent others. In each case, 50 per cent of respondents have been drawn from those currently engaged with SWESA/FRESA – leaving 50 per cent of subjects to be drawn from those that will potentially be engaged in the future. Sampling also reflects a range of seniority within organisations. A baseline assessment was conducted by SLIM by telephone during the first two weeks of November and it is anticipated that the panel will move to electronic data collection by the third round of questioning.

79 respondents participated in the baseline assessment, rating the current effectiveness of joint planning in the region as 3.9 out of 10. On the individual questions, responsiveness to newly identified needs was rated lowest (2.6) and the extent to which provision is informed by evidence was rated highest (4.9). The other scores were 4.5 for the extent to which training currently meets the needs of employers and individuals, 3.4 for the extent to which joint planning activities currently add value and 4.1 for flexibility relative to national constraints.

The value of **training budgets aligned with SWESA planning processes** will be reported as a single monetary value for the region. Note that the qualifying criterion will be alignment with SWESA planning processes,[7] rather than alignment with SWESA goals and priorities. Therefore, until these planning processes are up and running, a zero score will be included in the Balanced Scorecard. Key tests will include the degree of influence on partner planning, the allocation of partner funding and the development and provision of training in identified areas of need.

Internal Processes Focus	Baseline
Partner employee rating of the effectiveness of joint planning in the region (on a scale[8] of 1 to 10).	3.9
Value of the publicly funded training budget aligned with SWESA planning processes.	£0

Internal capability focus

The effectiveness of the internal processes, external engagement and overall leadership needed for SWESA to deliver long-term change will be heavily dependent on the collaborative capabilities of participating organisations. If it is to succeed, it must ensure that the networks and skills that are the underpinning bedrock of activities are fit for purpose.

In the first instance, the internal capability perspective of the Balanced Scorecard will concentrate on building SWESA capacity for delivering the skills and enterprise agenda in the region. Two measures have been developed to enable progress to be gauged:

Goal: To ensure that the SWESA and its constituent parts have the capacity to deliver the skills and enterprise agenda in the region.

- Partner employee rating of SWESA capability.
- Internal engagement: number of individuals actively engaged in SWESA activities and projects.

Once the early capacity building is achieved, the Balanced Scorecard will evolve in line with the development of SWESA. An increasing focus on innovation and knowledge management is likely.

The **partner rating of SWESA[9] capability** is being assessed through a second set of five questions in the quarterly poll (outlined above). In the baseline assessment, an overall score of 4.2 was achieved. On the individual questions, the effectiveness of innovation was rated lowest (3.3) and the extent to which SWESA currently has the ability to improve provision was rated highest (4.9). The other scores were 3.9 for the impact of SWESA leadership on building joint capability, 4.7 for communication and knowledge sharing and 4.3 for the usefulness of information made available by SWESA.

Internal engagement is being assessed through a quarterly stocktake/register of the number of individuals actively engaged with SWESA activities and projects – active engagement is defined as attendance at SWESA meetings (Board, Alliance & Research Forum) or participation[10] in SWESA projects and Task and Finish Groups. In the future, the SWESA Central Team will undertake the stocktake but EKOS has prepared the baseline assessment, concluding that 123 people were actively engaged with SWESA/FRESA during the July to September quarter.

Internal Capability Focus	Baseline
Partner employee rating of SWESA capability (on a scale[11] of 1 to 10).	4.2
Internal engagement: the number of individuals actively engaged in SWESA activities and projects.	123

Notes

1. The flexibility of the labour market and, in particular, its responsiveness to rapid changes.
2. Source: SW Healthy Labour Market Review, IES, May 2004, with updates by SLIM in November 2004.
3. The UK's Productivity Gap, ESRC, September 2004.
4. Note that Skills for Life baseline is NVQ level 1 (not foundation level 1, which is much lower).
5. Provisional figure based on a six-month return from SBS and the quarterly return of Leadership Southwest. It will be updated in the first quarterly report.
6. The measurement for participation in literacy, language and numeracy programmes is under development by the LSC and will be reported twice per year – starting with the first quarterly report.
7. A SWESA Task and Finish Group will be implementing joint planning and will play a major role in defining the criteria for alignment.
8. Current rating: 1–2 = very low; 3–4 = low; 5–6 = adequate; 7–8 = high; 9–10 = very high.
9. Note that the baseline assessment takes account of current FRESA capability.
10. In the future, active engagement will take account of participation in joint staff development programmes.
11. Current rating: 1–2 = very low; 3–4 = low; 5–6 = adequate; 7–8 = high; 9–10 = very high.

Appendix 2
Learning South West: Strategic Opportunities

The following tables show a list of potential opportunities Learning South West (LSW) is now considering. This is the first stage of decision-making relating to the organisation's overall strategic direction. Each opportunity was scored by Learning South West's senior management team from six perspectives. The scoring scale is from 0–6. Those opportunities marked low priority helped the team to identify the areas that LSW should stop doing.

Opportunity	Impact on Primary Stakeholders	Impact on Targets for Influence	Sustainability of intervention or network	Established Track Record and/or Internal Competency or Capacity	Policy and/or funding support from powerful actors	Low Reputation or Finance Risk	Priority
Muliti-sectoral Portfolio of CPD							
1 Becoming a Centre for Excellence in Teacher Training following Reform of Teacher Training	6	3 Implement Policy	6	6 Would need help	6	5	
2 Partner with Investors in People champion to develop 'smart business package' involving holistic thinking and creating a learning organisation (links to Greater Expectations)	6	5	4.5	5 Established track record only just beginning	2 Policy in place but no support	5 Key targets of influence think Skills Brokers will do this	
3 Support development of Foundation Degrees with HE and FE working together	6	5	5	3	2 Policy in place but no support	5	
4 Working with Plymouth to adapt their Linking thinking course to develop other accredited provision re sustainable communities with Creating Excellence	4	6	4	4 Higher score due to existing contacts	3	6	

5	Work closely With FE Providers to support impact of Foster review and new White paper	6	4	5	6	2 Funding may go straight to providers via QIA	4 Investing time while others are already doing it
6	Work with ABC to develop new professional qualifications for teachers, trainers and mentors to support unitised provision and Framework for Achievement	6	3	6	3	2	3

Opportunity	Impact on Primary Stakeholders	Impact on Targets for Influence	Sustainability of intervention or network	Established Track Record and/or Internal Competency or Capacity	Policy and/or funding support from powerful actors	Low Reputation or Finance Risk	Priority
7 Coordinate CPD between members, grouping members together to reduce costs	5	1	3	3	1	1	Low priority
8 Make new offer on Professional development to members	6	5 Because we are the first to think this way	6	6	1	3	
9 Run series of session on empowering professionals for staff across Youth and learning sectors – enabling them to work though the tensions. Seminars and e-debates, good dissemination. Effective peer networks with mechanisms to record and demonstrate involvement as CPD.	4	5	4	6 Assumes implementation by LSW team	2	2	
10 Workforce development in Children & Young people's Services – developing strategies and provision	6	5	5	5.5	2	3 Depends on time allocated to pursue this in isolation	

Opportunity	Impact on Primary Stakeholders	Impact on Targets for Influence	Sustainability of intervention or network	Established Track Record and/or Internal Competency or Capacity	Policy and/or funding support from powerful actors	Low Reputation or Finance Risk	Priority
New Qualifications for our stakeholders							
11 Develop modular youth work apprenticeship using e-assessment	6	4	5 More efficient to deliver regionally than through individual employers	6	5 Employers – Yes, Colleges – No	4 Risk of failure in delivery	
12 Life Beyond GCSE – Round Robin event for 40 schools and 4–5 awarding bodies	6	6	3	4 Capacity	3 Need to investigate	5	
13 Develop accredited qualification in Smart Business (developed through Greater Expectations)	5	4	4	5	5	5	
14 Develop package of qualifications and support for a 'learning to learn' qualification that would hopefully link to Framework for Achievement	3 Not sure who benefits	5	5	3 resource questions	3	4	Low priority – or later

15	Develop package of qualifications and support for new Framework for Achievement	5	5	6	5	6	6	
16	Develop CPD and qualifications re dealing with migration	4	5	2 Dependent on funding	3	4 Other players	2 Risky	Low priority
							6 Everyone is doing this	

Opportunity	Impact on Primary Stakeholders	Impact on Targets for Influence	Sustainability of Intervention or network	Established Track Record and/or Internal Competency or Capacity	Policy and/or funding support from powerful actors	Low Reputation or Finance Risk	Priority
17 Develop new Diplomas and provide training and support for their implementation	5	5 Use links with 14–19 advisers and providers	6	6	5	5	
18 Link Youth work to 14–19 Agenda	4	5	4	4 No gap in market	3	5	Low priority
19 Create qualifications re Olympics	5	3	1	4	3	4 ABC opportunity rather than LSW	Low priority
20 Pilot e-learning approaches in partnership with members and ABC to improve take-up	6	6	6	6	6	6	
Research							
21 Develop creative ways of measuring success and share good practice	2	4	6	6	1 Other players better placed to provide this	5	Agreed would only pursue internally

Opportunity	Impact on Primary Stakeholders	Impact on Targets for Influence	Sustainability of intervention or network	Established Track Record and/or Internal Competency or Capacity	Policy and/or funding support from powerful actors	Low Reputation or Finance Risk	Priority
22 Research into the extent to which current and emerging provision is supporting the Integrated Regional Strategy and other new policies that increasingly use holistic thinking	5	5	3	4	2	3	Low priority
Youth Work							
23 Continue programme of support, advocacy and development for youth work	6	5	6	6	3 Support from youth services, but not necessarily Children and Young people's Directors	4 Sustainable funding of youth services may end in 2008	
24 What can Youth Work tell the Regional Skills Partnership – can we translate best practice into other skills areas and relationships between brokers/employees/providers	5	5	1 Doesn't need to be sustainable	6	4	4 Dependent on funding	
25 Provide good practice guidelines on areas of Children and Young People's Services, mainly youth work	5	5	4	5	5	5	
26 Youth Evaluation with Regional Youth Parliament – offer participative evaluations service	4	5	4	6 Tessa and Sharon	5	5	

Opportunity	Impact on Primary Stakeholders	Impact on Targets for Influence	Sustainability of intervention or network	Established Track Record and/or Internal Competency or Capacity	Policy and/or funding support from powerful actors	Low Reputation or Finance Risk	Priority
Project Management							
27 Become regional project manager of choice for LSC ESF projects based on timely, low cost delivery with maximum added-value through high levels of regional ownership and excellent dissemination. This requires events and other strategies to market this new role.	2	5	5	4	4 Can use project funds to do some of this	5	
Employer Learning and Engagement							
28 Supporting improved employer engagement and partnerships by voluntary and community sector	4	4	3	5	1 Needs funding	3 If can get money not too risky	
29 Employer Engagement as in Greater Expectations	4	4	3	5	6	4	
30 ESRC research proposal into employee learning as contributor to business success	3 Research useful to providers and employers	5	5	4	4 Can use Greater Expectations as example	4 Not risky if funded	

Opportunity	Impact on Primary Stakeholders	Impact on Targets for Influence	Sustainability of intervention or network	Established Track Record and/or Internal Competency or Capacity	Policy and/or funding support from powerful actors	Low Reputation or Finance Risk	Priority
New Business Areas							
31 Become a provider where we do not compete with members, e.g. youth work apprenticeships	5	4	3	2 No track record but internal competence	4 Probably High	1 Risky	
32 Host Regional Education for Sustainable Development Coalition	1	3	2	5	1	2	Low priority till funding clearer
33 Regional Education for Sustainable Development Advisory Service	1 No voiced demand from FE Colleges or Youth Services	3	2 Lots of work to sustain	5	1 Not so far	2 Financial risk	Low priority

34	Act as neutral broker in commissioning for consortia of VCS and/or other providers of services	5 Big impact on volume of youth organisations and local authorities	5 'strategic'	2 Lots of networking activity required to attract support	4 Project management and building skills, youth skills	2 Unknown support and funding	1 tendering is risky	Low priority
35	Develop international youth work/learning specialisms	2 Impacts only few individuals	1 Too patchy to be strategic	1 Lots of work building international relationships	4 Good track record	1	1 Things go wrong on international youth trips	Low priority

Opportunity	Impact on Primary Stakeholders	Impact on Targets for Influence	Sustainability of Intervention or network	Established Track Record and/or Internal Competency or Capacity	Policy and/or funding support from powerful actors	Low Reputation or Finance Risk	Priority
Marketing and Membership							
36 Improved marketing materials and brand identity including revised statement of values and purpose and package of what we offer	1	4	4	2 Currently limited staff capacity	2	3 Need to get reputation right	
37 Position Learning South West as a best practice learning organisation	1	3	3	5	1	6	
38 Celebrate 60 years anniversary	2 Use to reflect on history and world in 2067	4	6	5	2	5	
39 Develop diary of events staff attending and coordinate and cross-reference networking and marketing opportunities	3	5	3	6	3	6	

40	Collaborate with ABC partners to develop national profile	3	5	3 Could be expensive	6	3	6
41	Offer bespoke consultancy to members as loss leader – develop clearer profile of each member's needs and strive to offer services to meet those needs	5	1	2 Free consultancy cost money and may create unsustainable expectation	4	2	4
42	Hire a marketing person	1	4	2	2	2	1 These costs will be hard to get funded

Opportunity	Impact on Primary Stakeholders	Impact on Targets for Influence	Sustainability of intervention or network	Established Track Record and/or Internal Competency or Capacity	Policy and/or funding support from powerful actors	Low Reputation or Finance Risk	Priority
43 Use House more to promote our activities – info board, posters etc	4	6	4 Needs to be updated	2	3	5	
44 Promote idea of partnership as well as membership	1	3	4	2	3	2 Might undermine notion of membership	Low priority
45 Develop new terminology around members and membership	1	1	5	3	1	2	Low priority
46 Relaunch membership with more specific benefits, regular communication, online forums and banks of resources	4	4	3 Need to provide resources	3	5	1	

House

							Low priority
47 a	Build more meeting space/ reorganise space to allow additional guests	2	1	6 Building investment should last	1 Carparking problems	1 Own money	5 Extra mortgage is small	
47 b	Improve eating facilities, storage without increasing guest capacity	3	2	6 Building investment should last	4	1 Own money	5 Extra mortgage is small	
48	Become a Smart business e.g. improve car-parking via improved community relations	2	1	3 Community relations need maintenance	4	1	5	

Opportunity	Impact on Primary Stakeholders	Impact on Targets for Influence	Sustainability of Intervention or network	Established Track Record and/or Internal Competency or Capacity	Policy and/or funding support from powerful actors	Low Reputation or Finance Risk	Priority
49 Become a Green host	4	3 GOSW/ Regional Assembly monitor this	3 Needs maintaining	6	3	6	
Internal Team Improvements							
50 Work together more muliti-sectorally and multi-disciplinary	3	4 More cohesive	6	4 Why hasn't happened before?	2	5	
51 Make Regional Youth Unit more integral to Learning South West	G3	4	3	3	3 Some concerns from youth work stakeholders	6	
52 Become an Investors in People Champion	2	3	5	5	4	5	

Board

53	Clearer Board and Project/Business Sub-groups with better ownership and Terms of Reference	1	5	3	2	5	4
54	Clearer job descriptions for Board members, recruitment process and responsibility to promote Learning South West	1	5	3	2	5	4
55	Hold Board and Staff Residential to improve mutual knowledge and communication	3	2	1	2	2 Expensive	2 Low priority

Index